Language Learning Practices with Deaf Children

Language Learning Practices with Deaf Children

Patricia L. McAnally, Ph.D.

Director of Training
University of Minnesota
University Affiliated Program on Developmental
  Disabilities
Minneapolis, Minnesota

Susan Rose, Ph.D.

Associate Professor
Department of Educational Psychology
University of Minnesota
Minneapolis, Minnesota

Stephen P. Quigley, Ph.D.

Professor of Education and Speech and Hearing Science
University of Illinois
Urbana-Champaign, Illinois

Chapter 6 by Peter V. Paul
College of Education
The Ohio State University

A College-Hill Publication
Little, Brown and Company
Boston   Toronto   San Diego

College-Hill Press
A Division of
Little, Brown and Company (Inc.)
34 Beacon Street
Boston, Massachusetts 02108

Library of Congress Cataloging in Publication Data
Main entry under title:

McAnally, Patricia L., 1927-
  Language learning practices with deaf children.

  Bibliography: p. 207.
  Includes index.
    1. Deaf—United States—Means of communication—Study
and teaching. 2. Children, Deaf—United States—
Language. 3. Deaf—Education—United States—English
Language. I. Rose, Susan, 1943-   . II. Quigley,
Stephen Patrick, 1927-   . III. Title.
HV2471.M22   1987   371.91'24   87-13232
ISBN 0-316-55343-3

Printed in the United States of America

C O N T E N T S

P R E F A C E

This is the third of three related books dealing with the development of language and reading in deaf children. The objective of the three texts is to provide future and practicing teachers of deaf children with basic theoretical and research knowledge as well as specific principles and practices for fostering the development of language and reading. *Language and Deafness* (Quigley and Paul, 1984b) provides research and theoretical information on language development; *Reading and Deafness* (King and Quigley, 1985) provides both research information and information on instructional practices in the development of reading skills; and the present text deals mostly with instructional practices in language development.

This book describes the variety of language development theories and practices that are used with deaf children without advocating any particular approach. Educated practitioners in any profession, and future teachers as well, should be familiar with all the major issues and practices in their field instead of being trained only as disciples in a particular doctrine. Specialization in a particular approach to language and reading development advocated by any teacher preparation program should follow a general introduction to all major approaches.

As was the case with the two preceding texts, the present book is concerned primarily with prelinguistically deaf children and youth. Although the term "prelinguistically deaf" is subject to various definitions and interpretations, it is used here in reference to persons who have sensorineural hearing impairments of 90 dB or greater that occurred prior to the age of 2 years. These individuals are likely to use vision as their major (or only) channel for receiving communication, and thus they are likely to be oriented visually rather than aurally to language acquisition. As is discussed in detail by Quigley and Paul (1984b, pp. 1–6), and more generally in Chapter 8 of the present book, this factor is of the utmost importance in distinguishing deaf children from children with other levels and ages at onset of hearing impairment, for whom audition is, or can be made, a major channel of communication. The distinction between visual and auditory orientation to language acquisition, with the caveat that this is often a matter of emphasis rather than exclusivity, has great significance for language development in deaf children. The eye, and various associated cerebral mechanisms, might perceive and structure communication differently from the ear, which is of obvious significance for both language acquisition and instructional practices.

Chapters 1 and 2 cover some of the accepted facts and known problems of language acquisition and instruction with hearing and with deaf children. Some implications for language development in deaf children are stressed. Chapter 3 is a history of instructional practices in language development with deaf children to show continuity of present with past practices and to illustrate the recurring cycles of major language development approaches with deaf children, such as the waxing and waning of natural (holistic) and structural (analytic) approaches. Chapters 4, 5, and 6 detail the major approaches of the present time: natural methods, structural methods, and ASL-ESL. Although the present forms of the natural and structural methods have undergone modern improvements (or at least changes), their basic principles have remained essentially the same for the past century. ASL-ESL, which is the development of English as a second language (ESL), has its roots in the 19th century but seems to be headed for a strong revival during the present decade. Chapter 7 presents some specialized aspects of language development, including inferencing and figurative language, and some current techniques for language and reading development, such as semantic webbing, paragraph networking, and the use of story grammars. Finally, a brief synthesis of the material of the book is provided in Chapter 8, where several points are stressed. First, it is stated that normal development of language depends, above all else, on fluent and intelligible communication between a child and a mature user of the language to be acquired. If fluent and intelligible communication is not established during the child's first year or two of life, language in any form will be acquired slowly and laboriously. Second, reading, although it eventually becomes at least partially a visual process, seems to require an established auditory, or at least articulatory, language as its foundation. This raises profound questions about the possibilities of success in reading for many deaf children. Third, the eye does not seem to be readily able to extract the structure of English from visual presentations, whether in print or in some form of manually coded English. This, too, has profound implications for the development of reading in deaf children. Finally, it is proposed that development of language in deaf children requires the judicious use of a variety of techniques, including both natural and structured approaches.

As is true with most professional work, completion of this book depended on many individuals in addition to the listed authors. We gratefully acknowledge the contributions of Lori Mack for her patience and expertise in typing the manuscript, to John Watham-Ocama for his assistance in library research, and to the Department of Educational Psychology at the University of Minnesota for support and commitment to the education of children with hearing impairments. In particular we single out for special thanks and recognition Charles Gramly for his consultation on Chapter 6 concerning the use of American Sign Language to teach English.

C H A P T E R 1

Language Development in Hearing Children

Language is the most important means for communication used by human beings. It is a rule-governed symbol system, generative in nature, through which individuals can represent their understanding of the world. Language is not restricted in this text to spoken language only, but it also includes the language of manual signs, including American Sign Language (ASL). Although most of this book is devoted to spoken language and its derivative written form, a chapter is devoted to American Sign Language (ASL) and its potential significance for educational work with deaf children.

THE ASPECTS OF LANGUAGE

Spoken language is generally considered to include four aspects: phonology, morphology, syntax, and semantics. Phonology is the sound system of spoken language. Children, in learning a word, learn the correspondence between a sequence of sounds and a particular referent, such as the word *car* and the object *car*. They also learn which speech sound changes are necessary to change meaning (e.g., in changing *car* to *far*). Morphology refers to the structure of words and the way affixes are added to words to alter meaning or to add specific information. For example, adding the prefix *un-* to the adjective *happy* changes the meaning; adding *-ed* to a verb indicates that the event occurred in the past. Syntax refers to word order or the way in which words are organized in sentences. Underlying the concept of organization is the more complex implication that the child understands the interrelationship of the words within the sentence. For example, in a subject-verb-object word order, the child must perceive which word indicates the doer of the action and which word indicates the receiver. The fourth aspect, semantics, is the study of the meaning of language. Bloom and Lahey (1978) stated that semantics is concerned with the meaningful relationships between words, groups of words, and sentences.

Recently another dimension of language, pragmatics, has received wide attention in the literature. Pragmatics refers to how language is used to gain what is wanted from the environment and to express communicative intents. A pragmatic view of language focuses on communicative interactions and intentions. The emphasis in pragmatics is on describing communicative competence, which includes linguistic and contextual elements rather than linguistic competence alone. Generally, pragmatics is considered a framework from which to understand syntax and semantics (Prutting and Kirchner, 1983). Much attention is given to the context in which a communicative interaction occurs, as a pragmatic view of language assumes that language use will vary with contexts and communication partners. This view also assumes that language is learned through communication for the purpose of communication and highlights the social aspects of language with the subsequent shift of attention to language use. To determine how effectively children use language, communication functions, such as asking and answering questions, expressing needs, and describing objects and events, are analyzed. The successful use of communication functions leads to the development of discourse and narrative skills, which allows the child to participate effectively in a variety of social contexts.

THEORIES OF LANGUAGE ACQUISITION

No theory has yet been able to account for the development of language behaviors in all of the areas of language. A theory of language must account for language behaviors at any point in development and for the processes that allow language growth. Thus, a language theory that is sufficient must explain why children say what they do when they are developing language and why they eventually speak like adults. Gleitman and Wanner (1982) suggested that the absence of a comprehensive language theory results from a lack of agreement on what either adults or children are doing when they produce and comprehend language. At present, there are four major perspectives on the acquisition of language, which are discussed briefly here. More detailed discussions of the theories can be found in *Language and Deafness* (Quigley and Paul, 1984b, pp. 56–64).

Behavioral Theory

Behavioral theories emphasize the influence of the environment in the language learning process (Skinner, 1957). For the behaviorist, the child is a passive learner who responds to stimuli in the environment and who does not purposefully self-initiate language learning. According to Skinner (1957), language is a verbal behavior that is dependent on reinforcement and subject to extinction, maintenance, discrimination, and generalization. Through reinforcement, sounds are shaped into words, and words are shaped into functional response units. The basic processes of learning (i.e., classical and operant conditioning or shaping) are assumed to direct and control the increasing diversity and complexity of the child's language behavior. Many behaviorists believe imitation is an especially important factor in language learning because it leads to mature language without laborious shaping of every response. When children successfully imitate new words and forms, the new behavior is maintained because reinforcement occurs either from adults or from the children themselves. The rate of language learning depends on the training techniques of the parents rather than on the maturation of the child, and the sequence of language learning is determined primarily by the environmental stimuli to which the child is exposed, for which he or she receives adequate reinforcement.

When 1-year-old children are observed, the behavioral theory seems to have a certain degree of validity. Young children no longer produce speech sounds that are not present in the environment (extinction of unreinforced behaviors) and do produce sounds like the syllables of their native language (reinforcement of successive approximations). However, there is much evidence to contradict this theory. The major argument against behaviorism is that it does not take meaning into account, and meaning must be considered in any theory of language. In addition, the theory of behaviorism does not account for the generative nature of language—that is, native speakers can produce an infinite number of sentences, many of which they have never heard (Quigley and Paul, 1984b). Bryen (n.d., p. 152) listed the following empirically verified phenomena as being unexplained by the behaviorist theory:

1. Many aspects of the language acquisition process are uniform in all children.
2. Children replace early correct forms (e.g., *came, went, feet*) with incorrect, overregularized forms (e.g, *comed, goed, foots*).
3. Although the children are exposed to certain sentences, they actually learn not these particular sentences but the underlying rules.

Linguistic Theory

Linguistic perspectives of language learning assume that language has a structure or grammar that is at least somewhat independent of language use. Grammars consist of finite sets of rules that allow for the generation of infinite sets of possible sentences. Linguistic rules are descriptions of the regularities of the language. All native speakers know these rules. Although they may not be aware that they know them and may not be able to verbalize the rules, nonetheless they apply these rules effortlessly as they use language. In linguistic theories, language acquisition is viewed as a process of deducing these regularities.

Chomsky (1957) argued that an adequate grammar must be generative to account for the number and variety of sentences that native speakers produce and comprehend. The grammar that Chomsky (1957, 1965) devised is known as tranformational generative grammar. This grammar includes phrase structure rules that parse sentences into constituent elements. It is concerned not only with surface structures of sentences but also with the deep structures that underlie the sentences. Chomsky believed that a speaker's meaning was not always conveyed in the surface structure but could be found in the underlying deep structure. For example, the meaning of the sentence, *They are visiting relatives*, is not revealed in the surface structure; however, determining the underlying deep structure clarifies the speaker's intent, which could be either of two possible interpretations:

They | are | relatives.

visiting

or

They | are visiting | relatives.

This distinction between deep and surface structures is one of the major contributions of transformational grammar.

One of the major apsects of Chomsky's theory (1968) is that children possess an innate predisposition to acquire language. The existence of innate structures is assumed from three factors: (1) the existence of linguistic universals; (2) the structure or form of the linguistic input to children; and (3) the speed of the acquisition of language. It appears that children must possess some innate predisposition that influences them to observe certain linguistic features, and these must be common to all languages.

Several research studies support Chomsky's hypotheses concerning language acquisition. These investigations have essentially followed two lines, one studying the concept of grammatical rules and the other searching for evidence of innate linguistic characteristics in humans. Results of studies investigating the concept of grammatical rules (e.g., Clifton and Odom, 1966; Gough, 1965; Savin and Perchonock, 1965; Slobin, 1966) supported Chomsky's distinction between underlying deep structure and surface structure. Other studies investigating cross-cultural and cross-linguistic perspectives have proved to be a rich source of data concerning the biological basis of language. If there is a biological basis for language, there must be common characteristics of language development observable in all children regardless of culture or language (Bever, Fodor, and Weksel, 1965). The results of several studies support the presence of these innate linguistic characteristics (e.g., Curtiss, 1981; Kuczaj, 1979; Lenneberg, 1966; McNeill, 1966b; Slobin, 1982; Springer and Deutsch, 1981; Umiker-Sebeok and Sebeok, 1980). Although evidence supporting a linguistic theory appears quite strong, there is significant contradictory evidence to be considered. Many developmental psychologists believe that the linguistic theories are too far removed from meaning (Bates and Snyder, in press; as cited in Gleason, 1985). Many view Chomsky's transformational generative grammar as an inadequate treatment of semantics. Currently, evidence is being accumulated suggesting that the major part of language acquisition involves semantic processes, and this reveals a flaw in the traditional linguistic approach (Maratsos, 1983). The linguistic approach generally minimizes the effects of different language environments. However, studies have indicated that children with minimal language stimulation in their natural environments learned very little language or speech by viewing television (Bonvillian, Nelson, and Charrow, 1976; Sachs and Johnson, 1972; Snow, 1977). Children appear to need more than just exposure to language; they seem to require some form of interaction with mature language users for normal language development (Bohannon and Warren-Leubecker, 1985).

Cognitive Theory

Cognitive theorists and semantic theorists argue that syntax is not separable from semantics and that semantics is more basic in language than syntax. Cognitive theorists oppose the idea that language is independent of other cognitive functions and argue that language is a mapping out of existing cognitive skills. These theorists believe that cognitive development is a prerequisite for grammatical and lexical development. Groundwork for the concept that language learning is based on general cognitive development was laid by Jean Piaget. It has been argued that most studies of cognitive development are useless for comparison with language development because cognition is studied through language (Cruttenden, 1979). The one framework of cognitive growth researched, in part, independently of language is that of Piaget (Piaget, 1954, 1971). The recent trend in cognition theory is to show that cognitive underpinnings exist but that after a short period of time, cognition and language exert some influence on each other. The nature of these influences (or the interaction approach) is still being explored (Schlesinger, 1982).

Sociocultural Theory

Sociocultural theorists, like semantic and cognitive theorists, also reject Chomsky's hypothesis of language as a system whose acquisition depends on innate linguistic structures. These theorists, however, differ from both semantic and cognitive theorists by emphasizing that the development of language is attributable to a child's interaction with other members of society. This view of pragmatics as a component of linguistics has emerged from this movement (Bates, 1976a, 1976b; Moerk, 1977). This component deals with such topics as logical and pragmatic presuppositions, the analysis of propositions, and the structure and functions of speech acts. The study of pragmatics is also concerned with communicative competence—in particular, the organization of discourse (that is, the manner in which conversations are opened, sustained, and terminated).

In general, sociocultural theory includes the following beliefs: (1) natural conversation is a valid source of data; (2) sentences are not the highest level of linguistic analysis; (3) social context is relevant to linguistic rules; (4) variability is a component of linguistic rules; and (5) language functions are diverse in nature (Ervin-Tripp and Mitchell-Kernan, 1977; Lucas, 1980; Mey, 1979). The main problem is to discover systematic rules in each of these areas (Quigley and Paul, 1984b). Contrary evidence is difficult to find because these theories have not been around long enough to be assessed adequately. Thus, many of the assumptions rest on untested and partial support gained from studies of the other approaches (Bohannon and Warren-Leubecker, 1985).

PRELINGUISTIC DEVELOPMENT

The preverbal child is a social being. Even within the first several days of life, infants have been shown to enjoy listening to, and responding to, speech events (Morse, 1972, 1974; Turnure, 1971). During this stage, as in all the language stages, the infant is not just a passive receptor who is merely absorbing language information. It appears that during the first year of life the child is actively processing the information he or she obtains and is learning much more about language during the early months than was previously believed.

Important cognitive events occur during the first year of an infant's life that are extremely important for the child's acquisition of language. Currently, the issue of the nature of the cognition-language development relationship and whether it is causal or correlative remains unresolved. The traditional thinking is that a causal relationship exists between cognition and language development, which would indicate that language acquisition follows the development of cognitive structures. Piaget proposed that cognitive structures provide the underlying bases for language development. For example, children begin to use names (e.g., ball) as they develop object permanence. However, the relationship of object permanence to language development has been questioned by several investigators (Bates, Benigni, Camaioni, and Volterra, 1977; Brown, 1973; Cornell, 1978; Moore, 1973), who have suggested that object permanence may not be a necessary prerequisite for the development of the first words. The use of words seems to emerge before Piaget's substage 6 of the sensorimotor period, in which object permanence appears, thus casting doubt on the presence of a causal relationship between cognition and language. If a positive correlative relationship existed, then, as object permanence develops, so would language develop, indicating that one variable (object permanence) does not cause the variation of the other (language development). Up to the present time, correlations between Piaget's cognitive stages during the sensorimotor period and communication-language behaviors have not yielded consistent patterns (Bernstein and Tiegerman, 1985).

Sugarman (1978) suggested that prerequisites to language development include cognitive and social schemes that are gradually combined into complex communicative sequences during the stages of sensorimotor development. The semantic structure of language according to Bruner (1975) is derived from social interaction events. Thus, children learn about speaker and listener roles through social interactions with adults, and Bruner suggests that the language to express these roles is mapped onto the child's developing social knowledge.

Interaction Between Adults and Infants

When adults speak to infants and very young children, their speech differs from that used when speaking to other adults. Phillips (1973), in a study of mother-child interactions, concluded that mothers' speech to children was significantly different in several respects. Sentences were shorter; fewer verbs, modifiers, and function words (e.g., conjunctions, prepositions) were used; fewer distinct verb forms (e.g., tenses) were produced; and vocabulary was less diverse and more concrete. Stern and Wasserman (1979) found that the prosodic elements of language (e.g., pitch, intonation) appeared to be more important than the words. Researchers who have studied speech by adults to babies have noticed higher overall pitch levels in a variety of languages, including English, Arabic, Spanish, and Latvian, than commonly occurs in adult to adult speech (Ferguson, 1964; Ruke-Dravina, 1977). Intonation patterns also seem to differ when an adult is speaking to a baby and include both extremes of high pitch and low pitch (Garnica, 1977). The rhythm of baby talk seems to be more regular than that of adults and is some-times described as having a singsong cadence (Moerk, 1972; Snow, 1977; Stern and Wasserman, 1979).

Phillips' description of mothers' speech to babies indicates that simple language structures are used predominantly. Dale (1976) sug-gests that simplification is an aid to learning. Very few passive and complex constructions are used in the mothers' language, thereby avoid-ing two kinds of sentences in which the deep structures are quite differ-ent from the surface structures. These sentence types will have to be learned later, but while the baby is in the initial stages of developing language, the impact is simplified. The mother's language, however, is not exactly at the level of the child's but is significantly more complex. Brown and Hanlon (1970) calculated that only 30 percent of the sen-tences heard by young children are simple, affirmative, declarative struc-tures. The remaining 70 percent are more complicated, indicating a variety and richness in the language used by mothers. The findings of Shipley, Smith, and Gleitman (1969) indicated that children are most attentive to utterances that are slightly beyond their own productive level, and Brown and Bellugi (1964) indicated that mothers tended to use language similar to the language their children would use 1 year later.

Repetition, both exact and paraphrased, was common in the lan-guage patterns used by mothers. Snow (1972) gives an example of how mothers present the basic message several times: "Pick up the red one. Find the red one. Not the green one. I want the red one. Can you find the red one?" Repetition, as most classroom teachers know, is an impor-tant aid to learning.

Differences in pitch and intonation patterns also seem to serve a purpose in language learning. Kearsley (1973) determined that infants respond best to high pitch levels. Other studies have shown that infants perceive and begin to mimic intonation patterns by 6 months of age (Chang and Trehub, 1977; Kessen, Levine, and Hendrich, 1979; Morse, 1974). If babies are more responsive to speech that includes variations in pitch and intonation patterns, it may be that adults use these charac-teristics because they have found that infants pay more attention to them. By maintaining the infant's attention, the adult may help to cement the emotional bond between adult and child (Gleason, 1985).

The speech directed toward infants must first attract their atten-tion. The attentive infant becomes quiet, turns toward the speaker, and establishes eye contact. Several studies have shown that eye contact is very important for establishing a bond between the baby and adult. Jaffe, Stern, and Perry (1973) have found that "gaze-coupling" between mothers and their 3-month-old infants resembles conversational turn-taking in adults. Some mothers also incorporated play routines into the looking behavior by alternately fixating on their infants's face and then playfully turning away.

It is not known whether the type of speech typically directed toward infants is necessary for normal language development because there are no studies of development in which such language input is absent. Gleason (1985) indicated that it is likely that visual and tactile stimulations also play an important role in establishing the bond between adult and child, and she suggested that these modalities can substitute completely for auditory stimulation, as, for example, in the development of deaf children. She also suggested that an infant requires a loving interaction of some sort for optimal development, and Sachs (1977) has stated that the language input of the adult typically is one source of that affectionate stimulation.

Infants participate in adult-infant interactions and do not remain passive, as was thought previously. Although the infants do not understand what is being said to them, they do react to the speech. It has been found that by 3 months of age, infants begin to show a high vocal responsiveness to vocal and visual stimulation by their mothers and a less excited response to stimulation by strangers (Roe, McClure, and Roe, 1982). The way the infant reacts to the adult's speech influences the adults' responding behavior. The adult knows that the infant does not understand what is being said, yet the adult behaves as if the child is understanding.

Snow (1977) studied mother-infant interactions and concluded that mothers responded to both verbal and nonverbal behaviors (e.g., smiles, burps, vocalizations) emitted by their infants and incorporated these behaviors into the conversation. The mothers seemed to regard these behaviors as intentional and treated them as the infants' turns in the interactions. Each mother seemed intent on allowing the child a turn in the conversation and would often pause after her own utterance, thereby providing an opportunity for the infant to respond. Initially the mothers accepted almost any behavior from the child as an attempt at communication, but as the infant became older, at approximately 7 months of age, the mothers accepted only higher quality vocalizations, such as babbling, not sounds such as burps. When the babies were 12 months old, the mothers attempted to interpret their children's vocalizations as words (Snow, 1977, p. 17):

CHILD: *abaabaa*
MOTHER: *Baba. Yes, that's what you are.*

The early language input of adults appears to influence the child's vocalizations. Lewis and Freedle (1973) found that if the mother vocalized to the infant, the response with the highest probability of occurring within a 10-second period was an infant vocalization followed by a smile. Clarke-Stewart (1973) found when observing older children (9 to 18 months) that the amount of verbal stimulation that a mother gave directly to her child was highly correlated with measures of the child's linguistic competence. The amount of maternal speech that was directed toward others and not toward the child did not correlate with language development. This result suggests that the quantity of direct adult-to-child language input is more important than the overall quantity of language that the child overhears.

Communicative Intentions Before Speech

During the last part of the first year of life, many children engage in behaviors that seem to be intentionally communicative even though most children are not yet using referential language. Bates, Camaioni, and Volterra (1975) related the example of a young child about 13 months of age. She was sitting outside the kitchen, looked at her mother, and said *ha*. As her mother walked to her, the little girl looked toward the kitchen, so her mother picked her up and carried her into the kitchen. The child pointed to the sink and the mother got her a drink of water. The child did not speak, yet her behavior seemed intentionally communicative.

Scoville (1983) listed several characteristics that typically mark the emergence of intentional communication.

1. Children gesture, point at objects, and make eye contact with adults.
2. Children often vocalize with consistent sounds and intonation patterns. These utterances are not imitated from adult speech but rather are communicative symbols invented by children. For example, in the previous illustration the child's use of *ha* was typical for situations in which she wanted something.
3. Children are persistent in their attempts at communication and, when not understood, will repeat their utterance and sometimes even change their behavior to communicate more clearly.

Early attempts to communicate can be categorized according to the functions they serve. Bates (1979) argues that there are two types of communication used by the preverbal child, a protodeclarative and a protoimperative. A protodeclarative behavior is one in which the child uses an object to gain the adult's attention. A protoimperative behavior occurs when the child gets another person to do something. In the earlier example, the little girl obtained something she could not get herself by pointing to the sink when her mother was attending.

It does seem that from quite an early age children attempt to communicate about objects and interactions using consistent sound patterns to call attention to what they are interested in and to influence other people's behavior (Gleason, 1985). By the end of the first year of life, the child is ready for the exciting milestone that his parents view as the beginning of language—the first word. In reality, the child has been preparing for this important event for many months.

SEMANTIC DEVELOPMENT

Cognitive Theory

By the time children begin to comprehend and produce language, significant development has already occurred in the area of cognition. As a result of his investigation, MacNamara (1972) stated that young children map language onto observations they have made about their world. They make these observations by participating in a wide variety of experiences in their environment. They do not learn about eating lunch because their mother says *It's time for lunch*. Rather, they already know that their daily routine contains such an activity, and, at some point, they realize that mother's statement refers to that familiar experience. Another example would be the child whose family has a dog for a pet. The child has experiences with the dog, petting, feeding, and playing with it, and observes certain characteristics of the dog. The child knows a great deal about the dog—for example, what it looks like, that it is furry, and that it barks, eats, and sleeps—before he or she actually learns to say *doggie*. Children know what milk looks like and how it tastes before they learn the word *milk*, and they know what their bed looks like and that they sleep in it before they learn to say *bed*.

Association Theory

One of the simplest explanations for how children attach meaning to their first words is that they do so through association. For example, the child is familiar with the family dog and if the parents point and say *doggie* when the dog appears, eventually the child will react to the word alone as if the dog were there. He or she will look around for it and be ready to play with or pet it. The word *dog* and the actual dog have been associated so that they evoke at least some of the same responses. Association theory may explain the earliest kinds of linking between words and objects; however, semantic development is much more complex than just learning a set of labels for objects in the immediate environment.

Semantic Feature Theory

Knowing the meaning of a word involves being able to understand that word in many contexts and to use it appropriately in a variety of contexts. This proposition involves the child's ability to store information about concepts and to apply that information in some way to new situations. Clark's (1973) semantic feature theory suggests that initially children do not use all features and characteristics when identifying an object. Clark asserts that children acquire meanings of words by sequentially adding specific semantic features. She concludes that perceptual features like size, shape, texture, and movement are abstracted most commonly by children at this early age. Children must determine which features are critical in establishing a category for a particular referent. At an early stage of lexical development, children commonly make errors in referent identification that are known as overextensions. These overextensions are a result of using a limited set of features. The universal examples of children who call all men *daddy* or all four-legged animals *doggie* illustrate the phenomenon of overextension. When doggie means "having four legs," the child is using fewer semantic features than an older child or an adult does for the word *dog*.

Initially, children use one or two features and gradually add semantic features until their meaning for the word matches the adult meaning. Overextensions are prevalent between the ages of 12 and 30 months. As children gradually add and apply more semantic features, they acquire knowledge about objects that belong and do not belong within a particular conceptual category. Overextension in child language has been cited more frequently than underextension, which is a meaning that is more restricted than an adult's meaning—for example, using *doggie* to refer only to the family pet and not to any other dog. Underextensions are difficult to detect in a child's spontaneous language. If he or she sees a dog and does not say *dog*, it may be that the child does not know the word is appropriate (underextension) or it may be that he or she simply chooses not to comment on the dog. Anglin (1977) presented data from an investigation of somewhat older children that suggested that underextensions occur as frequently as overextensions.

Prototype Theory

The prototype theory claims that children acquire core concepts that are the best examples of the categories they are learning (Bowerman, 1978; Rosch and Mervis, 1975). This hypothesis suggests that children develop a prototype against which all other exemplars are compared. The prototype is usually a member of a category that is a better representative than other members might be. For example, a German shepherd is a better representative of *dog* than a chihuahua; a robin is a better representative of *bird* than an ostrich. The prototype represents an underlying concept of "dogness" or "birdness," and other objects are compared to the stored mental representation. The closer the exemplar is to the prototype concept, the greater is the likelihood that it will be called by that name. Children acquire these core concepts when they acquire meaning and later begin to recognize members of that category that are distant from the prototype.

It is not known if features or associations or prototypes are used most frequently by children in acquiring meaning along with other strategies available to them. However, words that serve different semantic, syntactic, or pragmatic functions undoubtedly require different cognitive strategies (Gleason, 1985). It is probable that there are individual differences in cognitive style favoring one or another or a combination of these modes of semantic development.

Factors Influencing the First Words

Children's vocabularies grow at an astonishing rate, with an average of two to four new words being acquired each day during the ages of $2\frac{1}{2}$ to $4\frac{1}{2}$ years (Smith, 1926). By the time children begin to acquire a vocabulary, they have been exposed to an abundance of language and have had a wide range of experiences. It is interesting that children's initial expressive vocabularies have been found to be quite similar, despite differences in upbringing and environment (Gleason, 1985).

The words adults use when labeling objects for children influence children's early vocabularies. Adults tend to name objects by their general labels rather than by their specific labels. For example, an adult would point to a dog and say *dog*' rather than *German shepherd*, or say *flower* when pointing to a tulip. Adults sometimes purposely mislabel objects. Mervis and Mervis (1982) conducted a study in which 10 mothers and their 13-month-old children were given sets of toys to play with. The mothers named almost all of the toys for their children and occasionally misnamed some of them according to how their children might have categorized them. For example, a toy leopard was commonly called a *kittycat*, and a tow truck was called a *car*. According to Mervis and Mervis, children provide their parents with clues indicating how they might classify objects. Children initially treat all objects the same, mouthing, touching, and banging them, but eventually they begin to treat objects differentially. Children's differential treatment of objects indicates on a fundamental level how they are categorizing the objects. By labeling the objects for children according to the children's own categories, parents are probably showing how words are used, that is, objects that differ in minor ways but are of the same category share names.

In addition to the special vocabulary words directed toward young children, adults and older children (Shatz and Gelman, 1973) modify other aspects of their speech and language input, some of which probably aids semantic development. As stated earlier, speech to young children is ennunciated more clearly and slowly, exhibits a wider range of pitch and intonation, and has clear pauses between utterances; in addition, sentence elements are usually delineated clearly (Newport, 1975). Thus, it seems that language input to children contains words and sentences that are better formed than those in language directed toward adults. The clearer and simpler language could assist children in separating words from the flow of speech and aid them in becoming familiar with new words and in picking out those words that map meanings they wish to express (Gleason, 1985).

Adults usually speak to children about the "here and now" (Cross, 1977; Phillips, 1973; Snow, 1972) and about topics that are concrete; thus, the task of figuring out the referents of the words is kept within the inferential abilities of the children. Adults usually use a reduced vocabulary containing more content words and fewer verbs, modifiers, pronouns, and function words than when they are speaking to other adults. Words with simple and unambiguous meanings are predominant. As already stated, adults also tend to repeat key words in subsequent utterances when they are speaking to children.

In responding to the speech of young children, older listeners provide feedback to children on how well they have represented their intended meanings. The child's words are confirmed when they produce an appropriate or the desired result, as when the child yells *mommy* and mother comes. Gleason (1985) describes an incident in which the baby says *cracker* when she really wants a cookie and is quite disappointed when she is given a saltine. Feedback from other people that validates the adequacy of children's words can be an important source of information as children develop their semantic systems.

Children's early vocabularies seem to include words from a variety of grammatical classes, and the first 50 words contain representatives from all of the major grammatical classes found in adult language. Nelson (1973) studied the first 50 words used by children and found that, among the children studied, there were similarities in the relative proportions of word classes. General nominals, such as *doggie*, were the most commonly used words (51 percent) in the young children's vocabularies. The frequency of use of words from other classes included specific nominals, such as *Mommy* and pets' names (14 percent); action words, such as *up, give, bye-bye* (almost 14 percent); modifiers, such as *dirty* and *mine* (9 percent); personal-social words, such as *please* and *yes* (8 percent), and function words, such as *for* and *on* (4 percent). Nelson noted two conditions that appear to affect the words children use in their first vocabularies. She determined that children are more likely to include the names of referents with which they can interact, manipulate, or change. For example, words for food, toys, and articles of clothing that children can remove are used commonly by them (e.g., *cookie, car, socks*), whereas words for referents that children cannot manipulate or change are rarely used by them (e.g., *park, tree, sofa*). Children are much more likely to include the names of animals and vehicles than names of rooms or plants.

Production and Comprehension

Children's productive (expressive) vocabularies typically lag behind their comprehension (receptive) vocabularies. In Benedict's study (1977), the results indicated that children comprehended their first 50 words at about 13 months of age but do not produce 50 words until about 19 months of age. Researchers have noted several examples of accurate word comprehension in children who, at the same time, fail to differentiate words used for different class members in their productive vocabulary. Rescorla (cited in Gleason, 1985) found that one of the children in his study was able to identify a motorcycle, bike, truck, plane, and helicopter, yet at the same time she referred to them all as *car*. Nelson, Benedict, Gruendel, and Rescorla (1977) stated that children's ability to differentiate among more class members in comprehension than in production suggests that "the child's application of the (word) in production may then indicate far more about his use of language to serve as a categorizing function than it does about his understanding of a particular word meaning" (p. 9).

Attribution

It has already been noted that a large number (about 65 percent) of children's early words are nominals and about 9 percent are modifiers. Developmentally, children begin to use adjectives as single-word utterances, and later adjectives are used in the earliest multiword utterances. Among the attributes that children use between the ages of 16 to 21 months are adjectives such as *dirty* and *funny* (Bloom, 1973). Older children, of 21 months and older, use adjectives in two-word utterances, such as *tiny balls, dirty sock,* and *black hair* (Bloom, 1973). Bloom explains that references such as these to attributive values is not contrastive. The child was not saying *tiny balls* to differentiate from *big balls,* or *dirty sock* to distinguish that sock from a cleaner one. These early attributive forms were used more in a nominal or absolute sense in that a property (tiny, dirty, black) was not attributed to an object as much as it was used to name or identify the object (Bloom, Lightbown, and Hood, 1975).

Color Words

Bartlett (1977) and Carey and Bartlett (1978) studied the acquisition of color words and their meanings. The conceptual knowledge required to comprehend color words may be more complex than is assumed by teachers who include color words early in the curriculum. The conceptual knowledge required includes being able (a) to isolate color from objects, (b) to differentiate among hues, and (c) to notice similarities among related shades. The linguistic knowledge required includes recognizing that color words refer to the dimension of color (Bartlett, 1977). In their research, Carey and Bartlett (1978) found that if a first color word and its referent are already known, one or two brief exposures to a new color term are sufficient for the child to name the color and also to build on it from additional experiences 2 months later. In addition, they documented a variety of strategies used by children in integrating the new information into their vocabularies. Color words (Bartlett, 1977) may follow a unique pattern of acquisition in that the category of words may be recognized by children before the words are connected to their color referents. For example, when asked, "What color is this?" many 2-year-old children can supply a color word even though it may be wrong. Rice (1980) suggested that children may build the conceptual underpinnings for such knowledge through the kinds of interactions they experience with adults.

Pronouns

Baron and Kaiser (1975) investigated comprehension of pronouns that differ in person, number, and gender by a group of children 3 to 5 years old. The results indicated that pronouns are acquired by the addition of semantic elements. The data did not consistently show an order of difficulty of semantic components, indicating that semantic development may be influenced by experience, prior learning, or the different hypotheses children develop about word meanings. However, Wiig and Semel (1980) compiled several studies (Brown, 1973; Chipman and deDardel, 1974; Moorehead and Ingram, 1973) of normal acquisition of pronouns to obtain information about the relationships among the major stages in normal children's acquisition of syntax and selected pronouns.

Later Semantic Development

Semantic development in children from 4 through 12 years of age has been studied by many researchers; however, the research has not been integrated into a theoretical view (Palermo and Molfese, 1972).

Thus, the results of different studies may not be representative of semantic development in general. Because information on later semantic development is somewhat limited, only general comments are offered on this topic here.

Although vocabulary growth occurs prior to and during the school years, vocabulary size may not be an indicator of semantic sophistication. Vocabulary size does not increase in a strictly linear manner as children grow older (Dunn, 1965). Not all lexical items cause structured changes in the semantic system; some may add only redundant information. Gleason (1985) states that "semantic system development consists of increases in the number of concepts and words a child knows and in the range of mappings the child has worked out within and between the conceptual and linguistic systems" (p. 127). Thus, semantic development includes establishing semantic networks, which consist not only of an understanding of individual words but also a knowledge of how they are interrelated. These semantic networks are probably formed relatively late compared with other linguistic achievements (Francis, 1972; McNeill, 1966b)

SYNTAX AND MORPHOLOGY

Stage I

Utterances longer than a single word occasionally occur quite early in language production by young children, but during the last half of the second year, they begin to occur frequently in children's productive language. This new stage marks an important developmental milestone; two-word utterances are the beginning of the interaction of syntax and semantics. The development of multiword utterances has been described by Brown (1973) as occurring in five continuous but ordinal stages. (See Table 1-1 for a listing of Brown's language stages with comparable mean lengths of utterance and ages.) One problem in describing language development is that children do not develop language at the same rate; the age of acquisition of particular linguistic structures varies from child to child. A measure that is a more useful index of language development than age is the mean length of utterance (MLU). Determining a child's MLU involves counting the number of morphemes per utterance in a sample of the child's spontaneous language (See Brown, 1973, p. 54, for a description of the procedures.) MLU is useful in that children of the same MLU have made roughly the same amount of progress in language development even though their ages may be quite different (Foss and Hakes, 1978). Table 1-1 shows the MLUs associated with language stages and approximate ages.

Table 1-1 Brown's Language Stages with Comparable Mean Lengths of Utterance (MLUs) and Ages

Brown's Language Stage	MLU	Approximate Age
Pre-Stage I	0.00–1.00	0–18 months
Early Stage I	1.01–1.49	19–22 months
Late Stage I	1.50–1.99	23–26 months
Stage II	2.00–2.49	27–30 months
III	2.50–2.99	31–34 months
IV	3.00–3.74	35–40 months
V	3.75–4.50	41–46 months
Post-Stage V	4.51+	47+ months

Adapted from Miller, J. (1981). *Assessing language production in children: Experimental procedures*. Baltimore: University Park Press.

Early Stage I (MLU = 1.01 to 1.49, age = approximately 19 to 22 months) is characterized by the development of the basic semantic relations. Two-word utterances appear during this stage and include the combining of semantic notions present in the previous single-word utterances (e.g., action, object) and the emergence of new semantic relations. The meanings expressed during this stage continue to depend to a large extent on context. For example, if a young child says *Daddy shoe*, he or she could mean *Daddy's shoe* or *Daddy put on shoe*. Using contextual clues, the child's intent could be intepreted.

It is argued that children's two-word formulations contain only those semantic notions expressed previously in the single-word or successive utterance stages (Greenfield and Smith, 1976). Children at this stage seem to express previously mastered semantic concepts while attempting to gain mastery of new forms (Kretschmer and Kretschmer, 1978). The semantic relationships expressed by children during this stage are either functional (linear) relationships or grammatical (hierarchical) relationships. The functional relationships are characterized by utterances such as *no milk, there milk*, in which the entire utterance means no more than the meaning of each word. The grammatical relationships are characterized by utterances such as *drink milk, want milk*, in which the entire utterance means something more than the meaning of each word; a relational concept between or among the words is implied. Both of these relationships can be noted in the child's language production at the two-word stage, with the grammatical relationships becoming more dominant than the functional relationships by the end of the two-word stage.

In Stage I, children's language becomes somewhat freed from their actions, that is, they no longer must act on objects in order to talk about them, although they do continue to talk predominantly about the ''here and now.'' The semantic features children apply to many words still are not exactly the same as those used by adults; thus, they may continue the overextension of words, although to a lesser degree than during the single-word utterance period. During late Stage I, children generally acquire three more basic semantic relations: (1) dative or indirect object (*Give Mommy*), (2) experiencer and state (*doggie want, baby need, Mommy hear*), and (3) instrumental (*knife cut*).

Important questions in the two-word stage are whether children have knowledge of subject and predicate and whether this knowledge is similar to that of adults. Several researchers have suggested that knowledge of the basic grammatical relation between subject and predicate is possessed by children (Bloom, Miller, and Hood, 1975; Smith, 1975). Bowerman (1975) disagrees with this position, arguing that observation of word order alone is not sufficient to credit a young child with knowledge of grammatical categories. Pragmatically oriented theorists, such as Bates (1976b) and Greenfield and Smith (1976), argue that children establish a word order rule based on given new information rather than on grammatical categories. Thus, there appears to be disagreement concerning the possible presence of syntactic knowledge at the two-word stage. The debate regarding this aspect of children's language acquisition continues (Kretschmer and Kretschmer, 1978).

Stage II

During the three-word stage, or Stage II (MLU = 2.00 to 2.49, age = approximately 27 to 30 months), two important operations can be observed (Brown, 1973). First, an embedding process occurs in which children insert a functional relationship into a grammatical relationship. For example, the child might insert *no milk* into *want milk*, thereby producing *no want milk*. The second operation is conjoining, in which two grammatical relations that share a common word are combined. In the conjoining process, the common word is deleted. For example, *Baby drink* and *drink milk* might be conjoined in the three-word stage into the combination *Baby drink milk*.

Children during the three-word stage often begin to adhere rigidly to a subject-verb-object word order, even when it is not appropriate, as in passivization (de Villiers and de Villiers, 1972). This rigidity in comprehension is interpreted by some researchers as the overlearning of a syntactic rule. Pragmatically oriented researchers interpret it differently, however, their research findings suggest that children establish topic-comment relations that result in adherence to rigid word-order patterns in spite of occasional semantic contradictions, as in *car washed boy.*

Along with an increased sentence length, another important change during this stage is the gradual emergence of a few inflections and function words. These forms begin to appear between and upon the nouns and verbs used by the child. The acquisition of the major grammatical morphemes is a slow and lengthy process. Some are not fully acquired until the child enters school (for example, adverb derivation-*ly*), although the process begins early, as soon as the MLU nears 2.0.

Brown (1973) investigated the order of acquisition of 14 grammatical morphemes by three children. The most important finding reported was the similarity among the three subjects in the order in which these morphemes were acquired. Brown defined acquisition as the time at which the child used the morpheme in 90 percent of its obligatory contexts. The first morphemes to be acquired included the present progressive inflection (-*ing*), two prepositions (*in, on*), and the plural ending (-*s*). The last morphemes were the contractible copula (as in *He's sick, I'm hungry*) and the contractible auxiliary (as in *I've done that, He's gone*). de Villiers and de Villiers (1973) investigated the development of the same morphemes in a group of 21 children and found the same order of acquisition that Brown reported. Thus, the evidence indicates that English grammatical morphology develops in a predictable order.

Brown (1973) found that the order of acquisition did not relate to the frequency of occurrence of morphemes in the parents' speech but related to the linguistic complexity of the morphemes. Complexity can be defined as semantic complexity, the number of meanings encoded in the morpheme, and syntactic complexity, the number of rules required for the morpheme (Gleason, 1985). The earlier acquired morphemes are largely semantic in nature, whereas the later acquired morphemes are a combination of semantic and syntactic complexity.

Beyond Stage II

During the 3 years following Stage II (or approximately beyond 2.55 years of age), children's utterances show a rapid rate of structure development. A great deal of semantic development also occurs during this period, with children gradually expanding their frame of reference beyond the "here and now," allowing them to talk about things that occurred in the past, things that might occur in the future, and things that they have not directly experienced. They also begin to discuss the temporal and spatial relationships of objects and events, and vocabulary continues to expand at a rapid rate. Children's utterances become longer and more complex, expressing a larger amount of content within a single utterance. Two related kinds of structures make their appearance in children's simple sentences—first utterances containing negatives, then questions.

Negatives

Bellugi (1967) investigated the expression of negation in children and identified four phases in the acquisition of the full negative. Children's earliest negatives occur as single words and express the semantic functions of nonexistence, rejection, and denial—for example, *no, allgone*. During Stage I, multiword negative utterances usually appear with the negative at the beginning of the utterance, such as *no milk, not go*. From 3 to 7 months later, when the MLU is between 2.5 and 3.0, the form of the negative utterances changes, with the negative generally occurring between the subject and verb, as in the utterances, *I not going to be daddy, He no bite you*. The final period is usually reached during Stage V, when the negative utterances are quite similar to those used by adults, for example, *He shouldn't be eating, I'm not sad now*.

A major development occurs during Stage IV that results in the negative sentence structures so similar to those used by adults. That major development is the emergence of an auxiliary system that provides the auxiliary verb *do* for use in negative utterances. Another interesting development during Stage IV is the appearances of multiple negatives in one sentence, such as, *No one's not going to sleep now*. The tendency to produce multiple negatives lasts quite a long time, even into the early school years. It seems that children often use multiple negatives to emphasize the negative character of what they are saying (Foss and Hakes, 1978). It is interesting to note that in many languages the use of multiple negation for emphasis is acceptable, even though in English it is not.

Yes-No Questions

Initially children simply use a rising intonation on a declarative sentence to signal that they are asking a question, for example, *Mommy see?* and *You can't fix it?* Utterances similar to these appear during Stages I, II, and III, but by Stage IV, children begin to use auxiliaries, appropriately inverted, such as *Am I silly?* and *Do I look like a doggie?* They extend their use of auxiliary elements, including present tense *be, can, will,* and *do* in their question forms, but they also continue to use declarative statements with rising intonation as an alternative form for asking yes-no questions.

Wh-Questions

Another group of questions are those that begin with *who, what, where, when, whose, which, why,* and *how.* Answers to these questions are more complex than for yes-no questions and contain more information. These questions also require the rule of inverting the subject and the auxiliary, as well as the correct placement of the appropriate wh-word at the beginning, for example, *Why did daddy go?* Children intially ask wh-questions by completely omitting the auxiliary, such as *What that?* and *Where the ball go?* Later they include the auxiliary but do not consistently invert it with the subject, for example, *Where the glass of milk is?* Finally, children are able to incorporate all of the syntactic rules necessary to produce well-formed wh-questions. Wootten, Merkin, Hood, and Bloom (1979) found that *what, where,* and *who* questions were the first ones asked by the children, followed by *when, how,* and *why.* Studies of children's comprehension of wh-question forms indicate that *what, where,* and *who* are easier to understand and correctly respond to than *how, why,* and *when* (Ervin-Tripp, 1970; Tyack and Ingram, 1977; Winzemer, 1980).

Within a few months of beginning to produce structured utterances, children's utterances become progressively more complex and more similar in structure to an adult's. It appears that this development is systematic; essentially the same order for adding syntactic features occurs in all children. The nature of the changes that occur indicates that the children are learning general syntactic rules and applying them to their generation of utterances rather than learning particular utterance forms. When a particular syntactic feature begins to appear, it tends to appear simultaneously in a wide variety of utterances.

Foss and Hakes (1978) state that several kinds of evidence suggest that the development of children's utterances involves three kinds of changes.

> First there is an increase in the number, variety, and complexity of semantic concepts expressed in utterances. Second, there is an increase in children's knowledge of the syntactic structures and rules involved in producing utterances. And third, there is an increase in the capacity for performing the production processing required for producing complete well-formed utterances. Progress in all of these areas is rapid enough that by the age of 4 or 5 years children are producing utterances that are very similar to those of adults. (pp. 264–265)

As children continue to develop more sophisticated semantic and syntactic structures, they are also developing conversational skills and an understanding of how language is used. It is extremely difficult to separate the different aspects of language development that are interwoven in normally developing children. It is also difficult to determine which, if either, comes first—an understanding of pragmatic use of language or an understanding of the syntax and semantics of language. The simultaneous emergence of performance in both language forms and language use is possibly the most reasonable definition of normal language development (Kretschmer and Kretschmer, 1978).

Complex Sentences

By age 3 years, children can use a variety of simple sentences, such as, *This is a ball, Mommy bought the ball*. These sentences, as with most early sentences, contain one proposition; however, as children's language becomes more sophisticated, they begin to include more than one proposition within a sentence. Their sentence construction advances from a linear ordering of words to a hierarchical ordering within and among sentence elements.

Coordination

The first complex sentence structure to emerge in children's language is coordination. Usually, coordination appears first as children combine two propositions using *and*; for example, *This is a ball and Mommy bought the ball*. There are two kinds of coordination—sentence coordination, in which two or more complete sentences are conjoined, as in the example just given, and phrase coordination, in which phrases within a sentence are conjoined, as in the sentence, *Mommy bought the ball and the truck*. Several studies (Bloom, Lahey, Hood, Lifter, and Fiess, 1980; de Villiers, Tager-Flusberg, and Hakuta, 1976) indicate that both forms seem to enter children's language at about the same time, with the probable restriction that sentence coordination does not develop before phrase coordination.

Bloom and her colleagues (1980) found that at an early stage in the development of coordination, children use *and* in a semantically limited manner; however, as they progress, they add greater semantic and syntactic flexibility to their language. Bloom and her colleagues found that children used *and* to encode a variety of meanings, and these meanings developed in a fixed order:

1. Additive, as in *I play with this and you play with that*.
2. Temporal, as in *I'm going home and get a cookie*.
3. Causal, as in *Mommy put the cake in the oven and it cooked*.

Other meanings were also encoded but were less frequent and more variable among children.

Complementation

Bloom, Lifter, and Hafitz (1980) investigated the development of complement constructions in children's language and concluded that their order of emergence was based on the semantics of the verb. The results of their investigation indicate that complements emerge in children's language in the following order:

1. With state verbs or verbs that express a feeling or intention such as, *like, want, need* (example: *I want to watch TV.*)
2. With notice verbs which are followed by the complement *what*, such as *see, look, watch* (example: *Watch what I'm doing.*)
3. With knowledge verbs followed by the complement *that* or *what*, such as *know, think* (example: *I know what that is.*)
4. With communication verbs that require the complement construction *to* plus a verb, such as *ask, tell, promise* (example: *Ask daddy to come here.*)

Bloom concluded that the acquisition of complement constructions is a function of semantic constraints.

Relativization

Relative clauses can be categorized as objective clauses and subjective clauses, depending on whether they modify the subject or the object of a sentence. In the sentence, *I have a brother who is really tall*, the relative clause modifies the object. In the sentence, *The girl who called you is my sister*, the relative clause modifies the subject. Menyuk (1977) reported that objective clauses are acquired before subjective clauses. The objective clause usually emerges after 5 years of age and the subjective clause after 7 years of age. It seems that children find it easier to add a clause at the end of a sentence than in the middle, as this minimizes constraints on processing (Hakuta, de Villiers, and Tager-Flusberg, 1982; Slobin, 1973).

Several studies have investigated young children's comprehension of sentences containing relative clauses. Generally, the results are in agreement and support the notion that preschoolers find most sentences with relativization difficult to understand. A number of recent studies (de Villiers, Tager-Flusberg, Hakuta, and Cohen, 1979; Goodluck and Tavakolian, 1982; Hamburger and Crain, 1982) indicate that, as in production, children find object relative clauses easier to understand. Studies investigating the production and comprehension of sentences containing relativization indicate clearly that preschool children are just beginning to use and understand this construction. Their knowledge of the syntactic structure of this construction is incomplete at this time, and their performance with relative clauses is limited by processing constraints (Gleason, 1985).

Passivization

Passive construction sentences are used only rarely by young children; therefore, studies investigating the passive construction have had to devise formats that would elicit responses to the construction. Most of these studies have required the children to act out the sentences given by the experimenter. Passives can be of two kinds: reversible, such as *Susie hit Tom* (active) or *Tom was hit by Susie* (passive), in which both nouns could serve as subject or object; and irreversible, as in *Susie washed the car* (active) or *The car was washed by Susie* (passive), in which only one noun can act as the agent.

Bever (1970) conducted one of the earliest studies on passive constructions, comparing children of ages 2, 3, and 4 on their understanding of active and passive constructions. Some of the sentences were semantically reversible; some were irreversible. Bever found that children could understand irreversible passives before they could understand reversible passives. Only some of the older 4-year-old children could correctly act out the reversible passives. Bever also found that the 2- and 3-year-old children made systematic errors on the reversible passives. He concluded that the children used a word order strategy to decode the meaning and, thus, imposed a subject-verb-object sequence, ignored the auxiliary verb and preposition, and interpreted it as an active construction. For example, the sentence *Tom was hit by Susie* would be interpreted as *Tom hit Susie*.

Many subsequent investigations have confirmed Bever's findings, and most claim that children appear to understand the passive construction by age 5 years. However, Maratsos, Kuczaj, Fox, and Chalkley (1979) found that 5-year-old children understood passives with action verbs but did not understand passives with nonaction verbs, such as *Tom was liked by Susie*. Thus, it seems that the acquisition of passives is not complete at 5 years of age. Only by middle childhood is the passive completely understood and used productively.

SUMMARY AND IMPLICATIONS

During a period of only a few years, most children develop a rich and complex linguistic system, all of which is acquired with little apparent effort and with no formal instruction. Children quickly progress from expressing simple semantic relationships using only two words to expressing sophisticated concepts in multiword sentences. The course of language development is influenced by linguistic, semantic, and contextual factors directed by the pragmatic need to communicate in order to satisfy basic needs and desires. Detailed accounts of this development can be found in many books (e.g., Bernstein & Tiegerman, 1985; Bloom & Lahey, 1978; Dale, 1976; Gleason, 1985). The intent in this chapter was to give only a general outline of the development and its processes to emphasize a number of factors that have direct relevance for developing language in deaf children.

1. *The need to communicate precedes the ability to communicate.* Although parents usually regard the appearance of the child's first word as the beginning of language, much meaningful communication between parent and child precedes that event. Many children engage in preverbal behaviors, such as gesturing, smiling, pointing, vocalizing, and tugging, that seem to be intentionally communicative even though they do not involve use of referential symbols. Conversely, caregivers learn to respond to these behaviors and to interpret them into expressions of the child's intents. Although not yet well understood, these preverbal attempts at communication might be important and necessary precursors to verbal communication.

2. *Interaction is essential to language development.* Studies have indicated that passive exposure to communication is not sufficient for adequate development of language. Children seem to require some form of communicative interaction with mature language users to develop a normal command of language. It has also been found that language development is facilitated when this is a *loving* interaction between child and parent or parent-surrogate.

3. *Prosodic elements of language appear to be more important initially than words.* Studies have indicated that the initial basic carriers of meaning for infants are the suprasegmental aspects of speech, such as pitch, loudness, and intonation patterns. Understanding of words gradually develops from the stream of speech-sound input, and the ability to use words develops somewhat later.

4. *The form of adult input influences early language development.* Speech to young children by adults usually is enunciated clearly and slowly, exhibits a wide range of pitch and intonation, and has clear pauses between utterances; sentence elements usually are delineated clearly. In addition, adults usually speak to children about the ''here and now'' and about topics that are concrete, thus keeping the task of interpreting the referents of words within the limits of the children's inferential abilities. Adults use reduced vocabularies in speaking with children and

tend to repeat key words in subsequent utterances. Thus, language input to children by adults contains words and sentences that are better formed than those in language directed toward adults.

5. *Feedback to children on how well they have represented their intended meanings is important to language development.* For example, the arrival of the mother when the child yells *Mommy* provides reinforcement for the meaning of that word.

6. *Children's vocabularies grow rapidly and follow patterns.* An average of two to four new words are acquired each day during the ages of 2½ to 4½ years. Nelson (1973) noted that children, when acquiring their first 50 words, are most likely to use the names of referents with which they can interact or which they manipulate or change—for example, words for food, toys, and articles of clothing that they can remove (*cookie, car, socks,* and so forth).

7. *Children's syntax also grows rapidly and follows patterns.* During the last half of the second year of life, utterances longer than a single word appear with increasing frequency in children's productive language. This appearance of two-word utterances marks the beginning of the interaction of syntax and semantics. Brown (1973) developed the concept of mean length of utterance (MLU) as an index of language development, which is useful in that children of the same MLU can be considered to have made roughly the same amount of progress in language development regardless of differences in their ages. Using the MLU, Brown and others have plotted syntactic development through six basic stages up to 4 years of age and beyond. By 5 years of age or so, the typical child has acquired a complex syntactic system to go along with an extensive vocabulary, although both the semantic and syntactic systems are capable of expansion and refinement throughout life.

8. *At least some of the basic processes of language development in children with normal hearing are directly applicable to language development practices with deaf children.* For example, as discussed in the section on prototype theory, it is possible that children acquire core concepts that are the best examples of the concepts they are learning (Bowerman, 1978; Rosch and Mervis, 1975). If this is so, then, using the principle of "the best example first," a typical four-legged chair rather than a bean-bag chair should be used to begin teaching the concept of *chair.* Similarly, a robin would be a better beginning representative of the concept *bird* than would an ostrich. As another example, the principles of imitation and expansion as described by Brown and Bellugi (1964) can be applied directly to language development with deaf children. Imitation and expansion are described in detail in Chapter 4, which deals with natural methods of language development.

Quigley and Kretschmer (1982) summarized some factors essential to normal language development.

> If an infant has a reasonably intact sensory system, has no severe intellectual or cognitive deficit, is exposed to a reasonably stimulating environment, and has reasonably verbal parents or parent surrogates who provide a reasonably warm and loving atmosphere and communicate reasonably fluently with the infant, an auditory-based language system will be internalized effortlessly by the child. This internalized, auditory-based language system will serve as a foundation of the child's receptive and expressive language in early childhood and as the base on which reading and writing and all educational factors related to them will later be developed. (p. 10)

Quigley and Kretschmer use the word "reasonably" deliberately to emphasize that some disruptions in the processes can take place without language development becoming seriously disordered or delayed. But deafness produces a massive disruption of the processes and of subsequent English language development. The effects of this disruption and the implications for language development are considered in Chapter 2.

C H A P T E R 2

Language Development in Prelinguistically Deaf Children

M eadow (1980) noted that the basic deprivation of deafness is not the loss of sound; it is the deprivation of language. The acquisition of language requires fluent communicative interaction between children and mature language users as well as intact sensory mechanisms to transmit linguistic information to the brain. In most children this linguistic intake is transmitted through the auditory channel and is processed by a central mechanism, which usually is unaffected by a hearing impairment. Despite the use of amplification, manual communication, and written language, the linguistic intake of the deaf child remains impoverished and incomplete (Grewel, 1963; Liberman, 1974). Hearing aids do not fully compensate for hearing impairments; the auditory signal received by the child remains limited and distorted (Niemoeller, 1978). Visual perception of language differs from auditory perception in ways that are obvious and in ways that are not yet understood. Speechreading as a visual stimulus provides limited information, as many articulatory movements are not visible. Written language differs from spoken language in that many of the prosodic elements present in speech cannot be represented in writing (e.g., duration, rhythm, intonation). Such information may play a significant role in language acquisition by emphasizing the chunking of language signals into constituent units (Crystal, 1973; Lenneberg, 1966; Martin, 1972). In addition, prosodic elements are not always represented clearly or consistently in manual communication, particularly if the signer is not a native signer. Therefore, because of the limitations of visual perception of language, the quality and quantity of linguistic information received by most deaf children are deficient, which probably causes their linguistic percepts to be different from those of hearing children (Bochner, 1982).

INTERACTION BETWEEN ADULTS AND YOUNG CHILDREN

In Chapter 1, it was noted that adults' speech to infants is different from speech they use when speaking with other adults. Some of these differences included shorter, simpler sentences, more pronounced prosodic elements (e.g., pitch, rhythm), and more repetition and looking behaviors. Communication between caregivers and children also included mutual and loving interactions.

Disadvantaging conditions such as language delay and mental retardation in children seem to affect the language environment of the child. Mothers of children with these conditions seem to show some differences in the amount and type of communication and in the situations under which they communicate with their impaired children compared with communication patterns of mothers of nonimpaired children (Bondurant, 1977; Buium, Rynders, and Turnure, 1974; Wulbert, Inglis, Kriegsmann, and Mills, 1975). Research with hearing impaired children suggests that when parents learn about their child's deafness, communication interaction patterns between parent and child often change to less favorable patterns and may subsequently have a deleterious effect on language growth in the deaf child. The results of several studies that investigated communication patterns between hearing mothers and their deaf children suggest that the communication style differs from that used between hearing mothers and their hearing children. Gross (1970) found that mothers of deaf children spoke less, used atypical intonation patterns, and were less likely to use tutorial strategies and to give verbal praise than mothers of hearing children. Weddell-Monig and Lumley (1980) concluded from their investigation that mothers of deaf children generally were more dominant in their interactions with their deaf children, and more of their utterances functioned to control or to direct behavior (Cheskin, 1982; Gross, 1970). Beckwith (1977) maintained that if mothers use language primarily to control their children's behavior, the result may be less interest on the part of the children in attaining speech as a tool for controlling their environment. Weddell-Monig and Lumley (1980) offer the explanation that initially a mother may engulf her deaf child with language stimulation to compensate for the sensory loss, and in doing so, eventually and inadvertently begin to control the interactions until the child makes no independent attempts to continue the communication. Schlesinger and Meadow (1972) stated that the hearing mother of a minimally communicatively competent deaf child is "much more likely to appear inflexible, controlling, didactic, intrusive, and disapproving" (p. 107).

Meadow, Greenberg, Erting, and Carmichael (1981) found that the interaction between deaf mothers and their deaf children was generally different than that between hearing mothers and their deaf children. A major conclusion of Meadow and her colleagues (1981) was that the quality of mother-child interactions is related to the deaf child's communication competence. They found that the interactions and the communication "climate" of deaf mother–deaf child dyads were very similar to those of hearing mother–hearing child dyads. The interactions of these two groups shared common characteristics, such as extended, complex, elaborated, and child-initiated interactions and an apparent enjoyment of the communication. The deaf mother–deaf child dyads, like the hearing mother–hearing child dyads, were able to sustain interaction for long periods of time, elaborate on ideas in a reciprocal fashion and, in general, reflected a mature conversational and interactional style.

In summary, child deafness does have an effect on mother–child interactions. The communication style of hearing mothers with their hearing impaired children is noticeably different from the interactions of hearing mothers with hearing children, especially among mothers of deaf children with slowly developing language performance. In deaf mother–deaf child dyads, in which a mutually comfortable communication system is shared, the interactions are more complex and more similar to the social and linguistic interactions of hearing mothers to hearing children than to hearing mothers and deaf children.

COMMUNICATIVE INTENTION BEFORE DEVELOPMENT OF REFERENTIAL LANGUAGE

Gestures

Hearing children exhibit communicative intentions before speech or formal expressive language is acquired, usually by gesturing, pointing, and making eye contact. Several studies of hearing impaired children indicate that they also exhibit communicative intentions before speech or the acquisition of a formal gesture system and that they do so in a manner that is generally similar to the performance of hearing children. However, a few divergences may exist between hearing and hearing impaired children in their patterns of gestural development. Several early studies (e.g., Carr, 1971; Grewel, 1963; Heider, Heider, and Stykes, 1941; Myklebust, 1954) of hearing impaired children have acknowledged that gesture systems seem to develop prior to the development of a formal expressive language system. Most of these studies indicate that deaf children develop a restricted range of gestures that becomes more elaborated and highly organized. These gesture systems were not described in detail until the mid 1970s, when Feldman (1975) investigated the relationships between forms and the meanings of individual gestures, and Goldin-Meadow and Feldman (1975) studied the semantic relations expressed by young deaf children. The subjects in both of these studies had no prior exposure to sign language.

Feldman (1975) found that deictic gestures were the most commonly used and the first acquired of the two categories of gestures used by young hearing impaired children. Deictic gestures functioned in a manner similar to the words *this* and *that* in spoken language and consisted usually of pointing at an object, tapping the object, or performing a swinging motion toward the object. Feldman found that the subjects generally used deictic gestures to identify small objects rather than large objects or locations, which offers an interesting parallel to Nelson's work (1973) on the first words used by hearing children (see Chapter 1). The hearing impaired children also indicated by using deictic gestures who was doing or giving what to whom, which also parallels hearing children's early use of words—that is, to identify agents, patients (object is moved but agent is not specified; e.g., "*horsie* go in truck," or "put *horsie* in barn"), or recipients within an action sequence rather than to identify only the objects apart from their activities or interactions.

Specific gestures were observed in older children and appeared first as action forms to identify sequences, then as nonaction forms to identify attributes. The first symbols produced by hearing children are produced exclusively within action contexts. Feldman's subjects used what were termed *act-on* specific referent gestures (indicating action on objects, such as *give* or *hit*) before they used *act-by* gestures (actions that are performed by agents on themselves, such as the gestures for *laugh* and *cry*). The order in which these two types of expressions emerge in spoken language of hearing children is reversed. The reason for the discrepant order of use in deaf children may be that the *act-by* gesture is cognitively and formationally more complex than the *act-on* gesture.

In an investigation of the semantic relations expressed by young deaf children, Goldin-Meadow and Feldman (1975) classified the observed gestures into two basic classes of propositions: actions and attributes. An action proposition was usually used to request or to comment on an action. An attribute proposition was used to comment on the perceptual characteristics of an object. Action propositions were produced at earlier ages and more frequently than attribute propositions. The earlier and more frequent use of gestures expressing action propositions is comparable to an occurrence in spoken language, that is, one- and two-word verbalizations expressing action are produced at earlier ages in the developmental processes and with greater frequency than one- and two-word attribute utterances. Goldin-Meadow also found that deictic gestures always preceded characterizing gestures—that is, the subjects always pointed to objects before using more symbol-like gestures in a descriptive manner.

When the action propositions of the deaf children were analyzed, Goldin-Meadow and Feldman (1975) found that all of the subjects combined the same structural components to convey similar types of action propositions. In addition, semantic roles were organized in similar ways, such as patient + act and act + recipient. In the action sequences, subjects tended to omit any gestures indicating the agent of the sentence. Continued analysis of action and attributive sequences seemed to indicate that affective agent and patient may constitute a category apart from causative agent. If this categorization occurs generally in deaf children, it would seem that their gestural systems contain syntactic groupings that apparently are determined semantically rather than by word order constraints. In spoken English, all agents are considered to be similar and occupy the same syntactic slots within sentence structures rather than being grouped together on the basis of semantic similarity. If young deaf children use gesture systems having conceptual-syntactic categories that differ from spoken English, it is possible that making a transition to the spoken English system might be confusing and difficult (Kretschmer and Kretschmer, 1978).

Skarakis and Prutting (1977) described the semantic-pragmatic component of the spontaneous communication acts of four preschool hearing impaired children. Communication acts were defined as gestures and descriptions of facial expressions and actions as well as vocalizations and verbalizations. The communication acts were analyzed for semantic function and communication intents and were compared to communication acts of the same developmental level but in younger hearing children. The investigators concluded that, although the deaf subjects were older, they were exhibiting communicative intents and semantic functions that usually are considered prerequisite to mature communicative competence. The hearing impaired children apparently were following the same continuum of language development as hearing children but at a delayed rate of language development; there were no indications that their development was divergent from normal patterns of language development.

The studies on the development of gesture systems in young deaf children are limited in number but suggest some interesting trends. Gesture usage seems to parallel but also diverges somewhat from the expectations of normal language development. Similarities are shown by the strong emphasis on action strings over attribute strings. These action strings reflect understanding of semantic characterizations known to very young hearing children, that is, causative and affective verbs and recipients. Gesture systems of deaf children may tend to be organized with semantic rather than word order focus, which may affect the learning of spoken English in older deaf children.

SEMANTIC DEVELOPMENT

Vocabulary Development

Although most studies indicate that semantic development in deaf children is similar to, but slower than, that of hearing children, few investigators have described the characteristics of deaf children's first lexicons to determine if they are comparable to the characteristics of first lexicons in hearing children. Schafer and Lynch (1980) observed four prelingually deaf children during the period when expressive language emerged. The children were 15 to 34 months old, had hearing parents, and were enrolled in private preschool programs. Two children were enrolled in an oral program, and two were enrolled in a total communication program. Studies of normal children report that youngsters use from 20 words (Lenneberg, 1966) to 50 words (Nelson, 1973) by 18 months of age. The subjects in the Schafer and Lynch (1980) study were using only 0 to 9 words at 18 months. However, by approximately 22 months of age, the two children in the total communication program used 58 and 62 signed or spoken words (or both), respectively, and the two children in the oral program used 13 and 8 spoken words, respectively. Schafer and Lynch found a commonality in the words first used by the deaf children in their study and in the first words used by hearing children (Bloom, 1973). Like hearing children, the deaf children signed or spoke of people important in their lives (*Mamma, Daddy*); they signed or spoke of objects that they could manipulate, such as *shoe* and *sock*, and they named both objects and actions whose movement was apparent, such as *cat, dog, open, move,* and *hop*. This tendency was also reported in the investigations by Clark (1973) and Nelson (1973).

Some differences were noted between the deaf subjects in the Schafer and Lynch study and hearing children. The deaf children used words expressing color and number earlier than did the hearing children; this usage, however, could reflect a common trend in the language curricula of the total communication program and the oral program. An obvious difference was in the speed of language acquisition; the deaf children were delayed in language development compared with hearing children. This delay was most obvious in the onset of two-word utterances. The MLU of hearing subjects in the Bloom, Lightbown, and Hood (1975) study was 1.0 to 2.0 at a chronological age of 19 to 24 months. Schafer and Lynch (1980) found their subjects to be about 8 months delayed in acquiring language. It should be noted that these children were diagnosed as being deaf sometime after they were 5 months old and that the children in the total communication programs were not exposed to a signed language environment until after 12 months of age.

Results of the Schafer and Lynch study (1980) indicated that a significant difference existed between deaf and hearing children, which was apparent in the overall reduced linguistic output and the slower rate of linguistic development. These results were similar to those found by Caselli (1983) but did not support the conclusions reached by Schlesinger and Meadow (1972), Gardner and Zorfass (1983), and Stoloff and Dennis (1982), who reported larger lexicons and only a slight delay in developmental stages. However, the investigators of the few studies on the language acquisition of young deaf children all agreed that the developmental stages for language acquisition were the same regardless of the hearing status of the child. These studies also seemed to indicate that the use of sign language was effective for primary language development if (1) it was used consistently in the home, and (2) its practitioners used structures that followed the developmental patterns of hearing children.

Later Vocabulary Achievement

The vocabularies of deaf students usually contain far fewer lexical items than those of their hearing peers (Odom, Blanton, and Nunnally, 1967; Walter, 1978), their knowledge of common content words is deficient (Walter, 1978), and they have a great deal of difficulty with English function words (Odom, Blanton, and Nunnally, 1967). DiFrancesca (1972) stated that most deaf students 18 years old and younger score at or below a fourth grade level on vocabulary achievement tests. Several studies have been conducted to describe the vocabulary levels of deaf children and to compare them with the vocabulary levels of hearing children. The conclusions reached by the investigators (Cooper and Rosenstein, 1966; DiFrancesca, 1972; Simmons, 1962; Walter, 1978) have been discouragingly consistent—that is, that the vocabulary levels of deaf children are far below those of their hearing peers. Cooper and Rosenstein (1966) found that the average vocabulary level of deaf 18-year-old person was comparable to that of a 9-year-old hearing child.

Development of Semantic Structure

Several studies investigating the knowledge of words and word classes in deaf children and adolescents have been conducted and have indicated that within the limits of their vocabularies, deaf students have some understanding of the gross distributional properties of English lexical items (Odom, Blanton, and Nunnally, 1967; MacGinitie, 1964). However, their functional knowledge of semantic information and of finer syntactic properties of lexical items is extremely limited (Odom, Blanton, and Nunnally, 1967; Walter, 1978); many of the studies conducted used cloze procedures (deleting a word at specified intervals) to determine knowledge of words and word classes, and results indicated that deaf students frequently select words from appropriate syntactic categories (e.g., nouns, verbs, adjectives) to complete sentences, but they often choose inappropriate words from within those categories. They appear to exhibit a knowledge of category membership but lack the knowledge necessary to make appropriate judgments of semantic information involving finer syntactic properties of words (Bochner, 1982). Marshall (1970) found that contextual support somewhat improved deaf children's performance on cloze procedures, although even when maximum contextual support was provided, performance was still inferior to that of their hearing peers.

Green and Shephard (1975) used a semantic differential procedure in an attempt to describe the semantic structure of language in deaf students. The results indicated that the semantic system of deaf children contained dimensions evident in semantic systems of hearing children 2 to 5 years younger. Hearing children demonstrated a more diverse semantic system, which apparently enabled them to exercise more options when making semantic judgments. Several researchers (Hughes, 1966; Templin, 1950; Wright, 1955) have reported that deaf subjects experienced considerably more difficulty than hearing children in abstract tasks. Green and Shephard (1975) observed that the factors present in the semantic system of hearing children could be classified in terms of a concrete-abstract continuum; they were able to deal with abstract judgment as early as 7 years of age. Deaf subjects, however, exhibited a semantic structure heavily weighted toward or even restricted to those factors concerned with concrete judgments. The performances of hearing subjects were distributed more evenly over several factors.

Kantor (1980) investigated the acquisition of classifiers in American Sign Language (ASL) in nine young deaf children of deaf parents. The subjects were 3 to 11 years of age. The uses of classifiers are linguistically complex, requiring semantic, syntactic, and cherological (phonological) information for correct choice and function on the part of the user. Classifiers are structures not present in the English language and, thus, provide a means for investigating the acquisition process without interference from the child's exposure to English. ASL classifiers appear as part of syntactic forms (either the verb or the noun) and reflect semantic properties of their noun referent. The classifiers observed by Kantor in this study were *by-legs*, *vehicle*, and *stationary-object-taller-than-wide*. The order of acquisition of the three classifiers was *vehicle*, *tall-upright*, and *by-legs*. Children as young as 3 years of age recognized the environments requiring classifier usage. They never attempted to use a classifier in an inappropriate environment and always matched semantically the classifier type to its object domain. The three classifiers were acquired not as lexical items but as a part of a complex syntactic process, as is indicated by the fact that apparently acquired classifiers were not articulated in certain syntactic environments. The semantic and syntactic domain for each classifier widened as the children matured.

The child's acquisition of sign parameters did not appear to be a simple matter of incremental ability to control the weaker digits of the hand; rather, it appeared that complex interactions among the various components of the language influenced their acquisition. The children were able to use certain handshapes and orientations in many instances of nonclassifier signs, but they were not able to use the same parameters in classifier signs. For example, the children could use the V handshape for the sign *see* and the numeral 2 but not for the *by-legs* classifier. These data also indicated that there was a tendency on the part of the children to revert to early, motorically simpler handshapes when they were confronted with complex semantic and syntactic decisions. Kantor's study (1980) investigating a semantic-syntactic aspect of sign language acquisition suggested that hearing impaired children are capable of dealing appropriately with complex linguistic decisions at a very young age.

Later Semantic Development

Word association tests and semantic differential scales have been given to deaf children and young adults in attempts to gain insight into their vocabulary learning and lexical organizations. The basic finding has been that verbal associations of hearing impaired subjects differ from those of hearing individuals, with the word associations of deaf subjects frequently resembling those of younger, hearing children (Blanton, 1968; Koplin, Odom, Blanton, and Nunnally, 1967). The results of these studies suggest that deaf and hearing individuals differ with respect to the organization and acquisition of lexical information. Both sensory (the role of audition in experiencing the world and acquiring knowledge) and learning factors (the role of formal vocabulary teaching as opposed to natural verbal learning) have been mentioned as possible causes of this difference (Blanton, 1968; Nunnally and Blanton, 1966). However, Tweney, Hoemann, and Andrews (1975) indicated that word sorting data implied that the difference between the semantic organization of deaf and hearing adolescents is not generalized across the entire lexicon; rather, this difference appears to be limited mostly to semantic domains with which deaf people have little experience, such as words associated with auditory imagery. Regardless of limitations noted by Tweney and colleagues, differences do seem to exist between the performances of deaf and hearing individuals on verbal association, and these differences have been attributed to the effects of hearing loss on learning and information processing.

SYNTAX AND MORPHOLOGY

Stage I

Sometime during the last half of their second year, hearing children begin to combine words and produce multiword utterances. The two-word utterance stage is usually considered to be the beginning of interaction between semantics and syntax. At this stage in normal language acquisition, the mean length of utterance (MLU) becomes a useful index of structural achievement. Many investigators, when comparing children with various handicapping conditions to nonhandicapped children, use MLU rather than chronological age as the basis for comparison (Miller and Chapman, 1981). As already stated, the mean length of utterance is used because children of the same MLU have made roughly the same amount of progress in language development even though their ages may be quite different (Foss and Hakes, 1978). However, the appropriateness of applying MLU, which is intended as an index of spoken language, to sign language, which is visual and spatial in nature, has been questioned (Siple, 1978; Wilbur, 1980).

The difference between visual and auditory processing of language has not yet been determined, and it is not known whether comparable MLUs indicate comparable language levels. The problem of how to determine MLU in sign language further complicates the issue. For example, if a child signs *Look at me* using a directional sign, only one sign is made (*LOOK*, pointing at own face). This sign utterance could be counted as one morpheme because only one sign was made, or as three morphemes, if the English interpretation of the sign utterance "Look at me," is used. An additional problem that is encountered if the match between hearing and deaf children is based on MLU concerns the ages of the two groups of children. In most cases the hearing impaired children would be considerably older than hearing children of the same MLU, presenting additional confounding factors, such as different cognitive levels and home or school experiences. Despite these problems, because of an absence of other language measures and a lack of empirical data concerning deaf children and MLU indices, the mean length of utterance may yield the best information obtainable at this time. In fact, Bellugi and Klima (1972) and Schlesinger and Meadow (1972) suggest that deaf children learning American Sign Language may be comparable to their hearing peers at the early stages of language acquisition.

Most hearing children acquire a vocabulary of 20 (Lenneberg, 1966) to 50 words (Nelson, 1973) before they produce two-word utterances which usually occurs at approximately 18 months of age. As already noted, Schafer and Lynch (1980), in their study of deaf children of hearing parents, found that at 18 months of age their subjects had vocabularies consisting of 0 to 9 words and did not begin to combine words or signs until approximately 26 months of age and older. The results of other studies, which reported language development of deaf children of deaf parents or of hearing parents who learned some form of manual communication early and used it consistently, indicated that the deaf subjects began to combine words at 17 or 18 months of age (Caselli, 1983; Gardner and Zorfass, 1983; Schlesinger and Meadow, 1972; Stoloff and Dennis, 1982). When they began to use two-word utterances, some of the deaf children were reported to have vocabularies of 20 to 30 words (Caselli, 1983) or 100 and more words (Gardner and Zorfass, 1983; Schlesinger and Meadow, 1972; Stoloff and Dennis, 1982).

Few studies are available that describe the characteristics of multiword or multisign utterances of deaf children. Layton, Holmes, and Bradley (1979) examined the multisign communicative units of young deaf children of hearing parents by using the coding scheme of Bloom, Lightbown, and Hood (1975) and comparing the results with those for the hearing children in the study of Bloom and colleagues by noting the frequency count and the proportion of different relationships used by both groups. The results indicated that the deaf children used proportionately different semantic-syntactic categories than did the hearing children when they were functioning at equivalent linguistic levels. In comparing the deaf children's order of semantic-syntactic relations with that of the hearing children, several observations can be made. For all of the children, the *action* category had the highest ranking, while *action + place* had the lowest. The deaf subjects used more state, *negation*, and *notice* units and fewer *attribution*, *locative action*, and *existence* units than did the hearing children. The categories of *place, dative, intention, instrument*, and *recurrence* were not productive for any of the deaf children. However, Bellugi and Klima (1972) in their study of Pola, a young deaf girl of deaf parents, indicated that she used all of the semantic relationships exhibited by hearing children of a comparable age. Pola, having deaf parents, had been exposed to sign language from birth.

Several other studies (Collins-Ahlgren, 1975; Hoffmeister and Moores, 1973; Schlesinger and Meadow, 1972; Wilbur and Jones, 1974) reported satisfactory language development when consistent home use of manual communication was employed at an early age. The deaf children in the Layton, Holmes, and Bradley study (1979) had not been provided with such an opportunity to receive language information.

Skarakis and Prutting (1977) used a sociolinguistic approach to describe the semantic-pragmatic components of language in the spontaneous communication of hearing impaired preschool children. Results revealed that the hearing impaired children exhibited the same semantic functions and communicative intentions as those described in young hearing children's communications.

Stage II

During Stage II, hearing children begin to produce three-word utterances, and a few inflectional endings and function words begin to appear between and upon the nouns and verbs spoken by the child. Hearing impaired children exhibit similar characteristics at Stage II of language development, which usually occurs at a later age than it does for hearing children.

Hess (1972) studied the language patterns of a hearing impaired child and a hearing child whom she had matched on the basis of language levels. She collected spontaneous language samples during mother–child play sessions. Data analysis revealed very few differences between the deaf subject and the hearing subject in the development of syntactic structures. Hess concluded that the deaf child exhibited a sequence of acquisition similar to that of the hearing child, with two exceptions: (1) the deaf child showed less differentiation in the subject form class; and (2) the deaf child was slightly advanced in the acquisition of structures leading to a negative sentence structure. Smith (1972) investigated oral language comprehension of hearing impaired and normally hearing children by presenting grammatical strings and having the children identify appropriate pictures. The children were grouped according to mean length of utterance (MLU). The results indicated that both hearing and deaf children with lower MLUs focused on the semantic relationships being expressed. whereas those with higher MLUs used both the semantic and syntactic information in the strings. The younger hearing and deaf children seemed to treat the test sentences as word strings; the older children, hearing and deaf, were using an actor-action-object strategy to process the sentences. These findings are consistent with the results of Sinclair (1973) regarding the effect of word order on language comprehension.

Geffner and Freeman (1980) assessed the language comprehension of 6-year-old deaf children, of whom 95 percent were in total communication programs. The results of the study indicated that although the 6-year-old prelingually deaf children in this study were past the one-word and two-word utterance stages of language development and appeared to be in the process of acquiring syntax, they were doing it at a slower rate than their normally hearing peers. Bornstein, Saulnier, and Hamilton (1980) also concluded that the deaf individuals in their longitudinal study showed no apparent syntactic development until they were approximately 5 years of age. Although the studies of sign language acquisition in very young deaf children present a more optimistic picture, most deaf children are born to hearing parents (Meadow, 1980) and do not have the advantage of early exposure to sign language. For these children, a developmental lag in language acquisition appears to be common (Kretschmer and Kretschmer, 1978; Moores, 1978; Quigley and Paul, 1984b; Russell, Quigley, and Power, 1976; Wilbur, 1977).

A review of research regarding morphological development in deaf children yields few pertinent studies. The presence of morphemes in certain grammatical constructions and the way morphemes are combined into words are determined by the morphological rules of a verbally based language. All children, including deaf children, must follow the specific language system if they are to produce meaningful and grammatically correct sentences in that language. Cooper (1967) evaluated the English language receptive and expressive abilities of deaf children with second grade reading ability, older deaf children, and hearing children. He administered a 48-item test adapted from Berko (1958). The deaf subjects were selected from a school in which an oral-only communication approach was used. He found that the 19-year-old deaf subjects performed at a level that was similar to 7-year-old hearing children. On the receptive test, he found that the order of acquisition of selected morphemes was the same for the deaf subjects as for the hearing subjects.

Gilman and Raffin (1975) evaluated the expressive acquisition of some common inflectional morphemes in 20 hearing impaired children 8 to 12 years old who had been exposed to a morpheme-based sign system, Seeing Essential English (SEE I). The results indicated that a definite order existed in the acquisition of the morphemes tested. It was difficult to attribute the performance of the children to their exposure to a morpheme-based sign code because the reading levels of the children were highly correlated with the number of years the subjects had been exposed to SEE I. It could not be determined if the results were a consequence of reading ability or of their exposure to a sign system that differentiated the various inflectional morphemes. The investigators observed that the difficulties deaf children exhibit with morphology may be, in part, a product of the communication systems to which they are exposed.

Raffin, Davis, and Gilman (1978) administered a test of morpheme-based concepts to 67 deaf children (6 to 12 years of age) who were exposed to SEE I. The results indicated that these children acquired the inflectional morphemes in the following order: plural -s, past tense

-ed, present progressive -ing, possessive -'s, third person present indica-
tive -s, comparative -er, superlative -est, and present perfect -en. The
performance of the children in this study was consistent with the findings of Gilman and Raffin (1975).

The results of these two studies differ from those reported by Brown
(1973) for young hearing children. The order of acquisition for -ing and
plural -s was reversed. It should be noted that the deaf children, during
the stages of morpheme acquisition, were considerably older than the
hearing children when they were acquiring morphemes. In addition,
the differences observed between the results of the studies with deaf
children and those obtained with hearing subjects (Berko, 1958; Brown,
1973) may have resulted from differences in the educational experiences
of the children. The order of acquisition reflected by the performance
of the deaf subjects may have been related to the order in which the
various morphemes were introduced or practiced in the classroom. The
data from an investigation conducted by Looney and Rose (1979), for
example, indicated that systematic instruction enabled groups of deaf
children to make more significant gains in the acquisition of particular
morphemes than did a group of deaf children who did not receive systematic instruction.

Kluwin (1982) investigated the probable sequence of the comprehension of written English prepositions. He used Clark's scheme (1973)
for predicting the acquisition of prepositions by normally hearing children. Clark predicted the acquisition sequence on the basis of a semantic
featural analysis of the prepositions and the application of generalized
principles of language acquisition. According to this scheme, hearing
children first acquire locative (place) prepositions, then temporal, (time),
and finally manner (telling how or to what degree) prepositions. In
general, the deaf adolescents in Kluwin's study followed the same
sequence of acquisition as did the hearing children. Native adult
speakers of English can distinguish English from non-English words
on the basis of patterns called morpheme structure constraints. Hearing
children recognize violations in these patterns by 4 years of age. Wilbur
(1982) investigated the development of morpheme structure constraints
in deaf children. The subjects, deaf children from 8 to 15 years of age,
were tested to determine whether they extracted these patterns from
their exposure to written English. The results indicated that first, third,
and fifth grade deaf students, ages 8, 10, and 11 years old, respectively,
performed significantly below their hearing peers at approximately 8
years of age. However, at the seventh grade level, the difference had
disappeared. It should be noted that the deaf subjects were approximately 15 years old and the hearing subjects approximately 12 years
old. The similarity in performance between the deaf and hearing students by seventh grade does not mean that the students arrived at their

knowledge in the same way or that they were making judgments in the same manner. It cannot be concluded that the cognitive processes underlying the performance were identical for both groups.

The information derived from this study has important implications for teachers. Morpheme structure constraints of the type investigated by Wilbur (1982) reduce the amount of independent information that must be remembered for each lexical item. That the deaf subjects in this study were able to identify these morpheme structure constraints is encouraging. However, it is distressing that such constraints apparently were mastered late in development. The results suggested that deaf students were operating without optimal memory processes during the crucial educational years. A lack of efficient memory coding affects not only language development and reading but also performance in all academic subjects that rely on effective language and reading skills. Therefore, the development of good memory strategies should be a primary educational objective, and procedures for improving it should be investigated.

In summary, the few studies regarding English morphological development in deaf children indicated that the order of acquisition was similar to that of hearing children, although much delayed. The results also suggested that classroom teaching procedures might influence this sequence. However, because so few studies have been undertaken, any conclusions must be viewed tentatively.

Beyond Stage II

Negatives

Hoffmeister and Wilbur (1980) reviewed studies examining the acquisition of negation in deaf children who used ASL. In early stages, deaf children seem to use the sign for *no* and the negative headshake. The emergence of the signs *can't* and *not* characterizes the later stage of acquisition. The deaf children used the sign for *can't* before they produced *can*; this same sequence of production is common in hearing children. Hoffmeister and Wilbur (1980) concluded that these developmental stages were comparable to those of hearing children (Brown, 1973).

Quigley and several associates reported the findings of an extensive investigation of the comprehension and production of English syntactic structures by deaf children and youth (Power and Quigley, 1973; Quigley, Montanelli, and Wilbur, 1976; Quigley, Smith, and Wilbur, 1974; Quigley, Wilbur, and Montanelli, 1974; Wilbur, Montanelli, and Quigley, 1976; Wilbur, Quigley, and Montanelli, 1975). Four of the questions that guided the investigation and that are pertinent here concerned the order of difficulty of syntactic structures, establishment of syntactic rules, developmental stages of syntactic rules, and acquisition of distinct syntactic structures.

The investigators found that the order of difficulty of the syntactic structures was similar, but not identical, for deaf and hearing children. Progressing from least to most difficult, negation, conjunction, and question formation were the easiest structures for deaf children to acquire. These same structures were the three easiest for hearing children to master, but in reverse order. The result was predictable on the basis of transformational generative grammar theory; they involve fewer transformations from deep structure to surface structure than do other syntactic structures (McNeill, 1970).

For deaf children, more difficult structures were pronominalization, the verb system, complementation (e.g., I lost the watch *that you gave me*), and relativization (e.g., The boy *who hit the girl* ran away). Hearing children also found this group of structures more difficult than the first group, although the order of increasing difficulty for them was pronominalization, complementation, relativization, and verbs. Transformational generative grammar would predict that the recursive processes of relativization and complementation would be difficult for deaf children, partly because of the departure from the subject-verb-object surface order that deaf students tend to impose on sentences (Quigley, Power, and Steinkamp, 1977). Verbs are difficult for both deaf and hearing children because of the inherent difficulty of the verbal auxiliary. Deaf children's scores on verbs were further depressed by their difficulty with passive voice, which not only contains the auxiliary but also requires a departure from the subject-verb-object surface order for correct interpretation. Deaf students found the disjunction (John went to the party, but Susie stayed home) and alteration (You can have chocolate cake or pumpkin pie) structures to be the most difficult, whereas hearing students had much less difficulty with them. Quigley, Power, and Steinkamp (1977) suggested that the problem for deaf students may be explained by the complex semantic nature of sentences containing these structures.

The results of this group of studies indicated that deaf students frequently impose a subject-verb-object pattern on sentences even when it is inappropriate. Given a sentence such as *The boy who hit the girl ran away*, a deaf student is quite likely to comprehend that it was the girl who ran away. A similar tendency for surface reading of passive sentences, in which the child interpreted the sentence as an active one, was reported by Power and Quigley (1973). However, the results of a study conducted by McGill-Franzen and Gormley (1980) indicated better comprehension when a different test format was used. They assessed deaf children's comprehension of truncated passive sentences (e.g., *The crop was destroyed*) under two task conditions. Subjects were asked to identify the agent-object relationship in truncated passive sentences, which were presented in isolation in the first task and embedded within familiar prose in the second task. Neither age nor reading level was a significant factor in deaf children's understanding of truncated passive sentences. Older and younger deaf students, regardless of reading level, demonstrated significantly improved comprehension when sentences were embedded in text.

A second question that the studies by Quigley and colleagues addressed concerned the establishment of syntactic rules of standard English in the language of deaf children from 10 to 18 years of age. The results indicated that most of the structures were not well established even among the 18-year-old students. Only simple transformations, such as negation, question formation, and conjunction, had been mastered to any significant degree. In contrast, hearing students had mastered all but the most difficult structures by 10 years of age, and there were relatively few problems with those.

Psycholinguistic studies have indicated that syntactic structures, such as negation, progress through developmental stages in the hearing child rather than emerging suddenly in complete adult form (McNeill, 1970). The question concerning whether deaf children progress through the same stages was investigated in the group of studies conducted by Quigley and his associates, with the investigators concluding tentatively that English syntactic structures develop similarly in deaf and hearing children but at a much slower rate in deaf children. These results should be considered tentative because the deaf subjects ranged in age from 10 through 18 years, making it difficult to separate the influence of formal teaching from environmental development.

Although hearing and deaf children appeared to be similar in several aspects of language development, one important difference in syntactic development between these two groups should be noted. This was the presence in the language of many deaf subjects of certain distinct syntactic structures that seldom or never appeared in the language of hearing subjects. Two previously mentioned tendencies of deaf children in the production and comprehension of language apparently account for these distinct syntactic structures. Deaf children frequently imposed a subject-verb-object pattern on comprehension of English sentences, including sentences in which this order did not apply (e.g., the passive voice and in some forms of relativization). They also tended to connect the nearest noun phrase and the verb phrase, which led to misinterpretation of many sentences, such as those containing embedded relatives (*The boy who hit the girl ran away*). These two factors, which suggest that the deaf subjects were processing English as a linear rather than as a hierarchical structure, probably account for a large part of the deaf child's difficulty with the English language (Russell, Quigley, and Power, 1976).

Wilbur, Goodhart, and Montandon (1983) studied comprehension of nine previously uninvestigated syntactic structures using a comic-book format to provide pragmatically appropriate contexts in which to test comprehension of the nine structures. The nine English structures investigated were why-questions, conditionals (e.g., *If it rains, we will stay home*), nonlocative prepositions (*Mary bought the candy for her mother*), indefinite pronouns (e.g,, *somebody*), quantifiers (e.g., *each, some*), modal verbs (e.g., *can, should*), elliptical constructions (e.g., *yes, it is*), reciprocal pronouns (e.g., *each other*), and comparative constructions (e.g., *John is taller than Bill*). These structures were investigated to determine the order of difficulty for deaf children; no attempt was made to determine the order of difficulty for hearing children or to compare learning patterns of hearing and deaf students. The over-all conclusion of this study, that performance improved as reading level increased, was consistent with data indicating that performance improves with age (Quigley, Wilbur, Power, Montanelli, and Steinkamp, 1976; Wilbur, 1977, 1982) and with reading level (Fruchter, Wilbur, and Fraser, 1984). The results also provided general guidelines for determining the relative difficulty of various English syntactic structures.

An interesting conclusion reported by the investigators was that the five syntactic structures that contained substructures (nonlocative prepositions, indefinite pronouns, quantifiers, modals, and comparatives) all seemed to be learned more as separate lexical items than as unified syntactic structures. This observation could reflect the results of scattered teaching precipitated by curricular decisions, which did not reflect a natural developmental order for language acquisition (Wilbur, Goodhart, and Montandon, 1983). A second observation made by the investigators was that when structures were being acquired in piece-meal fashion (as with the five structures mentioned previously), models of language, such as transformational grammar, which postulate the acquisition of rules rather than individual lexical items, do not seem appropriate. However, it is possible that when children's exposure to their linguistic environment is incomplete, they might be unable to deduce the grammatical rules owing to insufficient information.

Questions

Quigley, Wilbur, and Montanelli (1974) found in their study investigating English syntactic structures in deaf students that the developmental stages in the acquisition of question forms were similar to those for hearing children. The comprehension of yes-no question forms was easier than the comprehension of wh- questions, and tag questions (*We'll go, won't we?*) were the most difficult to understand. This is the same order of emergence found by Klima and Bellugi (1966) and Brown and Hanlon (1970) in their studies of young hearing children. The deaf children seemed to differ from the hearing children mostly in rate rather than in order of acquisition. The deaf subjects in this study had not mastered all of the English wh-questions forms (e.g., *who* or *when* used as an object) even at 18 years of age; this appeared to be a common structure for the 10-year-old hearing children.

Coordination

Taylor (1969) found that deaf students frequently attempted to use the conjunction transformation between the ages of 10.5 to 16.5 years. Her students generally did fairly well; however, even the older students still made errors. Common errors observed were omissions (e.g., *Susie bought a skirt sweater*), misplacement (e.g., *Susie went to the shopping center and met a friend ate lunch*), or overapplication (e.g., *Susie ate a hamburger and french fries and pie and drank milk*). The deaf students seemed to make steady progress in constructing sentences using the conjunction *and* from age 10 through 18 years and found conjunction rules to be among the easiest to acquire. However, other forms of conjoining, such as using *but* and *or*, were more difficult, and little improvement was seen over the age range tested.

Complementation

In a study of the written language of deaf students, Taylor (1969) found complement structures that differed from standard English complement forms. Many of these variances, for example, confusion concerning infinitives (*to played, The baby began cried*) were similar to structures produced by young hearing children (Menyuk, 1963), but deaf children exhibited them at a much later age. The same types of variances appeared even in the writing samples of 16-year-old deaf students.

Of the three recursive processes in English (complementation, relativization, and conjunction), Quigley, Wilbur, and Montanelli (1975) found that complementation was the most difficult and conjunction was the least difficult for deaf students. They also found that there were some forms of complementation that deaf students did not even attempt. On the forms of complementation that could be tested, performance was only at the level of chance. In written language samples, the use of complements generally increased over the age range tested (10 to 18 years old). None of the students produced subject complements, but 22 percent of the 10-year-old deaf students used at least one object complement, increasing to 92 percent for the 18-year-old students. Nearly all of the complements occurred with action verbs; very rarely did they occur with verbs of perception, and none occurred with stative verbs.

In a test of grammaticality of complement structures, Quigley, Wilbur, and Montanelli (1975) used as test items variant complement forms frequently found in the written language of deaf persons. They concluded that not only do many deaf students produce such distinct complement structures in writing (e.g., *Susie went to shopping*), but they also, in a test situation, judge these structures to be grammatically accurate.

The current body of research concerning syntactic development of deaf students is not large. Possibly the most crucial contribution to emerge from these studies is the evidence that deaf children acquire syntactic structures in sequences similar to hearing children, that they follow similar within-stage sequences, and that they acquire rule-governed structures that differ from English syntactic structures.

SUMMARY

The Need to Communicate Precedes the Ability to Communicate

Hearing impaired children, just as normally hearing children, engage in prelinguistic behaviors that seem to be intentionally communicative. Several studies indicate that young deaf children develop extensive gesture and pointing systems in their determination to communicate their needs and interact with others in their environment. Hearing children begin to accompany their gestures and pointing with vocalizations using consistent sound patterns, which, by the end of the first year of life, become familiar words. This sequence does not occur for deaf children, but the need to communicate is as important to them as it is to hearing children. Studies indicate that many deaf children continue to use their gesture and pointing systems, extending and elaborating them. Kretschmer and Kretschmer (1978) suggested that these systems become highly organized and possibly rule governed to a point that such systems must be considered as functioning in a symbolic way.

Interaction is Essential to Language Development

Deaf children and their parents must become active partners in communicative interactions. For an optimal language learning environment, deaf children must participate in communication rather than being only the target for language stimulation. Unfortunately, passive participation frequently becomes a pattern when mothers, inadvertently overcompensating for the auditory deficit, bombard their deaf children with language stimulation and dominate the communication interaction. Deaf children should be encouraged to participate, and their attempts at communication, whether gestures, pointing, signs, or speech, should be accepted and incorporated into the "conversation."

Prosodic Elements of Language Appear to Be More Important Initially than Words

Prosodic elements have been described as the first linguistic features to which hearing children respond (Lewis, 1959), as well as the first linguistic features acquired by hearing children (Lenneberg, 1966), as is evidenced in children's babbling, cooing, and jargon stages of language development. Menyuk (1971) found that mothers, when interpreting their children's prelinguistic vocalizations (e.g., a child's use of *ha* accompanied by emphasis of different prosodic elements in different situations), respond to both phonological cues and prosodic features. Stark and Levitt (1974) found that mothers exaggerate prosodic features with respect to stress, pitch, intonation, and word duration. Menyuk (1971) and Bloom and Lahey (1978) suggest that such exaggeration contributes to the child's understanding of the literal meaning and implications of language.

Deaf children are unable to perceive and utilize these elements as hearing children do, thus adding another difference in their language environment from that of hearing children. There has been little or no research on the effects of the lack of prosodic stimulation on language acquisition in deaf children. Some linguists (Baker, 1980; Bellugi, 1980) who study American Sign Language (ASL) suggest that particular mechanisms in ASL substitute for prosodic elements. If this is so, native ASL users might be conveying information (ordinarily conveyed through prosodic features) to the deaf child through a different modality (e.g., facial expressions, eye blinks, tongue movements, or speed and size of sign movements).

The Form of Adult Input Influences Early Language Development

For language acquisition to occur, there must be fluent communicative interaction between deaf children and mature language users. Studies of hearing mother–hearing child dyads have described the characteristics of their interactions. Mothers adapt their speech to infants by making phonological, semantic, and syntactic modifications that appear to be beneficial to the language learning process. Mothers also use language that is slightly more advanced than their children's, and they gauge their expressive communications in large part by the feedback they receive from their children. Many studies have found similar characteristics in deaf mother–deaf child dyads. Unfortunately, this is not generally the case in hearing mother–deaf child dyads. The key ingredient that is lacking is a shared communication system. Such a lack largely precludes fluent and comfortable communicative interactions, and studies indicate that the dynamics in these dyads differ from those described previously. The effects that such a different language environment might have on young deaf children and their acquisition of language is not known. However, it seems highly likely that, because it differs greatly from natural language environments, it would not represent optimal learning opportunities for the deaf child.

Feedback to Children on How Well They Have Represented Their Intended Meanings Is Important to Language Development

Deaf children, just as normally hearing children do, require positive reinforcement to maintain or increase a behavior. A deaf child may want some milk and may communicate this need by pounding on the refrigerator door. When mother opens it and the child points to the milk, a communication has occurred. If the mother either picks up the milk, gives some to the child, and signs or talks about the milk, or picks up the milk, shakes her head, and says "no milk now, not now," she has provided feedback to the child, indicating that she understood the communication. The child, then, has a strategy and a fair amount of confidence that it will produce results again, and the mother will have continuing opportunities to help the child grow in language development. Conversely, if mother ignores the pounding on the refrigerator door, the child soon becomes discouraged and frustrated and "gives up" trying to communicate, and mother has lost the opportunity to advance the child's language learning.

Deaf Children's Vocabularies Grow Slowly and Follow Patterns

Deaf children of deaf parents who have early access to sign language have been reported to acquire vocabulary, in the early stages of acquisition, at a rate similar to that of hearing children (Schlesinger and Meadow, 1972). Vocabulary growth was quite rapid, and by 19½ months, one deaf child had a vocabulary of 142 signs. Another deaf child, whose parents were hearing and learned sign language, increased her vocabulary from 348 signs at 3 years of age to 604 signs 4 months later. However, the Schlesinger and Meadow study included observations of only four children, each having select characteristics, and the results cannot be generalized to apply to the entire population of young deaf children until many similar observations have been recorded. For the most part, deaf children's vocabulary growth is a slow, laborious process, as attested to by the results of several studies (DiFrancesca, 1972; Odom, Blanton, and Nunnally, 1967; Walter, 1978). The same is true with regard to the contention that deaf children who are consistently exposed to ASL at an early age will acquire vocabulary and syntax at a rate similar to that of hearing children. Until more empirical evidence has been acquired, this contention can be presented as a tentative conclusion, but it cannot yet be presented as fact for the general population. A few studies, however, do suggest that the kinds of words or signs produced first by deaf children are similar in kind to those produced by hearing children.

Deaf Children's Syntax Also Grows Slowly and Follows Patterns

Studies of early language acquisition in deaf children indicate that semantic and syntactic elements begin to appear in their two-word or two-sign utterances, and most studies found that deaf children express the same semantic relations in their multiword utterances that hearing children do. Deaf children usually begin combining words or signs at a later age than hearing children combine words, with some indication that deaf children do not use English syntactic information to any great extent until they are about 5 or 6 years old. The development of English syntactic structures in deaf children seems generally to follow the same stages and sequences as in hearing children, although these occur at a much slower rate. The studies by Quigley and colleagues indicate that most 18-year-old deaf students have mastery over only a few syntactic structures of English.

At Least Some Basic Processes of Language Development in Children with Normal Hearing are Directly Applicable to Language Development in Deaf Children

Most studies of language development in deaf children suggest that they progress through similar stages and sequences in language growth as hearing children, although at a much delayed rate. Therefore, the processes that occur in normal language development might serve as a guide for practices with deaf children. For example, the emphasis in language learning should be on communication. The teacher's language should be somewhat more advanced than the child's current level; the child must be encouraged to communicate and be reinforced so that communication attempts will continue. Teachers, like parents, should perhaps respond first to the child's communication rather than to language structure and provide new language information through natural language processes, such as imitation and expansion. Additional language practices are discussed in Chapter 4.

CHAPTER 3

Historical Overview of Teaching Methods and Materials for Deaf Children

Although electronics, computers, innovations in teaching, and new understandings of the physiological functions of the ear and brain hold rich promise for the future in teaching language to hearing impaired children, it is critically important that educators understand the developments of the past. If they are to move forward, they must build on the foundations of experience. Many of the "new methods" for teaching hearing impaired children are re-creations of past innovations. This chapter is a summary of teaching methodologies that have been used in education with deaf children from two perspectives: (1) chronological development of teaching methods, and (2) development of language materials and devices. Some of the material presented is adapted from the extensive reviews by Nelson (1947), Bender (1960), Schmitt (1966), Moores (1982), Kretschmer and Kretschmer (1978), and Quigley and Paul (1984b).

TEACHING DEVELOPMENTS BEFORE THE 20TH CENTURY

From ancient times through the Middle Ages, history records very little acceptance of deaf persons as rightful members of society. Because of their inability to speak and to use the language common to the general culture in which they lived, deaf persons were considered to be unable to learn, and they were regarded, for all practical purposes, as mentally handicapped. It was not until the early 1500s that Girolamo Cardano, an Italian physician, philosopher, and generalist scholar at the University in Padua, Italy, noted that the "deaf and dumb" were

53

undoubtedly capable of learning a form of language "by reason, even as in a picture; for by this means...actions and results are made known, and as for a picture the meaning of another picture is formed so that by reasoning it may be understood, so also in letters" (Bender, 1960, p. 48). Thus, Cardano theoretically established the principle that language and thought could exist without the presence of speech and hearing.

A Spanish Benedictine monk, Ponce de Leon (1520–1584), is credited with being the first recorded teacher of deaf children and the founder of the first school for such children. Although there are numerous testimonials to Ponce de Leon's successes in teaching "deaf and mute" individuals to lead productive lives and to enter a variety of professions, including the clergy, the sciences, and the military, information regarding his teaching methods is generally from third-hand reporting. It is said that he approached the education of deaf persons in much the same manner as suggested by Cardano. That is, in lieu of teaching speech as the initial and primary mode of communication, Ponce de Leon used writing in association with objects to convey language and meaning. Speech was taught on the foundation of the pupils' mastery of the written form (Peet, 1851). Ponce de Leon dedicated his life to teaching deaf children; however, he worked alone. When he died in 1584, his teaching strategies died with him. More than three decades elapsed after his death before the next generation of teachers was recorded in history.

A Spanish soldier of fortune, Juan Pablo Bonet (1579–1620), and Ramirez de Carrion, a tutor for deaf children, are reported to have used a method of teaching that included fingerspelling as the initial and primary means of communication. Articulation of sounds and syllables was taught prior to an emphasis on reading and writing. Bonet stressed the need for adapting the environment to provide communication models for the deaf student, and he initiated the instruction of family members and peers in the use of fingerspelling as an additional means of communication. Bonet is also credited with advancing the theoretical work of Cardano and Ponce de Leon in the application of teaching strategies to develop thinking and reasoning skills through experiential learning and natural language activities. Grammar was taught through formal and structured methods, which included memorization and drill in the syntax of Spanish (Bender, 1960).

John Wallis (1616–1703) and William Holder (1616–1698), both Fellows in the Royal Society, initiated the education of deaf children in Britain. Holder's instructional approaches resembled those of the Spanish masters, beginning with writing and the manual alphabet as a means of teaching language and speech communication skills. Holder stressed speech reading as an art and emphasized the use of context for the discrimination of word forms that were visually similar. Wallis documented his instructional approaches as beginning with the functional language system of his students; that is, he used the gestures of his deaf students as the foundation for communication. He associated the gestures with the written alphabet and then applied the manual alphabet. His approach to language instruction included very structured sequential steps, moving from the classification of nouns to verbs and systematically on to other parts and rules of language structure. George Dalgarno (1628–1687), a theorist in language and communication, contributed significantly to the field in England through his review of educational practices, although he never taught deaf students. Dalgarno advocated the use of fingerspelling as the primary mode of communication between mother and child. He strongly urged mothers of young deaf children to communicate with their children in naturally occurring settings and situations using fingerspelling. As the children progressed in the acquisition of language, Dalgarno advised a more structured grammatical method of instruction (Bender, 1960; Schmitt, 1966).

The historical records of language instruction for deaf children during the 16th and 17th centuries provide only very sketchy accounts of the early developments. Bender (1960, p. 83) noted that the pioneer ''teachers worked in isolation without reference to each other. Yet the teaching situations were ideal for best results. Each teacher had a few children, from the most cultured and intelligent families. He was well paid so as to devote his whole attention to the education of these children over a period of years.''

Developments in the 18th Century

Teaching deaf children began to flourish as a profession in the 18th century, as more and more children were provided with formal instruction. As teaching opportunities increased, so did the controversies over methodologies. The Spanish, English, French, and German teachers all entered into the struggle for superiority and success, and professional jealousies flourished.

Henry Baker (1698–1774) established the first school for deaf students in Britain, but, like so many of his colleagues in this era, he did not record his methods of teaching. Despite his proclaimed success with deaf children in teaching speech and language, his methods as well as his school died with him (de Land, 1931). Thomas Braidwood (1715–1806) established a second school in Edinburgh in 1767. Although Braidwood also attempted to keep secret his teaching methodologies, Francis Green, the father of an American deaf child, reported that Braidwood used fingerspelling, signs, reading, and writing in his teaching. Speech instruction was initiated through the articulation of individual phonemes and gradually progressed to syllables and whole words.

Johann Amman (1669–1724) was a Swiss physician who began teaching deaf children in Amsterdam and published his methodologies and findings. The availability of his practices probably influenced persons such as Wallis, Baker, and Braidwood. Amman's approach was highly structured and systematic. He began by labeling objects in the environment and proceeded to other grammatical categories and rules, including declension and conjugation exercises. After students mastered the vocabulary and grammatical rules, they were permitted to apply these to sentence structures. Perhaps Amman's most notable contribution was the use of the mirror in teaching speech to deaf persons in much the same manner as it is used today. His practice in teaching speech to deaf pupils was also applied to work with people with articulation defects, aphasia, and stammering; he perhaps laid the foundation for the development of the profession of speech pathology today (Bender, 1960).

Jacobo Rodriguez Pereira (1715–1790), who was born in Portugal and later moved to France, is credited with being the "greatest teacher of them all" (Bender, 1960, p. 73). Pereira was, perhaps, the first educator to develop an "Individualized Education Plan (I.E.P.)," which was tied directly to his teaching fees. Upon the attainment of stated goals and objectives with his deaf students, he would receive his fee. Pereira used a one-handed manual phonic alphabet for the teaching of speech and a system of signs for communication only until speech could be developed. Language instruction followed a natural approach, incorporating question and answer exercises and discussions regarding daily occurrences, daily letter writing, and auditory training for those with residual hearing. He used environmental cues and problem-solving strategies to develop the mind and reasoning in the deaf students. Instruction in the formal rules of syntax was postponed until the student had mastered reasoning and communication. The reputed success of Pereira and that of the French educator Charles Michel de l'Épée were credited with changing the commonly used label of "deaf-mute" to the "deaf–speaking ones" (Bender, 1960).

de l'Épée (1712–1789), a French lawyer and priest, was greatly influenced in his teaching by the works of Bonet and Amman. His language instruction was highly structured and stressed the development of grammatical rules. Sentences for required communication were memorized and repeated for intelligibility. de l'Épée, using those signs or gestures that were used by his students, developed an expanded sign communication system following the grammatical rules of French. (This is similar in principle to the system of manually coded English now in use in the United States and known as Signing Exact English or SEE II.) Although he did not emphasize original writing skills with his students, de l'Épée had great confidence in their ability to use language as a means of meeting their daily needs. He developed the first dictionary of signs not only to facilitate the instruction of his deaf students but also to provide them with more sophisticated tools with which to communicate their wants. The accounts of de l'Épée's teachings include the use of dramatization, writing about actions just completed, and signing recalled events. Unlike his predecessors and colleagues, the Abbé de l'Épée was eager to share his work, and he trained others to teach deaf children.

Following de l'Épée's death, Abbé Roch Ambrose Cucurron Sicard (1742–1822), who had been a teacher under de l'Épée, was appointed to continue de l'Épée's development and recording of signs, which eventually resulted in a two volume dictionary arranged in categories of ideas or concepts. However, Sicard's greatest contribution was his unique approach to teaching language to deaf persons. Initially, Sicard would act out or pantomime an idea with his pupils. He would then sign the idea using the grammatical word order of French. The communication was then written down. Unlike de l'Épée, who used prefabricated sentences for memorization by the students, Sicard used a coding system of columns and numbers to formalize language into patterns. These patterns were called the "Theory of Ciphers" and provided a structure in which deaf students could construct original sentences using French grammatical rules. This provided a means for generating sentences, which, albeit by formula, was an advance over the memorization of sentences used by de l'Épée and others. The sign language system Sicard developed grew to the point of becoming extremely unwieldy and ineffective; however, his Theory of Ciphers was brought to the United States through one of his deaf students, Laurent Clerc, and presented to the American Instructors of the Deaf in 1851 (Nelson, 1947).

Developments in the 19th Century

At the beginning of the 19th century there was continued emphasis on the teaching of language as a subject. Structured approaches with memorization of rules and grammatical forms dominated. Toward the middle of the century, education became available to more and more children with hearing impairments regardless of family status or wealth. Methods of teaching language to deaf children were reevaluated and critiqued by several highly respected scholars and teachers, which resulted in a gradual shift from structured to natural methods of language development.

Joseph Watson (1765–1829) advocated the use of fingerspelling and natural gestures to supplement speech, speechreading, and writing, and he advocated the natural approach to teaching language. He used conversation and natural interactions as the means for teaching grammar and stressed the need for "naming of perceptions as they arise" (Bender, 1960). Another 19th century proponent of the natural approach to language instruction was Guilio Tarra (1832–1889) of Italy, who advocated that the control and knowledge of the rules of grammar be the expertise of teachers who could model these rules for their students by planned communication with the students. In Germany, Johann Baptist Graser (1766–1841) advocated the placement of deaf children into more natural settings for education. He, as with today's advocates of Public Law 94-142, could find no rationale for the separation of deaf children from their families and from their peers. In response to his advocacy, Germany initiated mainstreaming for deaf students in the mid-19th century (Moores, 1982). Perhaps the most accomplished educator of deaf children in Germany was Friedrich Moritz Hill (1805–1874). Hill was committed to the concept that deaf children should learn language in the same manner as hearing children. His approach to instruction stressed "experience before expression" (Nelson, 1947). Hill developed and expounded on several teaching principles:

1. Deaf children should be taught language in the same way that hearing children learn it, by constant daily use associated with the proper objects and actions. (As an aid to this, Hill developed a set of charts, each containing 16 colored pictures supplemented by a series of special readers.)
2. Speech must be the basis of all language, as it is with hearing children. Oral language must be taught first through simple but natural conversations between teacher and child and between child and child.
3. Speech must be used from the beginning as a basis for teaching communication.

Hill did not exclude the use of natural gestures as a means of understanding, but he believed that they could be replaced by oral language (Bender, 1960). He was also a great activist in promoting his teaching strategies through teacher training. Hill believed that deaf children need to experience the functional use of language and that language should be used whenever the need arises and the child is motivated to communicate. He believed that by using the natural method of language development, referred to as the "mother's method," deaf children would gradually approach the same learning styles as hearing children and could be educated in the same setting.

Education in the United States, as in Europe during this period, focused on methods and modes of communication. An 18-year-old graduate of Yale University, Thomas Hopkins Gallaudet (1787–1851), who received training in Paris under the tutelage of Sicard, adopted sign language as a mode of communication and became intrigued with the ability of signs to convey abstract thought. Following the lead of the majority of European scholars, Gallaudet adopted a very structured approach to language instruction and used Sicard's method of illustrating language through the Theory of Ciphers. He returned to the United States and persuaded Laurent Clerc, a deaf teacher in Sicard's school, to return with him to help establish a school. Both men had a strong French orientation toward the education of deaf persons (manual communication and structured language methods) and had little exposure to other methods of instruction. The American School for the Deaf was opened in 1817 in Hartford, Connecticut, through funding solicited by Gallaudet and provided by the state of Connecticut. Although not all educators agreed with Gallaudet's approach, establishment of a state residential school program for the education of deaf children promoted the use of sign language in the United States.

Language instruction at the American School for the Deaf followed the beliefs and practices of Gallaudet and Clerc. Language was presented in a manner similar to how foreign languages were taught to linguistic scholars. Grammatical rules and sentences were committed to memory, vocabulary was presented in isolation, and each was then classified, memorized, and rehearsed. As a result of the introduction of Sicard's Theory of Ciphers concept, teachers at the American School developed a set of diagrams or line drawings to represent grammatical relationships and syntactic rules of English. This approach was referred to as the "Hartford System" and provided a visual representation of English as the foundation of language instruction. The Hartford System also advocated the sequential use of pantomime, gestures, conventional signs, and the manual alphabet, followed by the reading and writing of spoken messages.

Following the founding of the American School for the Deaf, residential educational programs were established in several states. As the profession attracted more and more highly qualified persons, training became more diversified. A number of teachers traveled to Germany and England to receive specialized methodological training in oral and auditory approaches to education. Two prominent American educators, Horace Mann and Samuel Howe, traveled to Germany and visited the educational programs for deaf pupils in that country. They were so impressed with the demonstrated results of the oral approaches used in the German schools that, on their return to the United States, they campaigned for the establishment of an oral school in Massachusetts. Other prominent educators specializing in deafness traveled to Germany and tended to be less impressed with the results noted by Mann and Howe. However, their general concern regarding the speaking abilities of deaf students did motivate the American School for the Deaf to add formal speech training and hire a teacher of speech as a key member of the faculty.

Through the efforts of Gardiner Greene Hubbard, a Massachusetts lawyer and the father of a deaf child, and the endowment of John Clarke, a residential school (The Clarke School for the Deaf) was established in Northampton, Massachusetts, in 1867. It was the intent of Hubbard that the Clarke School provide education for those children who became deaf after the age of 3 years and who could access language through the oral methods. At that time, oral approaches generally were considered ineffective for congenitally deaf children. Congenitally deaf children were expected to attend the American School for the Deaf and postlingually deaf children to attend the Clarke School for the Deaf.

Owing to the influence of the French method of teaching, nearly all the early approaches in language instruction in the American schools for deaf children were highly structured. Teachers during this time generally believed that the rote learning of vocabulary and grammatical rules provided the fundamentals for conversational language development. However, instruction did not provide the transition or application of the language principles memorized by the children to natural situations. It was assumed that generalization would occur once the rules were acquired.

Primary Lessons, developed by Jacobs (1858), superintendent of the Kentucky School for the Deaf, was a highly structured and systematic plan for language instruction. Preliminary skills were taught, including mastery of the alphabet and labels for 100 objects. Once the student had acquired these basics, nouns were presented in combination with adjectives, with the adjectives being repeated with various nouns, followed by the introduction of the verb "being." As the lessons progressed, the children were required to supply the nouns for prescribed sentences and phrases. The sentences were combined into stories or descriptions of pictures provided in the lessons. As the pictures were deleted, questions and original compositions were introduced, with modeling from previously presented narratives. Jacobs cited numerous advantages of his system over the structured approaches in vogue at the time. He suggested that *Primary Lessons* provided illustrations that simplified instruction and systematized teaching into small, graduated steps (Jacobs, 1858).

The most widely used language system in the mid-1800s was developed by Dr. Harvey P. Peet. Peet's system was founded on two basic criteria: (1) ideas preceded words; and (2) different concepts should be introduced one at a time (Nelson, 1947). As in Jacob's system, Peet proposed small, structured, sequential steps in the development of language. The system began with labels for familiar objects (nouns), after which adjectives were used with the nouns, followed by the introduction of the participle verb form. The children were presented with the language models through speech, the manual alphabet, and writing. The reading lessons reflected the language principles being taught. Question forms, such as *who, what, where,* and *when,* were introduced within each of the language lessons (Peet, 1869).

Several other teachers developed structured language systems during this time (Nelson, 1947); however, pleas for the use of less structured and less grammatically oriented methods were appearing simultaneously (Schmitt, 1966). Emphasis on teaching language through incidental occurrences, particularly during the early years of the child's development, was advocated by Turner in 1853. Porter (1869) spoke strongly for the merging of the natural and structured approaches to teaching language, encouraging more focused attention to the student's needs as determined by the situations and the settings. The practice and rehearsal of language in natural settings was thought to be the best means of language acquisition, according to the theories of Prendergast and Marcel (Fay, 1867).

Marcel (Storrs, 1880) developed a philosophy of instruction that was based on the observation that deaf children could comprehend short messages through facial expressions, gestures, and inflections. Thus, the wholeness of the message should be the foundation for language instruction. Sentences and phrases were presented in print, and the children were required to memorize the sentences. New sentences were introduced using the same basic sentence patterns that were already mastered, thus expanding the child's vocabulary in a functional manner. The sentence patterning model continued until the child was able to generate original sentences in grammatically appropriate sequence (Brock, 1868).

In a similar fashion, Prendergast (Fay, 1867) developed programs for language development that addressed the child's natural propensity for language. Prendergast stressed the need for language models that were of immediate use to the student and for which grammatical illustrations could be devised for clarity of meaning and use. He prepared guidelines for the teacher to present the child with relevant sentences or phrases. The child was required to imitate the sentence and rehearse and memorize statements for use in naturally occurring contexts (Fay, 1867).

The natural approach to teaching language was championed in the 1880s by David Greenberger, principal of the Lexington School for the Deaf in New York. He found the memorization of rules and structures distasteful and meaningless and encouraged the development of language through the use of sentences in daily activities with the children.

Accepting the principles of the "mother's method" advocated by Hill (Baldwin, 1925), Greenberger thought that the child was more likely to acquire language efficiently and effectively through the need for expression than through the imposition of expression externally. In lieu of prescribed vocabulary lists for instruction, he argued for words and grammatical structures in the context of the situation and needs of the child at the time (Greenberger, 1879).

In 1872, Alexander Graham Bell accepted the responsibility for the education of a 5-year-old congenitally deaf child. In his instruction, Bell used play, which he believed was the most natural thing for a young child to do, as his tool for motivating the use of language. Because the child could not access natural language through the usual auditory means, Bell provided visual language through writing. His written presentations were both informal, referring to the activities occurring, and formal, with the students practicing what had been experienced in play. Rhythms and intonations of speech patterns were illustrated by grouping words into patterns and varying the size of the script to indicate degrees of loudness or stress. (These techniques are similar to some employed later by van Uden, 1970.) Expressive communication by the child was not forced but was encouraged as the child needed it. While speaking in normal conversational sentences, Bell used an "alphabet glove" and visual speech to provide a wider range of access to the oral language occurring in the child's environment. It is reported that the child developed language in the same manner as hearing children, and by the age of 7 years, he was able to express himself in writing with very appropriate English structure (Bell, 1883).

Westervelt (Westervelt and Peet, 1880), a teacher at the Rochester School for the Deaf in Rochester, New York, was most likely influenced by Greenberger's and Bell's approaches and was also committed to the development of language in naturally occurring situations. In his work with deaf preschoolers, ranging in age from 4 to 7 years, Westervelt used play, games, toys, and daily activities as his "curriculum" for language development. The uniqueness of his approach, in contrast to Greenberger's and Bell's, was that he used fingerspelling as an initial mode of communication in addition to speech. Westervelt presented new vocabulary and phrases to the preschoolers by fingerspelling the entire phrase. Words were repeated and modeled for the students until the child began reproducing the fingerspelling and the spoken word. Westervelt found no prerequisite for teaching the fingerspelled alphabet to the youngsters. The communication system of speech and fingerspelling developed by Westervelt in the 1880s is currently referred to as the Rochester Method (Nelson, 1947) and was used in the Soviet Union in the 1950s under the name of neo-oralism (Morkovin, 1960).

Although an increasing number of individuals advocated the natural approach in language instruction, the majority of educators were reluctant to change and were skeptical of the methods used in natural language instruction. Many remained committed to structured methods. Various types of teaching techniques were used to help students comprehend the grammatical aspects of English. Visual displays were used as mnemonic devices for the practice of linguistic structures, a means of making rules of an auditory language visible.

Frederick Barnard was one of the first American teachers of deaf students to publish a system of grammatical symbols that represented substantives, assertion, attribution, and influence (Barnard, 1836). Six basic line and curve symbols were used to depict word relationships. Although the system may have been very effective for Barnard, a teacher at the American School for the Deaf in 1831, it proved to be too complex and cumbersome for use with young deaf children. Barnard abandoned his system and went on to become the President of Columbia University. However, the teachers at the American School, already familiar with Clerc's teachings, may have been influenced by Barnard as well. They developed a simplified system of diagrammatic lines, referred to earlier as the Hartford System.

Richard Storrs refined and adapted the Hartford symbols into a more systematic format. A set of 47 symbols provided the student with visual grammatical patterns and relationships. The Storrs Symbols (Porter, 1868; Storrs, 1880) were box-like figures that could be written above words or constructed so that the children filled in the ''formula'' with the appropriate grammatical structures. Using the common practice of memorization, language was learned by mastery of sequential principles of grammatical structures. Storrs contended that deaf children were unable to learn the complex structures of language through the natural methods but were able to memorize formulas or patterns of grammar that could serve their daily communication needs (Moores, 1982). The Hartford System and the Storrs System were extensions and translations of Sicard's Theory of Ciphers.

The Wing Symbols (*Course of Study*, 1918) were developed by George Wing, a teacher at the Minnesota School for the Deaf in 1883, and were published in 1887. The symbols consisted of letters, numbers, and line figures representing forms and functions of words in a sentence. The symbols represented four basic categories: (1) S = Subject and V = Verb, with three modifications of the verb ,including the verb as a transitive, intransitive, or passive; (2) O = Object; (3) AC = Adjective complement; (4) N = Noun and pronoun complement (Kretschmer and Kretschmer, 1978; Schmitt, 1966). Numbers were used for modifying forms, and six connective symbols and 14 special line figure symbols were used as indicators for verb tense, possessives, and other linguistic components. The Wing Symbols (Wing, 1887) emphasized the instruction of grammar through the relative position of each word in a sentence. The goal of using symbols, as stated in the manual (Nelson, 1947), was to give teachers a tool with which they could teach the essential components and functions of the modifying forms in the correct order in a way that could be easily understood by the students. It was also believed that the students would be able to memorize the *forms* of sentences, thus eliminating the memorization of specific sentences. The Wing Symbols were used as soon as the child was able to write. An account of the sequence of instruction can be found in the *Course of Study* (1918) and also in Nelson (1947).

One of the most popular systems in the late 1800s was introduced in 1893 by Katherine Barry and was called the Barry Five Slates (Barry, 1899). Her system was based on a grammatical, structured approach to teaching language. She attempted to develop a visual pattern of grammatical models so that deaf children could rely on sight rules just as hearing children relied on auditory rules of language. Five large slates were used to structure language into patterns similar to the five columns used by Sicard and illustrated in the Theory of Ciphers. Each slate represented one of the following: (1) the subject of the sentence, (2) the verb, (3) the direct object, (4) the preposition, and (5) the object of the preposition. A sixth slate was added later for expanded sentences, including time words and phrases.

At the beginning of language instruction, the children's names were recorded on the first slate, along with the names of familiar and required objects. The subject slate was labeled as the "Who and What" slate. The second slate was added for the instruction initially of the intransitive action verb, with the heading "What doing." The third slate, object of the sentence, posed the question "Whom" and "What." "Where" was used as the preposition heading for the fourth slate, and "Whom" and "What" headed the fifth slate as the object of the preposition. As the child mastered the elemental skills by completing the responses to the headings, numbers were used to replace the headings (Kretschmer and Kretschmer, 1978). Nelson (1947) noted that Barry's book was the first ever published and sold commercially that provided teachers with a total plan for the development of language with young deaf children. The Barry System was used in nearly every school for deaf children in the United States for many years and was immensely popular with teachers. *Fokes Sentence Builder* (Fokes, 1982) materials follow the principles of patterning set forth by Barry.

Other types of patterning systems were used in the late 1880s including Robinson's "key-system" in 1896, which used question form indicators to elicit language in patterned grammatical structure. Most of these systems tended to be unique to the developers and never seemed to be adopted by other professionals in the field. Underlying each of the systems was the hope that the visual representation of rules of language would provide the deaf child with the form and function of English that could not be accessed through the auditory channel.

THE 20TH CENTURY

At the beginning of the 20th century, the search for the most effective means of teaching language to deaf children gained momentum. The most frequently used and most widely known language training system in the United States in the early part of the century was developed by Edith Fitzgerald, a teacher at the Wisconsin School for the Deaf, who was herself deaf. The Key, as it was popularly named, was an expansion and an elaboration of the Barry Five Slate System. The objective in using the Key was to give deaf students a tool with which they could follow the rules of English, construct their own sentences, and evaluate their productions in composition (Fitzgerald, 1929).

The Key had six columns, each labeled with interrogative words and symbols that indicated grammatical structures and functions. The grammatical headings used were the following: (1) subject (*Who, What*), (2) verb and predicate words (=), (3) indirect and direct objects (*What, Whom*), (4) phrases and words denoting place (*Where*), (5) other phrases and word modifiers of the main verb (*For, From, How, How Often, How Much,*), (6) words and phrases telling time (*When*). The use of connective symbols adapted the use of connective phrases and clauses into the basic pattern outlined for the students. Fitzgerald claimed that the Key was a significant improvement over the Five Slates, as it could respond to greater complexity in sentence structures than Barry's system, was more flexible in application to various grammatical forms, and was more adaptable to the needs of the child. She also believed that the child familiar with the Key concepts and structures could be independent of the teacher for expression. The popularity of the Key extends into present day methods of teaching, and it can still be found in many of the instructional programs for deaf children. A more detailed discussion of the use of the Fitzgerald Key as a structured approach to teaching language is presented in Chapter 5.

Although the practices of Sicard and Clerc continued to influence the majority of educators of deaf students for nearly a century through the use of grammatically based and visually structured systems, a committed minority continued to advocate the need for more natural means of teaching deaf children. With an increase in the knowledge base of both child psychology and the psychology of learning and the need for a better means to teach language to deaf children, a growing number of teachers adopted the commitment of the Lexington School for the Deaf to provide deaf children with natural language. In the footsteps of her predecessor, Greenberger, Mildred Groht, an educator and principal at the Lexington School for the Deaf, introduced a "new" Natural Method, a somewhat radical approach for the era.

At the International Congress on Education of the Deaf in 1933, Groht outlined the principles and procedures of the Natural Method (Groht, 1933). She considered language as an evolving process that continued to develop through natural interactions and occurrences in the environment rather than as a subject to be taught and mastered. Fundamental principles that she advocated included the following: (1) vocabulary and language must be based on the child's needs rather than on prescribed lists of words and language principles; (2) natural language is acquired through practice in meaningful situations rather than by drill and textbook exercises; (3) language use is best taught through conversation and discussion, writing of various types, and academic and skill areas of curriculum; and (4) when language principles require explicit teaching, they should be introduced through natural situations, then explained by the teacher in real situations, and rehearsed by the children through the use of games, questions, stories and other motivating events. In her book, *Natural Language for Deaf Children*, Groht (1958) stated:

> The present available language workbooks and textbooks for the deaf have consisted of analytical drills and exercises. As a result, most deaf children and deaf adults have been given a stereotyped, parrot-like, and limited use of language—a language without spontaneity, naturalness, or individuality. A system of language teaching that develops the memory, not the mind, will not attain for the learner the ability to use the language most needful to him in each and every situation in which he finds himself. (p. xi)

Although Groht did not provide a curriculum for the development of language with deaf children, she did insist that teachers of deaf children should have fundamental understanding of principles of language development and that they be able to apply these principles in natural situations and settings. A more detailed discussion of the natural approach to language instruction and Groht's method is presented in Chapter 4.

Sister Jeanne d'Arc (1958) proposed an alternative to the Groht model of instruction, which blended the natural and structured approaches. She contended that linguistic patterning was required to facilitate the development of linguistic competence. Her procedures used command forms, requests, and questions with basic patterns and variations of these patterns. The first pattern used was the verb-what relationship (e.g., *Close the window*); next, the verb-where pattern was used (e.g., *Come here*); followed by verb-what-where, verb-adjective, verb-whom, and verb-whom-what. Although the language curriculum and the knowledge of the teacher were highly structured, language patterns were presented to the children in natural settings and within functional situations emphasizing a conversational format.

Beginning in the 1950s and 1960s, the study of language through psycholinguistics and child development had a significant effect on the teaching methods used with deaf children. Although the differences between natural and structured approaches remained, the content of language expanded from basic grammatical patterns into transformational-generative grammar and phrase-structure rules. The dimensions of language expanded beyond surface structure to the deep meaning of language contained in the syntax and semantics of linguistic structures.

As a follower of the works of Groht and of natural language development and as a student of the psycholinguistic era exemplified in the writings of Chomsky (1957, 1965), van Uden expanded on the natural approach of teaching language to include a naturally structured use of language with deaf children. In his book, *A World of Language for Deaf Children*, van Uden (1970) emphasized the "maternal reflective method," which he defined as a means of developing the child's language through natural communicative interactions between child and caregivers. Whereas Groht stressed expressive natural language, van Uden emphasized the receptive aspect. He was also committed to the oral-auditory approach and to using only one language with the deaf child—that being the spoken language of the general society. Through the use of naturally occurring conversations as the basis for language development, as well as experiences, diaries, storytelling, and reading, van Uden believed that the deaf child would acquire the rules of grammar in a natural way, just as hearing children do. His natural approach, however, did not obviate the use of structure. In the reflective language method, emphasis was placed on the teachers' using suprasegmental aspects of speech with phrase-grouping, rhythm, and basic sentence structures mirroring or echoing the vocabulary and grammar familiar to the child.

Like his European and American predecessors, van Uden was committed to the idea that language for the deaf child was necessarily acquired through reading, that is, conversations conducted through the reading of written conversations. His conversations with children were recorded in writing using various sizes of script and spacing of words as well as line drawings to reflect the rhythms of speech and the intonations of the spoken message. He sharply criticized the use of contrived situations for teaching specific vocabulary and had great disdain for structured approaches, such as the Fitzgerald Key or any similar box-like construction patterns. He believed that such approaches fixed language into externally prescribed forms. In addition to limiting language development, the direct teaching of structure did not allow the child to internalize communication and its intent. van Uden encouraged communicative interactions between students and teachers and between students and students; he also supported the need for students to observe the natural interactions of others, thus giving the deaf child the opportunity to develop language in the same manner as hearing children.

Language instruction at the Central Institute for the Deaf (CID) in St. Louis, Missouri, also reflected the natural approach to language development (Moog, 1970) and the dawning of the psycholinguistic era. The CID language program was shaped by the theoretical premise of Lenneberg (1966) and of Smith and Miller (1966) that human beings have an innate ability to acquire language. The foundation for the teaching of language was that deaf children, like hearing children, had an innate capacity for language and that, with repeated exposure, deaf children could acquire language in the same manner and to the same level as hearing children. The basic tenets of the CID language program were summarized by Moog (1970) as follows:

1. All children, including deaf children, have an innate ability for learning the system of language through examples of sentences, from which they are able to induce grammatical principles.
2. The hearing impaired child needs to be allowed to go through the natural stages of language development. Language should be taught in the sequence in which normally hearing children give evidence of learning it.
3. Articulation of elements should be developed as a separate skill fitted to the language being used by the child.
4. Nearly all hearing impaired children have some amount of residual hearing, which should be exploited to the fullest.
5. The technique of expansion and imitation should be used by the teacher.
6. The motivation for learning language is the satisfaction gained from acquiring the ability to manipulate the environment by verbal means.
7. Hearing impaired children should be given the verbal language they need for talking to and interacting with each other. Then they will find it useful and satisfying to communicate with each other verbally.
8. The language that is learned can be useful and meaningful because it is based on the child's daily experiences, activities, and needs. (p. 59).

Streng (1972), using transformational-generative grammar as described in the works of Chomsky (1957), advocated a structured approach to teaching language in a natural manner. Because she believed that deaf children could not learn language solely through daily interactions with others, she proposed that the teacher be required to provide the structure and to guide the child into the acquisition of the appropriate rules of language rather than allowing the child to develop faulty generalizations. She emphatically stressed in her teachings that young deaf children should ''be provided with correct models of language.'' According to Streng (1972, p. xvii), teachers must be able to analyze the rules a particular child is using to compare the child's rules with the correct ones and to pick out salient points for clarification so that the child can be aided in reformulating concepts about usage.

Heidinger (1984), like Streng (1972), proposed that deaf children be provided with natural experiences and exposure to language that meets the needs of the child. In Heidinger's view, it is the responsibility of the teacher or language clinician to structure language naturally. In her book, *Analyzing Syntax and Semantics*, Heidinger updates the work of Streng and presents language acquisition patterns using transformational-generative grammar precepts. She expands on Streng's presentation and includes the principles of modern linguistics, including morphology, syntax, and semantic functions. The book and associated practice materials are designed for the preparation of teachers and are valuable resources for teachers and clinicians. Blackwell, Engen, Fischgrund, and Zarcadoolas (1978) present a language development program within the same theoretical framework as that proposed by Moog (1970) and van Uden (1970); that is, that deaf children have the innate ability to acquire language and that language cannot be taught but rather must be acquired through interactions, modeling, and imitation. Using linguistic structures proposed by Chomsky (1965), Blackwell and colleagues (1978) developed a grammatically structured method of teaching language within a natural framework. This program, known as the Rhode Island Curriculum, was first developed and used at the Rhode Island School for the Deaf. It presents language within four levels of acquisition: (1) exposure, (2) recognition, (3) comprehension, and (4) production. Within each of these levels the students develop language through five basic sentence patterns following transformational-generative grammar rules (Chomsky, 1965).

The general principles for the acquisition of language incorporated into the Rhode Island Curriculum (Blackwell et al., 1978) include the following: (1) Direction of instruction should always be toward the development of rules, both grammatical and semantic, that should be kept constant over multiple presentations; (2) when presenting new linguistic principles, always present them in relation to real-life situations; vicarious or representational experience is not sufficient; (3) emphasis should be placed on helping the child develop a grammatical strategy; (4) errors in production should be tolerated, as they reflect attempts by the child to master linguistic rules; when such errors are made, children should be praised for their efforts and provided with a target model from which they can gain new information; and (5) linguistic comprehension and production should always be viewed in light of the perceptual-cognitive understandings of the child (Blackwell et al., 1978). An expanded discussion of the Rhode Island Curriculum is presented in Chapter 5.

A widely used approach toward language instruction evolved out of materials that were developed by a group of teachers at the Iowa School for the Deaf. The *Apple Tree* curriculum (Anderson, Boren, Caniglia, Howard, and Krohn, 1980) consists of a set of workbooks that were intended for use as supplemental and practice material for teachers using the natural approach to teaching language. (*Apple Tree* is acronym for A Patterned program of Linguistic Expression through Reinforced Experiences and Evaluations.) The workbooks, however, have been adopted as a complete program for language instruction by many teachers and at many schools for deaf children. King (1984) conducted a survey of programs for hearing impaired students and reported that the *Apple Tree* curriculum was perhaps the most widely used commercial language program in the United States. The program provides practice through exercises in comprehension tasks, manipulation of grammatical patterns, substitution of grammatical structures, and production of sentence patterns. Ten basic sentence patterns are presented in the materials (e.g., N + V + Adjective) plus two transformation forms, negation and questions. A more detailed discussion of the *Apple Tree* curriculum is presented in Chapter 5.

Kretschmer and Kretschmer (1978) proposed a "remedial" language development program for use with children who have established an English language base. The program begins with assessment of the deaf child's spontaneous use of language in a variety of natural settings and under a variety of conditions, including spoken, signed, and written. Instruction is focused on the interrelationships among the various aspects of language, including the pragmatic intent, structural organization, and application of selectional features that designate which words are compatible with one another. Discrepancies between the child's spontaneous language and standard English are identified as either developmental delays or variances from to the standards for the child's peer group. Kretschmer and Kretschmer (1978) proposed an extensive series of decision-making steps that the teacher needs to take prior to planning language intervention. Instruction is based on a three-dimensional model of communication, including the cognitive, linguistic, and pragmatic aspects of the English language.

The *TSA Syntax Program* developed by Quigley and Power (1979) was a result of 10 years of research at the University of Illinois on the language structure of deaf students. In response to teachers' needs for materials addressing the acquisition of sentence structure by hearing impaired children, the *TSA Syntax Program* was developed as a natural approach. The materials are intended to supplement instruction for hearing impaired students in the comprehension and production of syntactic structures. Teachers' guides provide basic information on syntactic development and a variety of games and other activities for developing syntactic structures in natural situations. Workbooks provide intensive exposure to particular syntactic aspects of language in more structured situations. Diagnostic guides for assessing student performance on the *Test of Syntactic Abilities* (Quigley, Steinkamp, Power, and Jones, 1978) and relating it to development of language structure assist the teacher in identifying the instructional objectives most appropriate for the individual student.

Satisfied with the current instructional methods used for teaching language, speech, and academics at the Central Institute for the Deaf, but dissatisfied with the overall lag of hearing impaired children in acquiring language skills in comparison to hearing children, Moog and Geers (1985) attempted to accelerate or intensify instruction through a special project referred to as the EPIC Educational Program (EPIC is an acronym for the Experimental Project in Instructional Concentration). In lieu of manipulating the methods of teaching language to deaf students, the EPIC program manipulated the variables for instruction, keeping the methods constant. Using current research on effective teaching principles, the EPIC program focused on three variables: (1) instructional time allocated to the teaching of speech, language, and academics, (2) opportunity to learn, and (3) direct instruction (Rosenshine, 1979). The structure of the school program was revamped to allow the changes in instructional practices. These changes included flexible scheduling to accommodate greater amounts of time for teaching language, speech, and mathematics based on the individual needs of the students. The students were organized into homogeneous instructional groups for each area of study to facilitate increased time on task and to intensify instruction. Another major area was the development of a hierarchy of skills in each subject area, including language, that allowed direct teaching and control of the content of instruction. The teachers, therefore, used a structured approach based on the skills to be mastered before proceeding to the next level of skills. The reported results of the project have been positive. Those students whose instructional programming was manipulated and intensified showed a significantly accelerated rate of progress over that of the deaf students who were not included in the EPIC program (Moog and Geers, 1985).

Discussion of the Development of Instructional Language Methods

For the beginning professional educator, a walk through the history of the development of methods to teach language to hearing impaired children must be confusing. The historical pendulum has swung through the era of oralism, manualism, oral-auralism, oral-aural-manualism, and oral plus. Instructional developments have focused on the recurring themes of natural approaches and structured approaches. With each swing of the pendulum, it was and is hoped that an improved method of instruction will advance the ability of the deaf child to access and acquire language for the purpose of communication. The methods of instruction selected by teachers for use with deaf students usually reflect the social trends and prevailing theories of language. The early educational approaches, beginning in the 1500s and dominating the field to the late 19th century, focused on the classical grammatical models of language, which used structured methods involving rules of syntax and parts of speech. Through the process of direct imitation, memorization, drill, and practice, the deaf child was expected to reproduce language using correct grammatical forms.

The natural approach to language development of deaf children represents the opposite end of the spectrum. It is based on the theory that the capacity to develop language is an innate characteristic for every human being, and that deaf children are exposed to language in the same manner as hearing children. Rules of language are not taught explicitly; instead, it is assumed that the deaf child will acquire the rules unconsciously, through exposure, imitation, expansion, and expression, without the need for rote memorization or contrived language drills.

LANGUAGE MATERIALS AND TECHNOLOGY

The education of deaf children has continually been influenced by developments in technology. In a constant struggle to compensate for loss of hearing, educators have turned to external devices as a means of making auditory-based language accessible to deaf children. Concurrently with the introduction of various methods for language development, language materials were being devised to support the instructional systems. A number of textbooks, curricula, teaching manuals, and readers illustrating specific skills to be acquired by the deaf child were made available for teachers. It is not possible to review all of the past and present teaching materials, but some of those that represent innovation and change in the field are discussed here.

Among the earliest language textbooks for deaf children were those of Peet (1869), whose textbook series began with an initial vocabulary of 50 words that the students were required to master in writing and fingerspelling. As the students progressed through a series of lessons, vocabulary, phrase, and sentence building were introduced sequentially in systematically ordered patterns (Nelson, 1947).

The Croker, Jones, and Pratt *Language Stories and Drills* series (1920, 1922, 1928) can still be found in classrooms and school libraries for deaf children. The series consisted of four volumes of language practice exercises. Each book presented sets of four-page lessons, which included the following: (1) a story with new vocabulary and examples of the language objective to be mastered, (2) practice in writing questions to answers already given, as well as review drills of previous lessons, (3) comprehension questions, and (4) exercises using the new language objective incorporated in the lesson. Nelson (1947) states that the series had three objectives: (1) to provide a systematic course of language instruction, (2) to give deaf children school books as attractive as those of their hearing peers, and (3) to save teachers hours of needless drudgery in preparing materials. The series originated at the Clarke School for the Deaf and was known prior to publication as the Northampton Drill Story Method. These books were a landmark in the development of media and materials for handicapped children and formed the foundation for many of the special education materials in use today.

A set of two teacher-guide textbooks for deaf children was prepared by Buell (1931), a teacher and principal at the Lexington School for the Deaf. The books focused on supplemental language exercises for the elementary and middle school classes, using the Fitzgerald Key as a core curriculum. Buell prepared the texts to assist teachers in developing exercises for reinforcement of language skills. Several other texts for teacher use were developed as teacher guides in support of specific methods of teaching, including the Barry, Fitzgerald, and Wing methods; however, materials for direct student use were rare.

Teachers used numerous language activities and exercises to supplement the lack of teaching materials and to increase opportunities for children to experience natural language situations. Nelson (1947) listed a series of language activities that were in vogue during the first several decades of the 20th century. Many of these are still used.

1. News items. This activity is widely used in eliciting the child's ideas. Vocabulary and language can be supplied to help the child express needs and desires.
2. Educational trips. Language principles are built around the things seen on trips of various types.

3. Action work. This is one of the most commonly used activities. It is simple and tangible and can be used effectively in teaching verbs, prepositions, and pronouns. A child performs an action and then tells and writes what was performed.
4. Action sequence stories.
5. Prose compositions of all types.
6. Vocabulary notebooks.
7. Topics. These can be developed through the use of actual objects, toys, pictures, and reading stories.
8. Experience stories.
9. Descriptions of persons or pictures.
10. Picture stories.
11. Letters, notes, cards.
12. General conversations.
13. Short stories.

General availability of instructional materials for use with deaf children did not become a reality until the establishment of the Captioned Films for the Deaf program by the federal government in 1958. The era of special media and materials and of resources for adapting existing media for deaf individuals had begun. In 1966, as an outgrowth of the popularity and demand for better teaching materials for use with hearing impaired students, four Regional Media Centers for the Deaf supported by the Division of Captioned Films for the Deaf, United States Department of Education, were established to train teachers, produce instructional materials, and provide a network for information and exchange among educators regarding the use of media in the classroom (Stepp, 1981). These centers trained hundreds of teachers in the techniques of developing overhead transparencies, movies, and slide productions and in programmed instruction techniques. Eighty percent of the materials developed by the teachers focused on assistive media for the development of language.

The University of Massachusetts was headquarters for one of the Regional Media Centers for the Deaf. In addition to producing a number of sets of overhead transparencies for use in language instruction, social studies, and reading, this center developed a Visual Response System (Wyman, 1969). The primary objective of the system was to make interactive communication visible. Each student and teacher was equipped with an overhead projector with individual screens hung along the perimeter of the room. The teacher would present questions on the overhead projector, and the students could respond, with the added advantage of being able to see other students' responses simultaneously. The Visual Response System can still be found in some schools.

Perhaps the most extensive programmed instructional materials were the Project Life (Language Instruction to Facilitate Education) filmstrips. Under the direction of Pfau (1974), more than 300 filmstrips were produced for grades K through 12 for almost every academic curriculum. The materials were designed to support and supplement specific skills introduced through classroom instruction, but, as with so many other supportive materials, the Project Life materials were used by many educators as complete curricula. The filmstrips were preprogrammed with opportunities for multiple choice responses. Using a specially designed projector unit, the students received immediate feedback for the correct response. In addition, student responses were recorded on a small card for the teacher's review. The materials were concentrated primarily on language instruction and the control of language forms to improve the comprehension of information and reduce the barriers of reading and language (Stepp, 1981). Project Life material is now available commercially as the *PAL* (*Programmed Assisted Learning*) *System* (1986). An ESL-Spanish alternative and a variety of subject areas have also been made available.

The *Reading Milestones* series (Quigley and King, 1981, 1982, 1983, 1984) is the only basal-type reading program that incorporates linguistic controls while focusing on the interests and experiences of deaf children throughout the series. Syntactic structures are identified clearly and introduced in graduated steps of complexity. New vocabulary is introduced at a controlled pace to ensure that the majority of the words are easily accessible to the deaf student. Idioms and inferences are also introduced in a progression of complexity. The careful planning and research that has underlain the *Reading Milestones* system is recognized by teachers of deaf children as well as other special education teachers. Currently, *Reading Milestones* is the series used most frequently with deaf children (LaSasso, 1985). The scope and sequence of the program are based on extensive research regarding the language comprehension and the syntactic abilities of deaf children (Quigley, Wilbur, Power, Montanelli, and Steinkamp, 1976). The series consists of 80 textbooks with accompanying workbooks subdivided into eight reading levels, ranging from beginning reading through grade 4. The *Reading Milestones* system includes placement assessments, teachers' guidelines, and instructional strategies for each level.

Stuckless (1981) introduced the possibility of using real time graphic display (RTGD) as a means of presenting language to deaf children and supplementing the reception of English. "Real-time graphic display is the presentation of language in printed or written form to one person as it is being generated orthographically or through speech by another" (p. 291). The Telecommunication Device for the Deaf (TDD) and captioned films are just two examples of real time graphics. Through the greater accessibility and flexibility of computer technology, the RTGD is currently being applied at the National Technical Institute for the Deaf as a supplementary system for communication in classroom lectures. As the professor speaks, a stenographer records the speech verbatim. A computer converts the stenographic shorthand into standard English and displays the print on a TV monitor for viewing by the students (Stuckless, 1983).

The first major computer assisted instruction project for the education of deaf students was PLATO, a teaching system that included data-based management, individualized instruction, and numerous learning and evaluation programs in mathematics and language. The earliest program, designed for grades K through 3, had the goal of improving visual memory (Watson, 1979). A much larger component was the Basic Skills Learning System designed for young adults with language, reading, and mathematics difficulties. PLATO was developed at the University of Illinois and later operated through a centralized mainframe computer supported by the Control Data Corporation (Richardson, 1981). Because of high cost, only a very limited number of sites subscribed to the PLATO system. More recently, PLATO programs have become available for use on microcomputers and may, perhaps, be used in larger school systems serving deaf students. A second major time-sharing computer assisted instruction program was established by Computer Curriculum Corporation. Programs again focused on mathematics and language instruction for hearing impaired students.

It was not until 1984 (Rose and Waldron, 1984) that computers became widely available as a communication tool for instruction with hearing impaired children. As in regular education, but perhaps with greater speed and urgency, the microcomputer and its technology offered more hope for teaching language to hearing impaired children than large mainframe computer systems. LOGO (Papert, 1980), a graphics software program, was used with hearing impaired preschoolers (Grant and Semmes, 1983) as a means of introducing problem-solving and creativity experiences without the need for complex language structures. Stone (1983) also used LOGO for problem-solving with children 8 to 13 years old. Student cooperative projects in drawing with the LOGO "turtle" were thought to facilitate language development. Using adapted hardware with changeable words and pictures, students can construct sentences, fill in predetermined sentences, and reproduce short stories with graphic stimuli.

Prinz and Nelson (1985) have developed a technology-based reading, writing, and communication system for preschool and early language learners. The ALPHA Interactive Language Series includes a microcomputer-videodisk interface with additional hardware adaptations that allows very young deaf children to select a communique by pressing a series of picture keys. The words or phrases appear in print, signs, and animated graphics. The design and flexibility of the system allow for the print and graphic expansion of vocabulary. The theoretical aim of the ALPHA system is to provide deaf children with an opportunity to learn language in the same manner as hearing children do while accessing language through the visual input system. The system provides for exploratory learning and interaction through printed, pictorial, and signed messages. Research results indicate that young deaf children between 2 and 6 years of age and multihandicapped children had a significant improvement in word and phrase identification, reading comprehension, and sentence construction and writing after using the system (Prinz and Nelson, 1985).

Interactive microcomputers linked to each other are being used in a few educational programs for deaf students to promote language development and writing skills. Using unique software, such as English Natural Form Instruction (ENFI) developed by Gallaudet University staff (Peyton and Batson, 1986), students can send messages to each other, interact with the teacher through print, comment on or question information sent, or develop their own prose and poetry and receive immediate feedback.

The advent of computer technology in the education of deaf students has produced great anticipation of improved educational achievement. Unfortunately, the rapid expansion and use of microcomputers has outdistanced basic knowledge of the most effective means of using these systems for developing language. Only limited development of software that is conducive to developing language beyond basic forms or syntactic rules has occurred. Users have also fallen short in adapting what is available (e.g., videodisk, graphic displays, print materials) to the educational needs of deaf students. Simply purchasing the hardware and software is not enough. As was the case for Ponce de Leon, de l'Épée, Fitzgerald, Bell, Groht, and thousands of other dedicated educators, nothing less than excellence in teaching can be successful for development of language in deaf children.

SUMMARY

Several threads wind almost continuously through the history of language development and instruction for deaf children from the earliest to the most recent times (Quigley and Paul, 1984b, p. 20). These are (1) structured approaches to language development, (2) natural approaches, (3) combined approaches, and (4) development of special language materials and technology.

Structured methods treat language analytically and prescriptively, emphasizing knowledge of structure as embodied in rules of grammar. Through processes of direct imitation, memorization, and drill, usually within the framework of a strictly sequenced curriculum, the deaf child is expected to acquire a grammatically accurate version of the general language of the society. Examples of users of structured approaches to language development have been de l'Épée and Sicard in France in the second half of the 18th century, Clerc and Gallaudet in the United States in the early to late 19th century, and Barry and Fitzgerald in the United States in the first half of the 20th century.

In the natural approaches, language is treated holistically, and development is planned to parallel the sequence of language acquisition in hearing children. The deaf child is expected to acquire language principles inductively and unconsciously through constant exposure to appropriate language patterns in situations that are designed on the basis of the child's needs and interests. Rules of language are not taught explicitly, but the approach implies that the deaf child will absorb the rules unconsciously through exposure, imitation, and expansion without memorization or language drills. Some of the foremost proponents of natural approaches have been Hill in Germany in the early and mid-1800s, Greenberger and Groht in the United States from the late 19th to the mid-20th century, and many individuals in many countries in the present era. Natural approaches to language development for deaf children are at present the most widely accepted and advocated (although not, perhaps, the most widely practiced) in the United States and many other countries. The natural approach is treated at length in Chapter 4.

According to results of a national survey of programs serving hearing impaired students in the United States (King, 1983), respondents used combined approaches to language development more often than any other approach. The percentages of respondents using combined approaches ranged from 36 percent at the preschool level to 56 percent at the intermediate level. Only at the preschool level did a significant percentage of respondents (34 percent) indicate that natural approaches were used exclusively. By the time children reach 8 to 10 years of age, the users of many programs seem to feel a need to supplement natural approaches with more structured language activities. Although the authors of some recently developed programs tend to label their programs as natural approaches, examination reveals that often they are natural approaches that incorporate structured activities to varying degrees; they are, in other words, combined approaches. This is not surprising. As Streng (1972), among others, has claimed, many deaf children do not seem to be able to acquire English solely through daily communicative interactions with parents, teachers, and others, and they need some structured activities to guide them in language acquisition. Some recent programs that appear to combine natural and structured approaches to language development are those of Streng (1972), van Uden (1970, the maternal reflective method), Blackwell and colleagues (1978, the *Rhode Island Curriculum*), Quigley and Power (1979, the *TSA Syntax Program*), and Anderson and colleagues (1980, the *Apple Tree Program*). These and other combined approaches are detailed in Chapter 5.

Use of educational media, materials, and technology has prevailed through the centuries as an integral part of language instruction with deaf children. Although teacher-made materials and the chalkboard have been and continue to be the dominant resources, the field of education for deaf children has demonstrated notable and unique leadership in instructional technology. Specialized reading materials such as the *Language Stories and Drills* by Croker, Jones, and Pratt (1920, 1922, 1928) and the *Reading Milestones* series (Quigley and King, 1981, 1982, 1983, 1984) emphasize student accessibility to print materials through systematic introduction of linguistic structures, vocabulary, and concepts. The application of programmed instruction, computer assisted instruction, and real time graphics display represents a significant development in attempts to provide effective learning environments for deaf students. The ALPHA Interactive Language Series (Prinz and Nelson, 1985) and the application of interactive microcomputers for the development of writing skills by deaf students are just a few examples of the continuing search for improved and innovative methods.

C H A P T E R 4

Natural Language Approach: Principles and Practices

In 1958, Mildred Groht published a book, *Natural Language for Deaf Children,* in which she advocated and described a language program that embodies a "natural" approach for deaf children from preschool through high school. Groht's rationale and conceptual framework were essentially in agreement with approaches that are now supported by early childhood educators. At the time the book was written, there was much less information on language acquisition than is available today. Groht's approach can be traced back to that advocated by Greenberger (1879) in the United States and Hill (Bender, 1960) in Germany.

Groht (1958) understood that the real purpose of language is communication, and that, for deaf children to understand this purpose, they must be exposed to language through communication that occurs naturally in the environment. She also understood the psychological need for communication. She stated that there must be communication between the child and family members for the child to feel secure, wanted, and a part of family life. The same is true in a classroom setting. Language should be developed through communicating in a natural way, making full use of the children's experiences, interests, and needs. Groht maintained that language presentations should "never be done through the use of extraneous materials, drill sentences, or artificial exercises devoid of personal interest and entirely outside the child's need for the language being taught" (p. 22). She further stated that if language were ever to be vital to deaf children, it must be acquired by them not as a lesson but as a "meaningful approach to a very necessary, useful and happy way" of understanding themselves and their environment (p. 8). She cited classic examples of obstacles that can defeat children's acquisition of language before they begin. Her list included overanxiety on the part of parents, overly formalized attempts at teaching vocabulary, and "deadly" repetition.

Groht believed that the development of language should be accomplished by making use of the experiences, interests, and needs of children as facilitators of comprehension and communication. Through careful observations and much communicative involvement with the children, teachers should become aware of words and structures needed by each child to communicate effectively, and, in communicating with each child, the teacher should emphasize through *meaningful* repetitions those words and structures needed. In doing so, the child would receive numerous exposures in meaningful situations and would eventually associate the object, action, or event with the appropriate word or words, and he or she would then begin to use the words and structures spontaneously. Groht (1958) encouraged teachers to observe young hearing children to gain a background for teaching language to deaf children using a natural approach. She listed 11 questions for teachers to answer as they observed the children. Many of the questions listed by Groht (e.g., How did the baby first use words? What were the first words?) are questions that linguists and psycholinguists began to study and respond to in the two decades that followed.

ASSUMPTIONS AND PRINCIPLES OF NATURAL LANGUAGE LEARNING

In the past, the language goals for deaf children and the appropriate sequence for presenting activities to accomplish these goals were determined primarily by the intuition of teachers. Teachers often have considered, either singly or in committee, the words and language forms that are either the easiest or the most important for children to learn. These lists of words and language forms then became the language curriculum for the program. A review of the literature on normal language development that has been published during the past 20 years makes it clear that the intuitions that teachers have had concerning the order of difficulty and importance of different words and syntactic structures do not agree with the kinds of words and sentence relations that young hearing children use when they first learn to talk (Bloom and Lahey, 1978).

Teachers' intuitions about language learning have often resulted in prescriptions for teaching the correct adult model of a sentence instead of allowing the child to communicate by using a form that is appropriate child language. The rationale for teaching the correct adult model of a sentence was to avoid the establishment of incorrect productions. Thus, when teaching sentences such as *The boy is running,* the child might be taught and expected to imitate the entire sentence. A hearing child learning language would most likely say *boy run,* and this utterance would be accepted by the parents as an appropriate communication. They would probably respond to the child, *Yes, the boy is running,* thus positively reinforcing the child's language attempts. The natural approach to language learning for deaf children would endorse the natural response method, which coincides with the underlying principles of this approach. The basic assumption underlying the natural approach to language learning, although unproved, is that hearing impaired children develop language by progressing through stages and sequences in a manner similar to hearing children. The underlying principles, which provide guidelines for developing language goals and intervention strategies, are the following: (1) language involves interactions among the components of content, form, and use; (2) information about normal language development is the basis for determining language goals and intervention strategies; (3) language is learned through communication; and (4) communicative competence is the ultimate goal of language development.

Principle 1: *Language Involves Interactions Among the Components of Content, Form, and Use*

The first principle emphasizes the notion that language goals and intervention strategies must take into account more than language form or the morphological aspects and syntactic structures. Children talk or communicate because they have something to say, and focusing on teaching form apart from meaning would be an empty and wasteful activity. Unless children attach meaning to the words and structures that they can generalize to other situations, they might not use the language forms outside of the teaching or learning situation. Semantic intentions or meanings that originate in the children's experiences underlie most of their utterances. In early language development, children do not learn sounds, words, and sentences and then find meaning for these forms; instead, children learn about objects and events, and then search for the forms to code those experiences (Bloom and Lahey, 1978). Therefore, a language program would not present forms in isolation or before the meanings that the forms represent.

Children's earliest attempts to master language are semantically, not syntactically, motivated. It is only after children have mastered the basic components of the underlying semantic relationships that they pay attention to syntactic elements such as word order. Learning a language depends to a large extent upon the experiential background of the child and the ability to represent experiences conceptually. Learning a language also involves more than learning meaning, or content, and form; it involves knowing how to use the content and form effectively in varying contexts and for varying purposes. Therefore, the language goals and intervention strategies must take into account the interactions of the three components of language: content, form, and use.

Principle 2: Information About Normal Language Development is the Basis for Determining Language Goals and Intervention Strategies

Both conceptual development and linguistic development occur in an orderly sequence, and each step in development is important and influences subsequent stages (Bloom and Lahey, 1978). Certain early two- and three-word phrases are necessary antecedents to the more advanced structures that will be used later. For example, as mentioned previously, children typically say, *boy run* before they say *The boy is running* and *that a doggie* before *That is a nice doggie*. What may appear to be the simplest structure in adult sentences may not necessarily be the first structure learned by children. For example, it is conceptually simpler for children to use utterances that consist of action-object (e.g., *push car*) than to use phrases that code plurality or the size or color of objects (e.g., *two books, big book, blue book*) (Bloom and Lahey, 1978). Success in presenting a language program will depend, in part, on following certain sequences, both cognitive and linguistic, in the course of development.

Because the natural approach to language learning is developmental, the child's language behaviors or productions, not chronological age, are used in determining language level. Intervention strategies are planned according to the language level of the child. Chronological age must also be considered, however, to ensure that materials and activities, while appropriate for the child's language level, are also appropriate for his or her age group. For example, if an older child is ready to learn noun plurals, the content categories and intervention strategies of the lesson should be age-appropriate, at the same time focusing on the linguistic form of pluralization.

Principle 3: *Language Is Learned Through Communication*

Parents do not plan and design language lessons and activities to teach language to their children. Rather, language is acquired by children comfortably and easily, in a social setting and in an unconscious manner. Young children acquire language because mature language users communicate with them. One of the foundation studies in psycholinguistic research, conducted by Brown and Bellugi (1964), described three processes in the acquisition of language that occur as very young children and their mothers communicate. These processes include children's imitations as responses to adult utterances, adult expansions as responses to child utterances, and the process by which children induce the regularities and rules of the English language from language information they receive.

As noted in Chapter 1, communication with the young child appears to be an important factor in language development even before the child can respond using a language form; this is borne out by recent literature on semantic and pragmatic development. Before children can use language to communicate, they must learn what communication is. They must learn that there is a purpose for communication, that of clarifying their own experiences and presenting them to someone else. Sugarman's studies (1984) have indicated that at least some of this learning occurs prior to language development. The need to clarify and present experiences to others may be partially what prompts the attempts for new, more effective means of communication—a first language (Sugarman, 1984).

Brown (1975) suggested that the most important form of concept learning for the infant is probably socially mediated. Parents, especially mothers, are the infant's first social contacts. They are the ones most responsible for the development of language in both the normal child and the hearing impaired child.

Greenstein, Bush, McConville, and Stellini (1977) examined the mother-infant communication dyad and its effect on language acquisition in hearing impaired infants. They found that affective aspects of mother-infant interaction were central to the language acquisition of the hearing impaired child. All other aspects of the mother's language input were less significant than the existence of a good mother-infant bond. This bond frequently was broken when a normally hearing mother learned of the child's hearing loss.

It is clear that communication plays several critical roles in a young child's life. Communication facilitates the bonding process between mother and infant; it enables young children to learn what communication is and its purposes, and the need or desire to communicate with people in their environment motivates young children to begin the process of language learning.

Principle 4: *Communicative Competence Is the Ultimate Goal of Language Development*

The fourth principle suggests that the final assessment of the effectiveness of a language program is how well the student can communicate in various contexts and for various purposes. During the past 30 years, three areas of language have been emphasized in the study of child language acquisition, and teaching practices have reflected these emphases. Initially, the focus was on syntax, or gaining knowledge of word order and the relations among words. Next, the emphasis shifted to semantics, or the relations between words and their referents. Most recently, it has focused on pragmatics, or the relations between words and how they are used by people. The focus on pragmatics marked an important theoretical change in the way language is studied. When the emphasis was on syntax and semantics, the linguistic competence of children was the subject of study, and the acquisition of linguistic forms (syntax and morphology) was the major goal of language programs. As the focus shifted first from syntax to semantics and then to pragmatics, the subject of study changed from linguistic competence to communicative competence. The shift emphasized the belief that the young child is learning not only linguistic structure but also the social values and rules underlying language in social interaction. Language is acquired and used in a social context. Young hearing children acquire language through communication for the purpose of communication.

The acquisition of expressive as well as receptive language depends on the social context in which the child develops. For expression, the acquisition of semantic and syntactic constructions is guided by the child's communicative needs. For reception, performance is guided by experiential background and communicative expectations, not by syntactic analyses. Accordingly, language acquisition and communicative competence appear to be identical during the early stages of normal development (Dore, 1974). For the young child, language *is* communication. Only with the development of metalinguistic functions do most children start to deal with language forms independent of their interpersonal meaning (Snow, 1984).

Pragmatic theories of language address language as it is used (Bates, 1976b; Searle, 1969) and characterize linguistic elements and contextual elements as forming communicative interactions. The goal of these theories is to characterize communicative competence, rather than linguistic competence only, and the basic unit of analysis is a communicative interaction. In a similar manner, language goals and intervention strategies must go beyond linguistic competence and lead to the ultimate goal of communicative competence. It is of little value for children to be linguistically competent if they do not use language effectively to express needs and ideas and to maintain social contacts.

FROM PRINCIPLES TO PRACTICES

Principle 1 Into Practice

The first principle, *language involves interactions among the components of content, form, and use,* suggests that the language program must be integrated into all activities during the school day as these activities provide natural occasions to use language. This principle further suggests that vocabulary words should not be taught in isolation and out of natural context, and that syntax and morphological endings should not be taught separately from meaning and use. Bloom, Lightbown, and Hood (1975) maintained that semantics and syntax are inseparable in the language of very young children; they cannot be viewed as independent of each other. Syntactic structure is embedded in semantic intent and, in beginning language intervention, should not be presented separately or in isolation.

When presenting language activities to young children, the teacher should be aware of the syntax in the child's utterances. The teacher first identifies the context and content of the child's utterances and can then determine the syntactic structure. For example, if a child looks up at the teacher and says, *horse water*, the teacher cannot determine the syntactic structure of the communication. However, if the teacher notes that the child is playing with the toy farm and has just moved the horse up to a tank of water (context), remembering the content of the utterance (*water*), the teacher can then assume that the syntactic structure of the utterance is probably subject-verb-object (*the horse is drinking water*). Eventually, the child's utterances will generate many forms of syntactic structure, and from these structures, which will be acquired within the pragmatic context of semantic intent, will emerge rules that are real and functional for the child. Knowledge of the language code has been described by Bloom and Lahey (1978) as content-form interactions, whereas skills involved in using the language code are referred to as content-form-use interactions. Goals for facilitating language learning must take into consideration both the contexts in which the content-form interactions are used, that is, the situations in which children speak or sign, and the purpose or functions for which they speak or sign.

It is believed that children initially learn about objects and events and then learn to name these experiences. Bloom (1970), Bowerman (1973), and Slobin (1973) have suggested that language maps onto the child's existing knowledge. These cognitive-semantic views suggest that, as noted previously, the basis for language development is what is real to children, that which they have experienced previously. In other words, children talk about what they know. Young hearing children have an abundance of experiences accompanied by a wealth of language input. Even with this advantageous background, hearing children are not expected to use expressive language until approximately 12 months after their language experiences begin, and two-word utterances are not anticipated until the child is 18 to 20 months old. In other words, hearing children have about $1\frac{1}{2}$ years to learn about their environment and to receive language information before they begin to use connected language. They, of course, continue to learn about their world as they continue to acquire language and talk about their experiences.

It follows, then, that young deaf children who do not have access to large amounts of language information should be allowed similar experiences and time spans before they are expected to use expressive language. Young deaf children entering preschool programs often have not had an abundance of experiences accompanied by language input that was usable by them. The children must first develop a familiarity with and understanding of objects and events and then "find" the forms to code those experiences and communicate them to others. Thus, during the first several months of preschool, the major goal of the language program should be to provide an abundance of usual and novel activities coupled with language input to expand the experiential backgrounds of the children. As children begin to figure out the language code and map content and form onto existing knowledge, they attempt communication.

Language learning does not teach children about things. Rather, the mapping construct would direct teachers to teach children to talk about things, relationships, and events about which they already exhibit some awareness and knowledge. For example, if a child plays appropriately with a car and a doll, the teacher can emphasize: *The car goes. The car goes fast.* and accept from the child, *Car go.* In the same manner, the teacher would talk about the baby sleeping, for example, *The baby is sleeping, The baby is tired*, and would accept from the child, *Baby sleep.* If the child walks to the teacher for help with boots, the teacher might say, *Do you want help?* and would accept *Help* or *Help me.*

Although observing the children for language information is important, it cannot be the only source of information from which language intervention is planned. The teacher must be aware of the developmental stages of language acquisition in hearing children and must plan experiences in the classroom that will encourage the use of appropriate pragmatic and semantic elements.

Principle 2 Into Practice

The second principle, *information about normal language development is the basis for determining language goals and intervention strategies*, suggests the sequence of goals for the language program as well as guidelines for intervention strategies. The teacher in the preschool classroom plans the language program so that the goals follow the normal stages and sequences in language development and the intervention strategies maintain a communicative interaction among and between children and teacher similar to the language input that is available to young hearing children in their home environments.

Information from Nelson's study (1973) provides guidelines that can be used to establish goals for the language program. Nelson found that most children acquire at least 50 words before they begin to combine two or more words. As noted in chapter 1, she also found that the most common category (51 percent) was that of general nouns, such as *doggie* or *ball*. Specific nouns were the next most common category (14 percent) and included nouns such as *Mommy* and *pet names*. The frequency of action words noted was also near 14 percent and included describing or demanding actions, such as *give, bye-bye,* and *up*. Less common (9 percent) were modifiers, such as *red, dirty, outside,* and *mine*. Personal-social words, such as *yes, no,* and *please,* made up 8 percent, and function words, such as *what* and *for,* made up only 4 percent of the vocabulary.

This information indicates that the first words used by children are highly selective. The important people in the child's environment and certain kinds of objects are particularly likely to be incorporated into the first vocabulary. Among the general nouns used, the most common are *juice, milk, cookies, dog, cat, shoes, ball,* and *car*. It is not surprising that the general categories represented in this group of words are food, clothing, animals, toys, and vehicles. It is also interesting and enlightening to look at the omissions from the list. Although *shoes* and *socks* are common, *pants, sweater, mitten,* and *diaper* are missing. Among the words for furniture, *table, stove, television,* and *window* did not occur, but *clock, blanket,* and *key* were fairly common. The words learned and used first by children seem to be the names of things that children can act on or manipulate easily (Nelson, 1973). The child's environment is not a large one, and change is important. The names of large objects that do not move or change, such as *tree, sofa, park,* are not learned first; those that move and change themselves, such as *cars, clocks,* and *animals,* are likely to be included among the first words. The preschool teacher of deaf children, when planning the language program for each child, should take into consideration the information known about the first words used by young children and incorporate and emphasize those kinds of words in the language activities.

As stated, Nelson (1973) suggested that children usually have at least 50 words in their vocabularies before they begin to combine two or more words. Brown (1970) examined records from a number of children acquiring English and other languages and concluded that the most common semantic relationships at the two-word utterance stage are the 11 listed in Table 4–1. They account for about 75 percent of Stage I utterances. Some other relationships that occur infrequently, however, are action-indirect object (give *Mommy*), instrumentals (*sweep broom,* meaning sweep with the broom), comitatives (*walk Mommy,* meaning walk with mommy), and conjunctions (*umbrella boot*).

Even at this early stage, different types of sentences are common. In addition to describing objects and events, children also ask questions and make demands. In hearing children, questions are often identical to statements except for a rising intonation, such as *Baby shoe?* Children using sign language would designate the question form as being different from a statement through use of facial expressions and body language. Children ask questions about locations (*Where Mommy go?*) and about names (*What that?*). Like questions, imperatives have a characteristic intonation or body language. Often the child's nonverbal behavior and the language context or situation communicates the intent to command.

In a language program for deaf children, the list of commonly expressed relationships in two-word utterances should serve as a guide for classroom teachers as they plan language activities. Language activities should target these relationships, ensuring that the child has exposure through experiences and through communication. Eventually the goal is for the children to begin to express spontaneously the 11 or more semantic relationships in their two-word utterances. Table 4–1 shows the commonly expressed relationships in approximate order of development, listed by frequency of occurrence. This order is derived from data presented by Brown (1973) and McDonald and Nickols (1974).

In the 1960s a wealth of information on language development in young children began to appear in publications. Some of this was presented in Chapter 1. One of the foundation studies, conducted by Brown and Bellugi (1964), described three processes that occur as very young children and their mothers communicate. (It must be

Table 4–1. Semantic Relations

Semantic Relationship	Syntactic Structure	Examples
1. Agent-action	N + V	Mommy push
2. Action-object	V + N	Push car
3. Nomination	that/it + N	That car
4. Notice	hi/see + N	Hi car
5. Possessor possession	N + N	Daddy car
6. Recurrence	more + N	More milk
7. Nonexistence	no/allgone + N	Allgone milk
8. Attribute	adjective + N	Big car
9. Entity-locative	N + N	Sweater chair
10. Action-locative	V + N	Sit chair
11. Agent-object	N + N	Mommy (put on) shoe
12. Conjunction (infrequent)	N + N	Umbrella boot

Brown, R. (1973). *A first language: The early stages*. Cambridge, MA: Harvard University Press; and McDonald, J. D. and Nickols, M. (1974). *The environmental language inventory*. Columbus: Nisonger Center, Ohio State University.

remembered that these processes require a "free and easy" communication between child and parents, which many deaf children do not have.) The first process is called imitation with reduction. In this process, the child is the active agent, imitating some of the mother's utterances, but reducing them by omitting some of the words. The following examples of imitations with reductions are taken from the records of two young children observed in the initial study (Brown and Bellugi, 1964, pp. 135, 137).

Model Utterance	Child's Imitation
There goes one.	*There go one.*
Fraser will be unhappy.	*Fraser unhappy.*
It's not the same dog as Pepper.	*Dog Pepper.*

Brown and Bellugi (1964) point out several interesting properties of these utterances that occurred in a normal, conversational setting between mother and child. One observation was that the child's imitations always preserved the word order of the model utterance. Brown and Bellugi interpreted the preservation of word order as an indication that children do not process utterances as a list of words, but as a total construction. A second observation that is important to note is that the child's imitations stayed within the range of two to four morphemes regardless of the length of the model utterance. This range was characteristic of the children's utterances in spontaneous language production as well as in imitations. The children seemed to be operating under some constraint on length, which compelled them to omit words or morphemes from the mother's longer sentences. The constraint is a limitation on the length of utterance that children are able to program or plan (Brown and Bellugi, 1964). The words that children use in their utterances are usually the contentives, or high-information words; the words they omit are the functors, or low-information words.

For preschool teachers of hearing-impaired children, these observations have important implications for natural language strategies. The observation that children process utterances as total constructions and not as lists of words suggests that the practice in some preschool classrooms of having a child imitate a sentence word for word will not accomplish the goal of sentence production, but may, in fact, hinder it. The following example illustrates the word-for-word imitation, sometimes referred to as the "Say It Again" technique (Lowenbraun, Appelman, and Callahan, 1980):

Teacher	Child
Say, Mother went to the store.	*Mother store.*
No, let's say a whole sentence.	

Say: Mother   *Mother*
    went   *went*
    to   *to*
    the   *the*
    store   *store*

Good, now say, Mother went to the store.   *Mother store.*

If children process language utterances as total constructions, as Brown and Bellugi maintain, fragmenting the sentence and presenting it as a list of separate words would likely hinder rather than facilitate a child's attempts to produce sentences.

The second observation concerning the constraint on the length of children's utterances also suggests that the "Say It Again" technique would not be effective. If children, when imitating or when producing spontaneous utterances, are operating under a constraint and cannot plan or program utterances longer than two to four morphemes, attempting to elicit longer utterances would likely be a futile and frustrating endeavor. An utterance within this range should be accepted as "good" language production for a child at this stage of language development. The language of children should not be judged by adult standards of language but by what is appropriate at the various stages of "child language." In this perspective, the utterance *Mommy store* would be considered "accurate child language" and would be accepted as such by the teacher.

The teacher, at this point, would likely initiate the second process discussed by Brown and Bellugi, which is labeled imitation and expansion. The adult, who is the active agent in this process, imitates the child's utterance, but expands it by adding functors and morphological endings to produce a grammatically correct simple sentence that is appropriate for that situation. Some examples of imitation with expansion that were collected in Brown and Bellugi's study (1964) are as follows:

Child	Mother
Baby highchair.	*Baby is in the highchair.*
Eve lunch.	*Eve is having lunch.*
Sat wall.	*He sat on a wall.*
Throw Daddy.	*Throw it to Daddy.*

By responding to children's utterances in a manner similar to that used commonly by mothers, teachers could add very positive aspects to the language program. Imitation with expansion serves as a communication check between mother (or teacher) and child. When the adult repeats and expands, it is akin to saying, "Is this what you mean?" If the adult correctly interprets the baby's communicative intent, the conversation continues. If the interpretation is not accurate, the child will repeat the utterance, perhaps more forcefully this time. The adult will most likely reassess the situation for more contextual clues and then try a different interpretation of the child's communication. This interaction maintains communication between the child and the adult and also exposes the child to turntaking in communicative interaction. The adult's responses serve as positive reinforcement to the child in the sense that the adult is conveying to the child, *I want to know what you say. What you say is important.* Brown and Bellugi suggest that imitation with expansion also serves as an effective tutorial technique. When adults provide the expanded statement, they are using language similar to that which the child will be using 1 year later. The mother is presenting new language information at a time when the child is attending and waiting for a response. The mother does not correct the child or ask the child to imitate the syntactic accuracy in the adult utterance.

The third process that Brown and Bellugi (1964) discuss is an attempt to describe how children induce semantic and syntactic structures from language that they hear. It is this process that perhaps accounts for most of language acquisition and that enables children to understand and produce novel utterances throughout their lives by using the general rule structures of language. This is largely a cognitive process, in which children begin to organize and categorize the language information they receive. In doing so, they are unconsciously searching for similarities and differences in the language information, or, as Brown and Bellugi (1964) suggest, they are searching for the syntactic regularities of the English language. The organizational structures that they develop from language input determine the generalizations they arrive at and apply in their language output. The reactions of the people in their language environment determine whether children maintain the newly tried general rule structure or modify it. For example, children induce from their language input that -*ed* added to the end of a verb indicates a past action. Children commonly make the generalization, or overgeneralization, that this is a general rule structure that can be applied to all verbs. Hence, the child will produce in expressive language verbs such as *walked* (which is a correct application) and also verbs such as *goed, runned,* and *breaked,* which are the result of an overgeneralization. As children continue to receive accurate irregular forms as language input (e.g., *went, ran,* and *broke*), they modify the rule previously formed and begin to distinguish irregular from regular verbs.

Some implications for preschool classroom teachers can be derived from the third process. In ''practicing'' language and in attempting to apply general rule structures, children often produce utterances that would be considered incorrect by adult standards. For example, if a child says, *I runned to school*, the teacher should tolerate the "error" and respond to the communication, possibly by replying, *You ran to school! Wow, you must be tired!* The child's use of *runned* should not be viewed in a negative manner but should be considered a very positive and exciting event. The use of *runned* most likely indicates that the child is attempting to assimilate and generalize information about the past tense of verbs. Perhaps the child had previously used *ran*, then "became aware" of the *-ed* ending on verbs and overgeneralized by adding *-ed* to all verbs to indicate past tense. A little later, the child sorts through the action words and relegates some to the category of "regular verbs, can add *-ed*, and irregular verbs, no *-ed*. Of course, children do not think in those terms, but that, in essence, is their conclusion. Hence, a child may initially use *ran* in utterances, then *runned*, and finally return to using *ran*; now, however, the child has a better linguistic understanding of what *ran* means and how it can be used. This example strongly emphasizes the need for preschool teachers of hearing impaired children to have extensive knowledge of developmental stages in language acquisition as well as the need for maintaining a positive and nurturing climate in the classroom that will promote and encourage conversation and communication. For hearing impaired children to assimilate language information, deduce general rule structures, and apply them to usual and novel situations (making generalizations), they must be afforded opportunities for many different experiences in which they can receive as accurately as possible an abundance of language information.

The first two processes that Brown and Bellugi (1964) discussed involved imitation. Often a child spontaneously imitates the utterance of another person, usually a parent. At other times an adult may ask the child to imitate an utterance or may elicit an imitation. Eliciting imitations is a common practice in some preschool classrooms and is used in the belief that the child, by imitating language, will learn and use language. This practice usually focuses on word order, or syntax, and morphological endings. For example, a child might say, *Doggie eat candy.* The teacher might respond, *The doggie ate the candy. Can you say that?* The teacher's intent is that the child imitate the sentence using the article, *the*, and the correct verb tense. (For a more detailed description of the role of imitation, the reader is referred to Bloom, Hood, and Lightbown, 1974.)

The evidence suggests (Bloom, Hood, and Lightbown, 1974; Kemp and Dale, 1973) that imitation, in the sense of a child's attempt to reproduce an adult utterance, does not play an important role in the acquisition of syntax. Many of the early utterances of children cannot be considered imitations or even reduced imitations of adult language—

for example, *allgone doggie*. Even when children do imitate adult language, they reformulate the sentences using their own grammars. It is unlikely that children can acquire new grammatical features through imitation when it is precisely these new features that are omitted in imitations. Therefore, the natural approach to language development in deaf children does not advocate extensive use of imitation, particulary not elicited imitation.

The following list summarizes the classroom practices derived from the second principle.

1. The sequence in which language goals are planned for inclusion in the language curriculum is determined by the sequence of stages and sequences within stages of normal language development.
2. Intervention strategies maintain a communicative interaction among and between children and teacher similar to the language input that is available to young hearing children in their home environments.
3. To facilitate the child's readiness for expressive language, the preschool teacher of deaf children will provide a variety of play experiences, including symbolic and cooperating play opportunities.
4. The teacher will accept "child language" as appropriate for each particular language stage and will not expect or require responses using correct adult syntax.
5. The teacher will frequently use an intervention strategy similar to language expansion of the child's utterance to maintain communicative interaction and to present new language information at a time when the child is attending and waiting for a response.
6. The teacher will respond to the semantic and communicative intent of the child rather than interrupting communication to require adult syntax in the child's utterance.
7. The teacher will provide an abundance of common and novel experiences to increase the children's experiential backgrounds and to serve as vehicles for language input and communication.

Principle 3 Into Practice

The third principle, *language is learned through communication*, provides the framework for the kinds of intervention strategies used in the natural approach to language learning. Using this principle, the preschool teacher of deaf children will provide a variety of experiences for the students, which will be accompanied by appropriate language input. These experiences serve many purposes, which include the following:

1. Children can learn what communication is.
2. They learn the many purposes of communication.
3. Experiences increase children's experiential backgrounds or their knowledge about their world and the development of concepts and relationships.
4. When children are involved in experiences, they are motivated to communicate their experiences to others, thus facilitating the process of language learning. Simply put, experiences provide children with something to communicate.

Because communication is the key to language learning, young children must participate in communicative interactions. This implies that the preschool teacher does not *teach* language in a structured setting, nor does the child play a passive, static role in a formal teaching or learning situation. Early childhood educators seem to be in general agreement that language activities should be presented in a natural context, which for preschool children is often a context of play. The language activities should have two emphases; first, the activities should be real and meaningful for children and should afford opportunities for them to communicate with another person about what they already know, and, second, the activities should be planned so that the children will also gain new knowledge about their environment and how to talk about and use the new information. The classroom teacher becomes a language facilitator and a communicator more than a language teacher.

Often language learning opportunities occur incidentally in the preschool classroom, and the teacher should be aware and take advantage of these situations. For example, if children indicate through gestures or grabbing that they want something, the teacher should begin to present the sign *want*, which can be used by children for the communicative function of expressing a need. They should then be encouraged to sign *want milk* or *want eat* instead of pointing or grabbing. These strategies are encouraging the development of a semantic relationship, *action-object*. Names are usually learned quickly by young children, and they should be taught their own names and those of their classmates. These names can then be used in a number of pragmatic and semantic functions such as describing an event and agent-action (*Susie fell*) or describing an event and agent-object (*Susie airplane*). Teachers must be alert to the current and future needs of children as they develop their communication skills and focus on concepts that will be the most functional for the children. Teachers should establish learning situations that will provide many natural opportunities to model language as they communicate with the children. They should also provide a nurturing environment, in which the children are comfortable and secure enough to experiment with language and practice what they are learning.

Principle 4 Into Practice

The fourth principle, *communicative competence is the ultimate goal of language development*, precludes a narrow focus that is solely on linguistic competence in a language program and ensures that language learning activities will lead to the practical, functional goal of enabling the children to use language effectively in all of their different environments. This principle assumes that, for children to attain communicative competence, they must necessarily also attain contextual and linguistic competence. Thus, this fourth principle emphasizes the critical need for a well-rounded, comprehensive language program, without which the ultimate goal of communicative competence cannot be reached.

An aspect of the language program that should not be overlooked is the provision of activities and contexts that will promote generalization. Language learning that does not "transfer" from the classroom to other environments will not lead to communicative competence. Several practices can be employed that promote the occurrence of generalizations. Language learning should occur in real-life situations or in situations as near real life as possible. Representative or vicarious experiences often are not clearly or accurately understood by young children and are, therefore, not generalized and applied to similar, but novel, situations. Thus, language learning contexts should not be concentrated exclusively on pictures, which often are heavily relied on by teachers of deaf children. A picture may not enable the deaf child to develop an accurate concept of the pictured object. Concepts learned through real experiences that actively involve the child and that provide activities that promote the development of generalization skills will more likely be generalized, used, and communicated about in new and different situations by children, thereby indicating a broader, more flexible understanding of the concept.

Adequate and appropriate reinforcement of a concept is also important. The teacher should reinforce a concept as it occurs at different times and in different situations throughout the school day. In addition, attention should be given to how a concept is immediately reinforced. When children participate in language activities and respond appropriately, the teacher should reinforce the response by allowing a natural consequence to occur. For example, if the child successfully communicates *I want a cookie*, the child should not be given a sticker on the hand for reinforcement but should receive the natural outcome of such a request, a cookie. The sticker reinforcement may increase the rate of that response in the classroom setting, but it does not allow the child to understand how the request functions in natural social contexts (McLean and Synder-McLean, 1978).

Modeling, encouraging, and reinforcing language responses using a natural approach is becoming increasingly prevalent in current language programs (Hart, 1981; Hart and Rogers-Warren, 1978). A rationale for changing to more natural teaching contexts stems from evidence that new responses learned in contrived and structured classroom settings often do not generalize to environments outside the classroom (McLean and Snyder-McLean, 1978). Such interactive language contexts require a great deal of planning on the part of the teacher. However, the contexts can be structured around a number of different activities that are common occurrences in children's lives, such as preparing snacks in the preschool and normal play activities; for older children, food preparation, clothing care, or grocery shopping are good activities.

INSTRUCTIONAL ACTIVITIES FOR TEACHING NATURAL LANGUAGE

Preschool Instruction

The following lessons are presented as samples of typical preschool activities. The primary language goal for all the lessons is to provide information and activities to enrich the experiential backgrounds of the children in a natural communicative setting. Because content, form, and use are interactive elements of language, they are not separated and focused on in different lessons but are an integral part of each lesson. The context for each lesson should be real life situations and activities in natural settings and the primary intervention strategy is communicative interaction among students and teachers. The students must be actively involved in each lesson, and each lesson must provide opportunities for the children to make generalizations. For all field experiences the teacher should make a visit beforehand or talk with a contact person at the site to determine what the children will be able to see and experience. The procedures are similar for all lessons. The teacher initiates and maintains communication and questioning and includes all the children in each activity and conversation.

Sample Goal: To develop the concept of apple.

SUBUNIT 1: Field trip to orchard

Lesson 1: Pre-visit preparation

Objective:
- Prepare children for field trip

Strategy:
- Planned situation as opposed to "teaching to the moment"
- Communicative interaction between teacher and learners in speech/sign
- Questioning
- Discourse

Procedure:
- Teacher shows a picture (preferably a photograph) of an apple tree and asks: "What is this? Do you know? Can you tell me? What is this?"
- Children: Tree.
- Teacher: "You're right—this is a picture of a tree! (points to apple) What's this?"
- Children: (Some may respond *apple,* some may respond *eat,* some may not respond at all.)
- Teacher: Yes, this is an apple. Look in my bag here— what is in the bag?"
- Children take turns peeking in the bag. Responses may be: *apple, eat,* or no response.
- Teacher takes an apple out of the bag and compares it to apples on the tree in the picture. Teacher: Tomorrow, we will go somewhere. You will come to school in the morning. Then we will ride a bus. We will see many apple trees. We will buy some apples and bring them back to school. Maybe we will eat apples tomorrow. Do you like to eat apples?
- All children have an opportunity to respond.
- Teacher and children find "tomorrow" on calendar and mark by drawing an apple on calendar.

Lesson 2: Trip to orchard

Objectives:
- See apple trees.
- Pick apples off the trees.
- Buy apples in the orchard store.
- Buy apple juice.

Strategy:
- Field experience
- Communication
- Discourse
- Questioning

Procedures: • The teacher or teacher aide should take instant-developing photographs during the trip, so children see the pictures together with the real thing.

• When the children are approaching the orchard, the teacher should comment about what they see (e.g., many trees, apples on the trees, size and colors of apples). Each child could pick an apple and the teacher could discuss "good apples" and "bad apples."

• Teacher and children go into the orchard store and see and discuss the apples.

• Most orchard stores offer samples of different kinds of apples so the children can taste the different ones.

• Teacher and children buy apples and juice to take back to school.

Lesson 3: Teacher and children develop written experience story by discussing each photograph. They eat apples and drink juice.

SUBUNIT 2: Field trip to grocery store produce department
Lesson 1: Prepare children for trip (walking trip).
Lesson 2: Trip to grocery store.
• Note different kinds of apples
• Buy apples at store

SUBUNIT 3: Make fruit salad
Lesson 1: • Teacher aide takes instant-developing photographs.
• Class discusses size, shape, and colors of apples.
• Teacher peels apple and children can inspect the inside (color is different, there is a core, there are seeds).
• Teacher chops up apple.
• Teacher-aide cuts up oranges.
• Each child peels and cuts up banana (with plastic knife). Add sugar and apple juice and all can eat fresh fruit salad.
Lesson 2: Teacher and children develop experience story by discussing each photograph taken. Children can add their own artwork to the story.

SUBUNIT 4: Make caramel apples

SUBUNIT 5: Make applesauce, apple pies, or apple juice
After this unit is completed, the children should have a fairly well developed beginning concept of *apples* and their various forms and uses. In addition, they will have participated in many enjoyable experiences

and conversations and will have received an abundance of language input during these pleasant and fun activities.

Instruction for School-aged Children

Muma (1971) summarized 10 basic types of instructional strategies used by clinicians and teachers for language instruction. Four of the models applicable to natural language instruction as they relate to school-aged deaf students are presented in this section with a brief discussion of research findings that support or refute the methods used.

Correction Model

Child: *Daddy go work*
Teacher: *No, daddy went to work.*

The correction model is perhaps the oldest method of language instruction used by teachers. In the model, the teacher, either in speech, signs, or writing, indicates that an error has been made and provides the correct form or functional term. Research regarding the use of the correction model has suggested that it generally is ineffective (Brown and Bellugi, 1964; Mellon, 1967). Forman and Spector (1980) reported using the correction technique with hearing impaired students at the National Technical Institute for the Deaf. Structured drills in English phonology, syntax, and morphology were completed followed by the use of English in conversational speech. Incorrect utterances were recorded by the clinician and given to the student to correct. More difficult structures were corrected directly by the clinician and explained to the student. No evidence of effectiveness was reported.

Expansion Model

Child: *Play swing.*
Teacher: *Jenny played on the swing.*

As discussed earlier in this chapter, Brown and Bellugi(1964) described syntactic expansion modeling as a phenomenon of parenting. Parents, communicating with their child, will typically imitate the communication of the child and insert those syntactical characteristics that were omitted by the child. Cazden (1965) studied the effects of expansion modeling with disadvantaged youngsters. She reported that the children receiving explicit expansion-modeling demonstrated noticeable growth in specific grammatical structures.

Simple Expatiation Model

Child: *Daddy go.*
Teacher: *Daddy's gone. Jenny go too. Mommy go. Jenny come.*

The expatiation model addresses the teacher's use of structures that are within the repertoire of the child. Cazden (1965) found that young children demonstrated form and content gains when teachers restricted their modeled utterances to those basic sentence patterns and transformations that were exhibited by the child.

Alternative Model

Child: *Daddy go.*
Teacher: *Yes. Did daddy go to work? Where does daddy work?*

The alternative model as described by Muma (1971) confirms the child's language use and probes into the function or semantic value expressed. Referring to the child's statement, the teacher questions the rationale and the "deep meaning" or underlying logic of the statement. Blank and Solomon (1968) demonstrated the effectiveness in the development of inferential cognitive skills and abstract thinking with early elementary school youngsters.

In addition to the direct intervention strategies mentioned, effective teaching strategies are also critical to language learning. Berliner (1984) identified three major strategies that effective teachers use. The first critical variable is content or the opportunity to learn. Effective natural language instruction provides a curriculum in which the teacher knows what needs to be taught and presents content to the student in a manner that will ensure that the child is able to access the content and experience success. It is within this area that the education of deaf children has been nonuniformly structured. The EPIC study conducted at the Central Institute for the Deaf (Moog and Geers, 1985) clearly demonstrates the effectiveness of using a specific language curriculum that is carried across grade levels and academic areas. The teacher has a clear understanding of the goal of instruction and is able to access the content and experience success.

"Allocated time" and "engaged time" for the opportunity to learn form the second critical variable in the attainment of effective teaching. Crandall and Albertini (1980) increased the number of hours per week allocated to English language instruction with postsecondary school deaf students. In addition, teachers were explicitly instructed to increase the quantity of utterances that occurred in discourse with the students. The effect of increased academic time and increase in time engaged in using language had positive effects on the students' ability to use English.

The third area of instructional effectiveness includes teacher directed classroom learning. Teacher monitoring of student performance—that is, providing feedback to the student and providing clarification and directions as well as questioning student performance—is strongly correlated with achievement. Although the natural language approach frequently is misinterpreted as "whatever happens, happens," actually the natural language approach requires a great deal of purposeful planning, direction, and guidance by the teacher. The students acquire language through the events arranged in the natural settings. The natural approach to language instruction advocates learning to use language by using language.

The following are descriptions of language activities that can be applied to foster natural language development in the context of discourse or social-conversational intent. Each of the activities can be adapted in form, content, and use to capitalize on the child's individual language strengths and needs. Many of the activities have been adapted from *Language Arts and Reading, K–13: A Handbook for Teachers* (Moffett and Wagner, 1986) and from practical experiences. Sample language lesson plans and scripts are included to illustrate practical implementation programs.

Elementary School Programs

CLASSROOM DRAMA—PLAYING WITH OBJECTS. Early elementary school youngsters can create a wealth of language-demanding interactions through the use of objects and things. "Learning Centers" that include a toy store, a play kitchen, or similar areas can lead to numerous forms of role playing. Bags of hats, jackets, and other clothing props can be made available for "dress-up" time. Children can assume roles that are appropriate to their dress and engage in conversations that would characterize the costume.

CONCENTRATION ACTIVITIES. "Simon Says" is a very popular activity with highly verbal hearing children. Deaf children can engage in similar games. The teacher or a student leader gives a set of directions. The students must follow the directions. Adaptations may include alternative directions for the group or for an individual student, which serves to maintain everyone's attention. Practice asking for permission can be added by requiring the student(s) to ask, "Mrs. Smith, can I take four big steps?"

TOSSING IMAGINARY OBJECTS. The teacher tosses out an imaginary ball and names a person to catch it. Students standing in a small circle toss the imaginary ball, naming another student, "Tonya, catch the ball." Variations can include adding adjectives, thereby changing the characteristics of the ball to a heavy ball, a big ball, a small ball, a tiny ball, a giant ball, or a beach ball.

UNISON. Walk in a circle as a whole class. Keep the activity short and slow. Let the students develop follow-up unison activities using their imaginations and language skills to describe alternative forms. Begin walking slowly. Pretend you are growing taller and taller as you walk, then shorter and shorter. Pretend you are walking up a hill, walking down stairs, holding on to the rail, climbing a ladder, or walking on slippery ice. You may be walking on marbles or in a wind storm. You can ride in space or walk through water or carry buckets of water. How does it feel? How does your body feel? What can you say? How can you help your friend?

PRETEND TO DO. Children can practice sequencing events, using expressions of shape, size, weight, odor, and so forth, through the re-creation of activities in pantomime. Pretending to eat various types of foods, such as spaghetti, ice cream, jello, soup, or peas can provide a wealth of natural language that fits into any food unit.

OPEN A PRESENT. Pretend to open a present of something you really want. One student describes the "present" while the others try to guess what it is.

WHAT AM I? The teacher or the students describe familiar objects, animals, places, people, or whatever classification group you may be focusing on in a particular instructional unit (e.g., *I am very, very hot. I can make the snow melt. I can make things burn. What am I?*). A variation of this theme can be "Where have I been?" or "Where am I going?"

WHOSE SHOE? Students each place one of their shoes in a large box and the other shoe into individual brown bags. Each student is given a shoe bag. The students may orally or manually or in writing describe the shoe in the bag. When the other students think they can identify the type of shoe described, they can locate the matching shoe from the box.

GETTING FROM HERE TO THERE. Each student is provided with a map of the "neighborhood" or the school building. A pack of cards is provided with pictorial representations and the printed names of various landmarks (e.g., mail box, school, church, gas station). The teacher or a student has a 'master map' with all the landmarks in place. With all the students starting in the same place, the teacher gives directions regarding the placement of the landmarks (e.g., *Walk 3 blocks, turn left, walk 1 block. The mailbox is located on the southwest corner.* Or *The mailbox is on the corner next to the school.*) Students may ask questions for more information or clarification.

MAKING DIRECTIONS COUNT. Each student (or the teacher) writes out on an overhead transparency (or you may want to use the microcomputer) three directions (e.g., *Walk to the window. Open the window and close it. Sit on the floor.*) When all the directions are written, a student selects one set of directions, reads it to the class, and puts the directions down. The student must then follow the directions exactly.

RECIPES. Making recipe books can be an ideal way of taking language home to Mom and Dad. Students can identify recipes they would like to make. Enter the recipes in their books and illustrate each step in the directions. Have younger children find pictures in magazines that illustrate the directions, or get the instant camera out and take pictures of the items and actions.

INTERVIEWS. Getting to know other people in the school or the community can be an extremely valuable experience for deaf children. Interview questions can be prepared in advance through class discussions. Students can practice interviewing protocols through questioning peers and summarizing discussions. Peers can provide feedback and evaluation of the accuracy of the information reported. Interviews with crossing guards, bus drivers, interpreters, and other teachers are just a few interesting possibilities. Completed interviews can be prepared in writing for a class newspaper or presented to the class in a panel discussion.

SURVEYS. People are questioned on such topics as favorite foods, opinions on popular issues, and career vocations. Give students the opportunity to apply mathematics, social studies, and science as well as natural language. A sixth grade hearing impaired class prepared a questionnaire on opinions about smoking and knowledge about hearing impairments. The questionnaires were distributed in classrooms throughout the school. Before the completed questionnaires were returned to the students, estimates were made regarding the results. Questionnaires were tabulated by the students, and percentages were computed. Bar and point graphs were made to illustrate the results. The class prepared a final report on each of the topics and submitted it to the principal.

CONCEPT BASED SHOW AND TELL. A variation from the traditional Show and Tell theme is to plan concept-based Show and Tell time. Children may be directed to bring something yellow during week one, blue during week two, and so forth. Other concepts may focus on things found in the kitchen, things we write with, pets, favorite people, or relatives. As the students describe their Show and Tell items, transcriptions can be made of their reports. These make excellent reading stories that can be illustrated and put into a reading book.

Lesson Plan

INSTRUCTIONAL OBJECTIVE: The student will be able to use the relative terms "more...than," "fewer...than," and "the same" in descriptive dialogue.

MATERIALS AND EQUIPMENT: Large sheets of newprint. Different colored packs of self-stick notes.

Draw a horizontal line toward the bottom edge of the paper and a vertical line at the left edge of the paper representing a graph.

INSTRUCTIONAL PROCEDURES
1. Ask all the boys to raise their hands. Give each boy a yellow post note.
2. Ask all the girls to raise their hands. Give each girl a blue post-note.
3. Instruct each student to put the square on the paper in the boy or girl column.
4. After all the squares are posted, ask, Are there more boys than girls? Are there more girls than boys? Are there fewer boys than girls? Are there fewer girls than boys? Using the column length to demonstrate "greater than" and "fewer than."
5. Repeat the same activity with the color of hair of each child: brown, black, blonde, and red.
6. Repeat with other factors, letting the students lead the discussion and questioning.

Junior High and Senior High Programs

Wiig (1982a) developed *Let's Talk—Developing Prosocial Communication Skills* for use with preadolescent and adolescent students. The assessment protocol and accompanying curriculum emphasize functional communication skills through interaction. The curriculum is divided into five major areas of pragmatics: ritualizing, informing, controlling, feelings, and imagining. Each of the categories is defined by a set of behaviors. For example:

Informing Statement:
SIMPLE: *The boy is tall.*
COMPLEX: *The boy who is taller than Jack lives on the corner.*
Question:
SIMPLE: *Are you tired?*
COMPLEX: *Did you say that you are tired?*
Content question:
SIMPLE: *Who is that?*
COMPLEX: *Who's the person who is sitting to the right of my aunt?*
Reason question (why):
SIMPLE: *Why?*
COMPLEX: *Why did you ever buy that car?*
Query name:
SIMPLE: *What is that (called)?*
COMPLEX: *What is the name of that object/person/car?*
Ostentation (showy or pretentious display):
SIMPLE: *That's the one I like.*
COMPLEX: *The car that is parked next to yours is the one I like.*
Response to content or reason question:
SIMPLE: *Jane is my friend.*
COMPLEX: *Jane is sitting next to your aunt. She is my friend.*

The instructional curriculum emphasizes common communication functions, such as asking for the location of necessities, telling about abilities, and leaving TDD (phone) messages.

ADVERTISING ME. Students can develop a collage by finding pictures and print in magazines that best describe themselves. Illustrations can include interests, feelings, skills, hobbies, and dreams. The students can write an autobiography to accompany their collage. A variation is to have students develop a collage of another student and write a biography of that student.

DRAMA. Students can write their own script—perhaps about their experiences as a deaf student—or develop a script about the accomplishments of deaf people. Short plays can provide an infinite number of opportunities of language use. Short classroom dramas can be videotaped and viewed by the families of the students as well.

STORY-TELLING. Story-telling is an excellent language setting for adolescents. A story can be started by one student and continued at varying intervals by other students. A mystery story can be started on the microcomputer print or graphics program. Students can add to the story in various ways. One day may focus on describing the setting.

On the second day the characters are described. On the third day the plot can be set. All students can participate by making contributions.

DECISION-MAKING. Numerous language events can be centered on the decision-making demands placed on adolescents and young adults. "What if . . ." cards can be made by the teacher or the students (e.g., "What if someone offered you a joint?"). Student responses can be written and then presented for discussion or entered into a microcomputer. Other students can review the summation of the responses.

FLOW-CHARTING. Flow-charting is another excellent tool for language instruction and decision-making skills. Students can map out all the activities in which they engage in a given day and identify those areas in which decisions need to be made.

These suggested activities are only a small sampling of items that can be used to promote natural language development and social communicative behaviors. The structure, content, and form of language used in each of the situations is under the control of the teacher. Each situation calls for the teacher's expertise and guidance in providing language models that are accessible to the student and that ensure a model for success in language growth and applicability.

Lesson Plan (adapted from Wiig, 1982a)

INSTRUCTIONAL OBJECTIVE: The student will be able to request repetition of a spoken or signed message using correct English form at appropriate times in the conversation.

MATERIALS AND EQUIPMENT: Language cards with the following expressions: What? Huh? Again? Please repeat that. Please explain that to me. Please repeat that word again. Please repeat that part again. I'm sorry, I didn't see you say that last part, please repeat it.

MOTIVATING ACTIVITY: Begin the class by mumbling to the students or covering your mouth until all the students are attending (and complaining).

INSTRUCTIONAL PROCEDURES:

1. Record comments students made in response to the motivational activity.
2. Introduce language cards with various ways students can request repetition.
3. Model the experience with another student using various forms of asking for repetition.
4. Students practice with each other.

EVALUATION: Observe students in a variety of situations.

SUMMARY

Language is learned through communication for the purpose of communication. When very young children are taught language through structured lessons, the basic purpose for learning language—that is, to communicate with others—often is obscured in the imitating and patterning activities. For deaf children to understand that language is a way of influencing their environment and the people in their environment, they must be exposed extensively to language as it is used in communication. Most of the language activities in preschool classrooms should use the interests and experiences of children along with naturally occurring events as vehicles for the comprehension and production of language. The basic assumption underlying the natural approach is that when acquiring language, deaf children progress through stages and sequences in a manner similar to that of hearing children. In planning language goals and intervention strategies, teachers of preschool deaf children should use information about normal language development as guidelines and plan activities that will encourage interactions among the language components of form, content, and use. All activities should promote communicative competence, which is the ultimate goal of the language program.

The natural language approach can also be used effectively beyond the preschool classroom, although some lessons, more structured in nature, are often combined with the natural approach at the primary level. The teacher often provides an experience in which the children can participate and communicate with the teacher and their classmates. The teacher usually has specific language goals in mind and incorporates them into the conversation with the children. After the experience is completed, the teacher may use a somewhat structured format as a follow-up to the experience and as a reinforcement of the targeted language.

As children become older and their metalinguistic abilities have begun to develop, the order and balance of the natural and structured approaches are often reversed, with the structured lesson focusing on specific language principles presented first. The experience follows the structured lessons and is used to reinforce the new learning and to model its use in a natural, communicative setting. As language intervention strategies move from a natural approach to more structured approaches, it becomes increasingly important to remember that children, both younger and older, learn language by using language. They learn language so they can communicate; to promote language learning, they must be given opportunities to communicate so they can practice and experiment with their growing language knowledge.

C H A P T E R 5

Structured and Combined Approaches to Teaching Language

Two major approaches to language development have been used with deaf children: the natural approach (indirect method of instruction) and the structured approach (frequently referred to as the formal, grammatical, or analytical method). In the natural approach, as discussed in Chapter 4, the implicit study and acquisition of language take place through interactions occurring within the environment. The structured method involves explicit instruction in the components of language and a visual coding or symbol system that represents the order or relationships within each component. The structured method of teaching language dominated the field of education for deaf children through the 1940s (Nelson, 1949). Today, in the majority of programs, combinations of the natural and structured approaches are used frequently. Programs differ in their emphases on either the natural or the structured components; rarely is there pure use of one approach or the other. King (1984) conducted a national survey of 233 educational programs serving deaf children in the United States. Approximately half the responders reported that they did not have an identified philosophy regarding the methodology to be used in teaching language to deaf children. About one third of the programs used the natural approach during the preschool years. This commitment to the natural approach decreased significantly to 6 percent at the primary level and 4 percent at the high school level. The structured approach to language development was used by approximately 10 percent of the high school programs and only 5 percent of the preschool respondents. The predominant method used by nearly half of the respondents from grades 1 through 12 was the combined approach, which made use of a structured plan along with selected characteristics of the natural approach.

A common feature of the structured approach includes the use of a visual coding or symbol system, which King (1984) refers to as *metalanguage*. "*Metalanguage* is language used to talk about language; and the symbol systems used in programs for hearing-impaired children provide teachers and students with a means to talk about language. Terms and symbols such as *noun, verb, pronoun, relativization, sentence pattern 3, NP + V,* =, *sentence, question,* and ⌐⎯⎯⎯⎤ are all examples of meta-linguistic symbols" (King, 1984, p. 313). Eighty percent of the respondents stated that they used some form of metalanguage in the instructional process. Sentence patterns, parts of speech, and *Apple Tree* sentence patterns (Caniglia, Cole, Howard, Krohn, and Rice, 1975) were the forms of metalanguage used most commonly.

This chapter presents in detail three of the most prominent language curricula used in the education of deaf children today. Briefer reviews of several other current combined and structured approaches are then presented. The first curriculum reviewed is the Fitzgerald Key, a structured approach to teaching language. The second curriculum, The *Apple Tree* (Caniglia et al., 1975) is perhaps the most widely used commercial curriculum in programs for deaf children (King, 1984); it represents a combined approach of traditional structured grammar with the transformational grammar theories. The third curriculum reviewed is the Rhode Island Curriculum (Blackwell et al., 1978), which is based on transformational generative grammar as proposed by Chomsky and the cognitive perspective of Piagetian theory.

ASSUMPTIONS AND PRINCIPLES

The assumption underlying language learning through the structured or combined approach is that language development depends on experiences with meaningful language combined with a structured organization of language form for the expression of those experiences. Because the English language is acquired primarily through the auditory system, "An initial understanding of the deaf child's situation thus involves the recognition that, by nature of the handicap, he is denied access to meaningful spoken language in use, and, therefore, the normal evolution of meanings and structures cannot take place" (Brennan, 1975, pp. 463–464). Providing the deaf child with carefully constructed models of English through teacher modeling and metalinguistic forms implies that the child will be able to acquire normal language skills. The assumptions inherent in the structured or combined approaches include the following: (1) the deaf child is able to acquire the structure of language through imitation of models (Watson, 1967); (2) repeated exposure to specific structures of language will enhance the child's rate and skills in the use of correct English form (Brennan, 1975); and (3) external and explicit cues, such as metalinguistic symbols, will provide the deaf child with a reference or reinforcement mechanism that can be used as a guide for linguistic construction or correction. The underlying principles of the structured or combined approaches for teaching language are as follows: (1) language modeling must occur not only in language class but as an integral part of content areas as well; (2) the child must be given the opportunity to receive frequent exemples of the sentence patterns or targeted language forms; (3) structured stimuli must be provided so that the child has the opportunity to perceive the patterns of language and eventually produce the targeted patterns; and (4) acquired language patterns must be applied to novel stimuli to ensure generalization of language use in a variety of situations (Fey, 1986).

Wiig and Semel (1980) developed a set of principles applicable to the structured methods of language instruction. The teacher of hearing impaired children may find these principles particularly helpful in the development of instructional units and activities focusing on morphological and syntactic skills.

1. Unfamiliar words and sentence formation rules should be presented according to normal language developmental sequences or established orders of difficulty.
2. The words featured in the phrases, clauses, and sentences used for intervention should be highly familiar. They may be selected from vocabulary lists for age or grade levels at least 3 years or grades below the child's current vocabulary age or grade level.
3. Sentence length in number of words should be kept to an absolute minimum. This may be achieved by limiting sentence length to five to 10 words and phrase by keeping or clause length to two to five words. A minimum sentence will depend on the syntactic complexity of the units to which the rules apply.
4. Pictorial or printed representation of words, phrases, or clauses should be given for all spoken sentences. Pictures or referents for content words with referential meaning may be used in association with printed representations of non-referential or function words.

5. Unfamiliar words or sentence formation rules should be introduced in at least 10 illustrated examples. The examples should feature different word selections.
6. Knowledge of word or sentence formation rules should be established first in recognition and comprehension tasks and then in formulation tasks.
7. The knowledge and control of word and sentence formation rules should be established first with highly familiar word choices. They should then be extended to contexts with higher level or less familiar vocabulary or with unfamiliar concepts.
8. The knowledge and use of words and sentence formation rules should be tested in at least 10 examples that feature vocabulary not previously used. (pp. 122–123)

These principles are discussed within the context of the curriculum presented in the following section.

The Fitzgerald Key

The Fitzgerald Key has been the most enduring method for teaching language to deaf children, and it was the most popular method until the 1960s. More than two thirds of the schools for deaf children surveyed by Nelson in 1949 reported using the Fitzgerald Key as their primary tool for language instruction. As recently as 1979, the Kansas State School for the Deaf revised its reading and language programs on the basis of the Fitzgerald Key (Hudson, 1979). In classrooms for deaf children today, the "Key," as it is commonly called, remains visible on chalkboards and sentence strips.

The Fitzgerald Key was developed by Edith Fitzgerald and published in her book, *Straight Language for the Deaf*, in 1949. The key is a highly structured approach to language instruction "in keeping with the tenets of the structuralist linguists that words are the basic building blocks of sentences and that sentences are *formed* by left-to-right combination of words into strings" (Russell, Quigley, and Power, 1976, p. 7); however, Fitzgerald was committed to the use of language and language instruction occurring in the natural environment. She strongly supported experientially based instruction in naturally occurring routines. The Fitzgerald Key graphically displays syntactic relationships that are commonly acquired through the auditory mechanism. It was developed to provide children with rules that were visually accessible. Through the use of the Key, a deaf child could write a sentence by visually following the English rules of syntax. In addition, the deaf child could use the Key to correct composition errors (Kretschmer and Kretschmer, 1978; Moores, 1982; Pugh, 1955).

The Key consists of six columns, as is illustrated in Table 5-1. Each column is labeled with a set of symbols or headings that represent linguistic structures and functions within the sentence. Column 1 functions as the subject or noun phrase and is labeled with the interrogative terms *Who* and *What*. Column 2 contains the verb or verb phrase and subject complements, predicate adjective, predicate noun, and predicate pronoun. This column does not have a heading but uses symbols placed below the words in the column to indicate a verb and verb phrase (══════), an infinitive ═════, and a predicate adjective (┌────┐), predicate noun (_____), and predicate pronoun (──┬──). Column 3 functions as the direct and indirect object of the sentence. The column headings include questions *Whom* and *What*, *Whose* for the direct object; and *What* and *Whom* coupled with the parentheses symbol ( ) to indicate the indirect object form. Columns 4, 5, and 6 are adverbials or phrases modifying the main verb. When the full Key is used, Column 4 is the locative adverbial or the adverbial of place and is headed by the term *Where*, whereas Column 5 specifies frequency and causal modifiers of the main verb, *How much, How often, For, From, How, How Long* and *Why*. Column 6 is the adverbial of time and is labeled with the question heading *When*.

Rather than exposing the deaf child to the entire Key initially, the students are introduced to the Key words *Who* and *What*. Instruction begins with the classification of real people and real objects common

Table 5-1. The Fitzgerald Key

Who: Whose: What:		What: ( ) Whose: Whom: What:	Whom:	Where:	How much: How often: How long:	For: From: How:	When:
	═══ ┌──┐						▽─7

From B.L. Pugh (1955). *Steps in language development for the deaf. Illustrated in the Fitzgerald Key*. Washington, DC: The Volta Bureau.

to the deaf child's environment as either *Who* or *What*. Pictures of people, animals, and things in addition to their names are used in the classification process. Color cards are placed under the interrogative *What Color* and numerals are classified under the heading *How many* along with the quantifiers a (an), some, one, and two.

Once the child has acquired a strong foundation of nouns and adjectives, the Key is then introduced using the verb column. Fitzgerald (1949) recommends beginning with the pronoun *I* in the *Who* column and engaging the child in a real experiential situation. Thus, as the child is participating in a real activity, the sentence can be recorded using the Key as the guide for construction. As the child progresses and masters the sentence patterns illustrated in Table 5-2, the verb "to be" is introduced, together with the predicate adjective ⌐‾‾¬. Predicate nominatives _____ are provided only after the child has mastered the predicate adjective. As Pugh (1955) notes in her illustrations of the use of the Fitzgerald Key, each of the steps in the Key must be introduced as the opportunity for use presents itself. Thus, a programmed or "one, two, three method" of using the Key with deaf children is not advocated. Rather, as opportunities arise in the classroom setting, vocabulary and events can be classified within the structure of the Key following the heading classifications. Teachers must be keenly aware of linguistic patterns and competent in their ability to analyze sentence forms when using the Key appropriately.

Sentence patterns are expanded to include the noun phrase and intransitive verbs followed by the use of the subject *Who*, transitive verbs, and adverbial phrases. Adverbials of time and place can be

Table 5-2. Early Use of the Fitzgerald Key with Young Deaf Children

Who:			Whom:	What:	Where:	When:
	=== ⌐‾‾¬					
I	see			a car		
I	went				to school	on Friday
I	laughed					
Mary and I	laughed					
Mary	is	tired				
Mary	was	sick			in school	yesterday

introduced in conjunction with the daily calendar activities and storytelling. Conjunctives are introduced as part of the daily activities of the children and are indicated by the symbol placed under the conjunction. For example:

Who:	
Harry	screamed.
I	screamed.
Harry and I	screamed.

Complex sentence structures are illustrated within the Key by embedding clauses under the words they modify and within the same columns as the head words, and adding a conjunction (⌐――――¬) at the beginning and end of the key to accommodate compound sentence structures. Complex sentence structures are illustrated in Table 5-3, following the classifications within the Fitzgerald Key.

As already stated, the Fitzgerald Key became an extremely popular tool among teachers of deaf children. As its use continued to grow, several adaptations were made to accommodate the growing needs of deaf children. Thomas (1958) expanded the concept of the Key to include eight basic sentence patterns that children frequently encountered in reading textbooks. In addition, she added an adverbial phrase symbol and a symbol for time. The order of modifying adjectives was expanded to include a series of question headings rather than the listing provided in the Key. Sister M. Walter (1959) developed an array of instructional tools to accompany the Fitzgerald Key patterns, including

Table 5–3. Complex Sentence Structures Using the Fitzgerald Key

Whose:	Who: What:		What: ( ) Whose: Whom:	Whom: What:	Where:	How much: How often: How long:	For: From: How:	When:
	══ ⌐―――¬					why:		
Minnesota Farmers	are selling			their farms		because they cannot pay their loans.		
The lawyer	drew up		a sales	contract	in his office	for $50,000 dollars.		
The lawyer	will give			the money	to the farmer	to buy more land		when the loan comes through.
Sally's father who lives next door	is	a lawyer						

a desk wheel where students could classify, match, and build sentences in accordance with classifications and patterns set within the Key.

Using the categorical headings of the Fitzgerald Key and the philosophical commitment to patterning, Sister Jeanne D'Arc (1958) and Sister M. Buckler (1968) described the Patterned Approach to the development of connected language skills used at St. Joseph's School for the Deaf in St. Louis, Missouri. The patterns of commands were selected as the foundation for building more complex structures in the English language. Using the theme ''Hear it!, Use it!, Read it!, Write it!,'' patterns from the Fitzgerald Key were organized around the commands most frequently used in the child's environment. Table 5–4 lists the seven basic structures.

The first pattern begins with the verb *What* pattern. For example, *Get the book. Pour the juice. Find the cat. Put on your coat.* Given the command, children are shown what to do, then they follow the command and repeat the linguistic phrase. Expansions of each of the basic patterns occur through the introduction of carrier phrases.

Mother said, ''Pour the juice.''
My father said, ''Put on your jacket.''

As the child progresses through the various patterns, expansions and supplementary patterns may include the following (Buckler, 1968, p. 92):

I know how to _____ _____ .

It's fun to _____ _____ .

Remember to _____ _____ .

_____ _____ please.

Did you _____ _____ ?

Table 5–4. The Patterned Approach to Connected Language Development and Examples

	Pattern	Example
I	Verb + What	*Clean the windows.*
II	Verb + Where	*Come home.*
III	Verb + What + Where	*Put your coat in the closet.*
IV	Verb + Adjective	*Be good.*
V	Verb + Whom	*Help your mother.*
VI	Verb	*Work.*
VII	Verb + Whom + What	*Give me a can of pop.*

From: Buckler, M.S., Sr. (1968). Expanding language through patterning. *Volta Review, 70,* 89–96.

Short stories are prepared through a combination of directives and basic sentence patterns. The following scenario is based on the children's preparation for an experience trip to the Circus Parade:

On Saturday we will _____ _____ .

go to the parade	bring money for popcorn
ride on the bus	see many bands
go to the circus parade	hear many bands
see many clowns	watch big horses
see many elephants	bring blanket
see my Mom	sit on blankets
see lions	have fun
eat popcorn	

When simple basic patterns of the English language, that are familiar to children are used, language learning can be fun and progressive (Buckler, 1968).

In summary, the Fitzgerald Key, along with variations and expansions into the patterned language systems, provides the deaf child with a framework or system for the comprehension and production of the English language. One of the major problems with the patterned approach is that teaching must be carefully planned and integrated into the environment. All too frequently, the child is allowed to respond to the surface structure or to the pattern without consideration of the use of language in functional terms. Another problem encountered by teachers using the structured or patterned approach is that not all English language rules fit into a linear sequential pattern presented in formats such as the Key. The teacher must have a thorough understanding of linguistics and the rules of grammar to facilitate the instruction of complex language forms.

Although Fitzgerald did not suggest a specific order in which to present language structures, a common order emerged in language curricula, owing largely to the influence of Pugh's book (1955), *Steps in Language Development for the Deaf: Illustrated in the Fitzgerald Key*. This textbook was widely used as a guide for the order of presentation of language structures to deaf children. When Pugh wrote her book, little was known about the stages and sequences of language development. However, as information became available, language curricula were seldom changed to accommodate the new findings. For example, after children have developed a vocabulary of nouns, the next step presented in Pugh's book is the development of the concepts, *how many* and *what color*. Clark (1974), in her research on how children develop concepts, concluded that very young children most commonly abstract perceptual features, such as size, shape, and texture, first. It would seem logical, then, that the first adjectives to be emphasized in a language curriculum should deal with size, shape, and texture rather than number and color. In normal language development, children first use adjectives as single-word utterances, such as *big* or *dirty*, and then use them in two-word utterances such as *big balls*, *dirty sock*. Later, an utterance such as *That a big ball* is used, and, finally, *That's a big ball*.

Pugh suggests that after listing *how many* and *what color* words under appropriate headings, the child should say sentences with subject + verb + object word order—for example, *I see a ball*. The next step is to say a sentence such as *I see a red ball*. This is quite a large jump from single word to complete sentence and does not coincide with normal language development sequences. Issue could also be taken with the order of presentation of syntactic structures. The first point to be noted is that children do not progress from single word (*ball*) to a complete sentence (*I see a ball*). A second point to note is that very young children who are developing language normally are not expected to speak a complete sentence when they first start to use connected language. They are allowed to progress through normal sequences, such as *put chair* → *put sweater chair* → *put sweater on chair* → *put the sweater on the chair*. According to Pugh, in addition to using the sentence, *I see a red ball*, the ball should then be taken away and the deaf children should learn to say *I saw a red ball*. In normal language development, verbs are not learned in that order, that is, present tense and then past tense. A common sequence in early verb usage is *boy run* → *boy running* → *boy ran* → *the boy running* → *The boy is running*.

In addition to lack of consideration of ''child language'' utterances and the ''out of order'' sequence of presentations, this approach also strongly emphasizes language form, or syntax and morphology, and it particularly concentrates on correct word order. This emphasis on word order may foster or cause a tendency on the part of deaf children to view a sentence as a linear structure rather than as a hierarchical structure, thus precipitating common misinterpretations of certain structures. For example, the sentence, *Billy was hit by Susie*, is often interpreted by deaf children as *Billy hit Susie*, because they use linear word order as a clue to meaning, imposing a subject + verb + object interpretation and thereby deriving an inaccurate meaning from the structure.

Apple Tree Program

A Patterned Program for Linguistic Expansion Through Reinforced Experiences and Evaluation, more commonly referred to by its acronym, the *Apple Tree* (Caniglia et al., 1975) program, was the joint effort of five teachers at the Iowa School for the Deaf. Using their experiences as teachers of the English language for profoundly deaf children, coupled with the structured approach to teaching language, they developed the *Apple Tree* program to focus on the development of 10 basic sentence patterns as a foundation for a deaf student's language base. The program is designed to present these patterns through a sequential, spiraling system; that is, single elements to be learned are presented in small sequential steps and reinforced in subsequent lessons. A prerequisite skill required for the student prior to the introduction of the *Apple Tree* program is a "meaningful vocabulary base" (Caniglia et al., 1975, p. ix). It is suggested that students be able to name persons in their environment, label animals and things such as food and household items, and label verbs or action words that are common to the student's activities. Adverbs such as "when" and "where," particularly those related to calendar activities and the school-home environment, in addition to pronouns, are included in the prerequisite content. The criteria for performance of the suggested prerequisite skills are not specified. Specific vocabulary introduced to the students is determined by the teacher and should be relevant to the needs and environment of the child. Practice exercises at the beginning of the program include the use of familiar nouns, verbs, and adjectives in directive phrases with pictorial representations (e.g., *circle the apple, color the mittens blue, draw a big balloon*).

The first basic pattern introduced to the student is $N_1 + V_{(be)} +$ Adjective (e.g., *The car is red*). This pattern was selected as the basis for the program because characteristically it is a very redundant pattern, and it lends itself to use in naming and describing people and objects in the student's immediate environment.

Sentence patterns 2 and 3 follow the identical $N_1 + V_{be}$ pattern as in the first pattern. The adverbial *Where* is introduced in pattern 2. The third pattern consists of $N_1 + V_{be} + N_1$. Patterns 4, 5, and 6 are clustered to introduce the present progressive and past forms of verbs. In pattern 4, the new verbs are introduced through the modal *can*, keeping the noun phrase and verb following the modal consistent. Once the child has acquired the use of the modal *can*, present progressive, past progressive, and simple past tenses are introduced. The present progressive form of the verb *be* is taught prior to the simple past tense or the past progressive because it allows the child to use the already known forms of the verb *be* used in patterns 1, 2, and 3. The adverb phrase is repeated in pattern 5 and expanded to include the *Where* + *When* phrase in pattern 6.

The third cluster of patterns 7, 8, and 9 repeats the $N_1 + V$ structure and introduce the direct object (N_2) to the students. The adverbial phrases of *Where* and *Where* + *When* are added to the basic pattern $N_1 + V + N_2$ in patterns 8 and 9. The last pattern introduces the indirect object and is added to the pattern presented in the previous nine elements of the program. Table 5-5 illustrates the basic structures with linguistic samples used in the *Apple Tree* program.

The program was designed so that each of the successive sentence patterns introduced to the student becomes increasingly difficult, with minimal frustration in the learning process. New principles in the linguistic structures are introduced one at a time, building on those items that the student already knows. Through this stepping stone, or spiraling, approach the author's intent is to provide the students with a systematic framework for the English language.

In addition to the prescribed program of syntactic structures, the *Apple Tree* program provides an outline for instructional procedures that includes five fundamental steps (Caniglia et al., 1975):

1. Comprehension: Development of the child's understanding of the vocabulary, concepts, and form of the structure.

Table 5-5. *Apple Tree* Language Patterns

1. $NP_1 + V_{be} +$ Adjective
   The bird is black.

2. $NP_1 + V_{be} +$ Where
   The bird is on the tree.

3. $NP_1 + V_{be} + NP_1$
   The bird is a crow.

4. $NP_1 + V$
   The bird can eat.

5. $NP_1 + V +$ Where
   The bird can eat outside.

6. $NP_1 + V +$ Where + When
   The bird can eat outside every morning.

7. $NP_1 + V + NP_2$
   The bird can eat worms.

8. $NP_1 + V + NP_2 +$ Where
   The bird can eat worms in the grass.

9. $NP_1 + V + NP_2 +$ Where + When
   The bird can eat worms in the grass every morning.

10. $NP_1 + V + NP_3 + NP_2$
    Mother bird can give baby bird a worm.

From: Anderson, M., Boren, N., Caniglia, J., Howard, W., and Krohn, E. (1980). *Apple Tree*. Beaverton, OR: Dormac.

2. Manipulation: A procedure to help the child understand the structure of the language.
3. Substitution: A teaching procedure that allows the child to use the known to explore the unknown.
4. Production: Results when students have comprehended and internalized the structure form so efficiently that they can reproduce it spontaneously.
5. Transformations: The rearrangements made in the simple sentence patterns.

The purpose of the first step, comprehension, is to provide experience that enables the child to build vocabulary. This vocabulary is presented in functional or natural settings to assist the child in the internalization of the concept or deep meaning of the target vocabulary. As stated within the authors' definition of the term "comprehension," this instructional phase also includes experience with different types of structures in which the key vocabulary is embedded. Directives, question forms, possessives, and reflexive and possessive pronouns are all used in the development of the comprehension of adjectives for inanimate objects. The strategy proposed in the comprehension phase of instruction emphasizes the receptive skills of language acquisition. The authors note that comprehension activities are too frequently neglected in the process of teaching language to deaf children. Writing or expressive use of the vocabulary or the sentence patterns is not encouraged until the child has had sufficient experience with the form and function of the concepts being taught. In addition, the comprehension phase is included as a vital part of instruction at the preschool level and continues to be used throughout the educational experience with increasing complexity. The teacher is required to assess the student's needs and interests and selects the type and amount of vocabulary accordingly. Varying experiences should be provided with each vocabulary word and concept to ensure the child's learning. The presentation of vocabulary should be in keeping with the designated sentence pattern.

The second instructional strategy applied in the *Apple Tree* program is manipulation. Assuming the child has acquired the concept or meaning of the vocabulary words used, the manipulation phase provides the student with varying visual patterns of the language structure in which the known lexicon can be applied. The intent of the manipulation phase is the internalization of the structural configurations in which the words can be used and those configurations in which the words cannot be used. For example, the student may be given a set of word cards to arrange into a set pattern as follows.

Mary	is	happy.
John	is	sad.
Harry	is	lazy.

At a more advanced level, manipulation may include the following:

John and Mary	went	to their grandmother's house.
Did John and Mary	go	to their grandmother's house?
Where	did	John and Mary go?

The cards are prepared by the teacher according to the skills of the child. Sentences can be divided into their various components following the basic sentence patterns to be used in the instructional process.

Substitution is the third instructional phase. Once the child has established patterns or rules for the appropriate placement of known vocabulary, single elements of the structure are substituted, introducing new or unknown elements. An example of the substitution practice using sentence pattern 1 is:

Mary is happy.
She is happy.
John is sad.
He is sad.

At the more advanced level, the substitutions may include:

John wants to work.
Mary wants to stay home.
I want to watch TV.

Through the substitution process, in conjunction with the use of naturally occurring events and the students' personal preferences and opinions, relationships of words to one another and their placement into known patterns are established.

The fourth instructional phase is the spontaneous production of the sentence structures learned as a result of the preceding phases. Given various stimuli, such as a specific activity, a picture story, or the placement of an object in the room, the student writes a sentence using the patterns and vocabulary learned. Student workbooks that accompany the *Apple Tree* program provide a variety of illustrations and structures for the production of sentences following specific patterns. Short stories are also available in which students can complete preconstructed sentences.

The final phase of instruction is the transformation of the basic sentence patterns. The *Apple Tree* program includes two basic transformational patterns: the negative transformation and the question form. The negative tranformation pattern is limited to the addition of the word *not*. For example:

> The apple is red.
> The apple is not red.
> John is sad.
> John is not sad.

At the more advanced level:

> We will go to the store this afternoon.
> We will not go to the store this afternoon.
> Ms. Pat sang a song at the party.
> Did Ms. Pat sing a song at the party?
> Ms. Pat did not sing a song at the party.

Question forms are introduced very early in the *Apple Tree* program through modeling by the teacher. Using sentence pattern 1, the student is bombarded with questions, *What is red? Who is tall? Which door is open?* Within this most basic question form, the child is able to substitute nouns and pronouns for the question word and later simply substitutes the question form for the nouns and pronouns. The question word becomes the noun phrase, and the period becomes the question mark. More complex question transformations require the rearrangement of words and perhaps the addition of new words. For example, using sentence pattern 5:

> Mr. Brown ran in the Boston Marathon.
> Mr. Brown did run in the Boston Marathon.
> Did Mr. Brown run in the Boston Marathon?

Question forms are taught in conjunction with the substitution and production phases of instruction once the child has mastered the basic sentence pattern.

The *Apple Tree* program is a structured approach to teaching language using naturally occurring situations and settings to provide stimuli and specific vocabulary for the program. The time required to achieve competence in the use of the patterns outlined in the program depends on the child's maturation and ability as well as the opportunities provided in the instructional process. The Teacher's Manual includes strategies and suggested activities for teaching comprehension, manipulation, substitution, production, and transformations in a progressive sequence through the use of 10 basic sentence patterns. Pre- and post-tests for each of the patterns are provided in the manual to evaluate student performance. Student workbooks are provided for each of the 10 sentence patterns that reinforce the activities and vocabulary suggested in the teacher's manual. Additional reinforcement materials have been developed by Townson (1978) that include short stories and sentence production using the basic patterns. A series of *Apple Tree* Story Books (Cole, 1979) is also available to supplement language instruction.

Rhode Island Curriculum

The Rhode Island Curriculum (Blackwell et al., 1978), developed by Blackwell and teachers at the Rhode Island School for the Deaf, uses naturally occurring events, curricular topics, and academic areas of study to develop language within the framework of transformational-generative grammar (Chomsky, 1957). The curriculum incorporates acquisition stages of cognitive development (Piaget, 1955) and attempts to foster linguistic knowledge and spontaneous language through explicit experiences with language models and situations (Kretschmer and Kretschmer, 1978). On the basis of the early work of Streng (1972), five basic sentence patterns and a prescribed framework for language instruction are used to internalize rather than memorize syntactic structure and semantic development. The curriculum may best be described in three components. The first major component is the framework for the language program (Blackwell et al., 1978) that provides the instructional procedures integrated into the entire curriculum. Exposure, recognition, comprehension, and production, including reading and writing skills, form the basic steps for language acquisition by deaf children. The second major component is the division of the curriculum into three developmental levels of language learning: (1) the preschool-kindergarten level, (2) the simple sentence level, and (3) the language complexity level. The third component is shaped by the academic subject areas, including mathematics, science, social studies, and the arts. It is the integration of these three dimensions that Blackwell and his associates refer to as the ''Language and Learning Curriculum for Hearing Impaired Children.'' The discussion here is limited to the components of the framework for instruction and the developmental levels of language.

The process of language development involves a sequence of four interrelated steps: (1) exposure, (2) recognition, (3) comprehension, and (4) production (Blackwell et al., 1978). These steps are used as the ''framework'' for the establishment of language goals and for a logical order of presentation of targeted skills for student acquisition. The first step in developing language with preschool deaf children requires consistent exposure and experience with language as a tool for communication. Exposure to the functional use of language may include a variety of media, such as storybooks, experience charts, interactive games, and dialogue between teacher and student. It is not necessary at this stage of development for the child to understand or respond to all of the language forms and functions used by the teacher. Rather, the goal of the exposure to language is to provide students with experiences that are structured by the teacher. During the preschool and kindergarten years, the Rhode Island Curriculum guidelines include exposure to the basic sentence patterns, prepositional phrases, personal pronouns, and transformations, including negation, question forms, and the auxiliary form of the verb *do*. Functional or pragmatic aspects of language include exposure to turn-taking routines, language-play activities, and use of declarative, interrogative, and imperative sentence types.

The second step, recognition, is the ability of the child to identify a unit of language—that is, a word, phrase, question, or larger segment—as familiar. ''Recognition might be defined as an awareness that something perceived has been perceived before'' (Blackwell et al., 1978, p. 26). For example, young deaf children may recognize the pattern of a question form, although they may not comprehend the semantics of the question. Given the question, *How old are you?*, the child may respond appropriately, indicating comprehension of the question pattern and the semantics, or the child may say, *Yes!* in response to the pattern or form only. Through recognition of the linguistic structure, the child demonstrates his or her familiarity with a specific pattern of language. The third step, comprehension, is an integral part of recognition. Comprehension is defined as the child's ability to understand language, including the form, function, and meaning. In contrast to recognition, in which the child indicates familiarity with a linguistic unit, comprehension requires that the child ''know'' the content of the language presented. The challenge presented in steps 2 and 3 is the ability of the teacher to identify the child's competence in recognition and comprehension skills. This can only be done through the fourth step—production. Student's behavioral responses through writing, speech, sign language, pantomime, and gestures are all indicators of recognition and comprehension in addition to being indices of the student's skills in the use of language production. As with all children, the deaf child's ''actual production and performance of language will be somewhat delayed in comparison to his competence in the receptive areas of recognition and comprehension'' (Blackwell et al., 1978).

Writing and reading also have a significant role in shaping the framework for language development. Reading is a process that includes exposure, recognition, and comprehension, whereas writing is part of the production process. Writing is subdivided into three planes: (1) the linguistic plane, (2) the compositional plane, and (3) the functional plane. The linguistic plane addresses the form of linguistic structures and their developmental sequence as they appear in writing. Linguistic parameters in writing are illustrated in Blackwell's curriculum (Blackwell et al., 1978, pp. 29–30) in a sequential or developmental order, beginning with early scribbling through complex sentences. The compositional plane focuses on the deep structure or semantic value of the written material. Compositional skills include the labeling of illustrations, short messages, and extended paragraphs in which sentence organization and emphasis have an effect on the meaning of the linguistic structures used. The functional plane addresses the differences in linguistic structures used for functional purposes and in varying modes—that is, the recognition that the linguistic structures used in writing differ from those used in speech or signing. The functional plane may include letter writing, recording a message, taking notes, or using a TDD.

The developmental levels of language learning within the Rhode Island Curriculum begin at the preschool-kindergarten level. The model followed during this phase of instruction emphasizes language exposure and experiences, with the teacher functioning as the primary arranger of input. The primary goals at this level of instruction include the following:

1. Development of the concept of self, and how the child relates to others and to the environment.
2. Exposure to or production of, the concept of self, others, and the environment through simple sentence structures. This may include names of persons, places, animals, and objects that are familiar; exposure to question types, including who, what, where, and when; verbs resulting from personal and shared experiences.
3. Development of a sense of word order or pattern recognition, particularly the basic structure of Noun Phrase–Verb Phrase.
4. Ability to recognize different language structures and comprehension that these different structures serve different functions—for example, stories, commands, questions.

The second level of language learning focuses on the simple sentence level or the acquisition of five basic sentence patterns, which generally occurs during the preschool years through approximately 6 to 7 years of age. The patterns represent kernel sentences from which complex sentences can be constructed. Competency with the kernel sentence structures also permits complex sentences to be analyzed and understood on the basis of their kernel structure. Complex structures are introduced at approximately 8 years of age, once the child has mastered the basic patterns. These sentence patterns, outlined in Table 5–6, are interrelated but do not represent a progressive succession. Rather, each of the patterns is used as a contrast to the others as part of a teaching strategy to demonstrate semantic relationships that are influenced through syntactic structures.

Sentence pattern I (NP + VP) is the most basic pattern and is usually introduced very early in the child's language development experiences. In this pattern, as with all the others, emphasis is placed on the semantic relationships within the structure outlines. ''The child must acquire the ability to identify who or what is acting, what the action is, and who or what is being acted upon. . . . This is the essence of acquisition of linguistic structure'' (Blackwell et al., 1978, p. 70). Within sentence pattern I the emphasis is placed on name of actor and action. Adverbials may be introduced at the beginning or the ending of the sentences. Semantic relations for actor and action can be introduced with question forms *where*, *when*, and *how*. The following are examples of the semantic relationships:

Dad worked. (actor + action)
Dad worked at night. (actor + action + when)
Dad worked in the office. (actor + action + where)
Dad worked on his computer. (actor + action + where)
Dad worked quietly. (actor + action + how)
Yesterday, Dad worked in the office. (when + actor + action + where)

Table 5–6. Rhode Island School for the Deaf Curriculum: Five Basic Sentence Patterns and Examples

Pattern 1	*The boy*	*laughed.*	
	NP	V	
Pattern 2	*The boy*	*bought*	*candy.*
	NP$_1$	V	NP$_2$
Pattern 3	*The boy*	*is*	*nice.*
	NP$_1$	LV	Adjective
Pattern 4	*The boy*	*is*	*my cousin.*
	NP$_1$	LV	NP
Pattern 5	*The boy*	*lives*	*in Africa.*
	NP$_1$	LV	Adverbial

From Blackwell, P.M., Engen, E., Fischgrund, J.E., and Zarcadoolas, C. (1978). *Sentences and other systems: A language learning curriculum for hearing-impaired children.* Washington, DC: A.G. Bell Association for the Deaf.

Pattern II (NP_1 + V + NP_2) illustrates the actor + action + object relationship as well as the distinction between *who* and *what* forms. Comparisons within the kernel sentence structures of pattern II and sentence pattern V (NP + LV + Adverbial) can be made, highlighting a sequence of events with the object of the action—for example, *Tim read a book, Tim is in his room.* Pattern III (NP + LV + Adjective) uses the actor as the focal point, with the introduction of descriptors or attributes of the actor linked together by the linking verb or the verb of being, such as *Tim is busy.* Sentence pattern IV (NP + LV + NP) relates the actor to another attribute or the changing of one thing to another—for example, *Tim is a good reader.* Pattern V (NP + LV + Adverbial) contrasts with pattern I in the use of adverbials and with pattern II in the sequencing of events.

While the students are being taught the patterns, the instruction is never focused on the rote acquisition of structure but rather is focused on the internalization of form and the semantic relationships in the word order of each pattern to facilitate the expression of needs and events that the child has experienced. A typical lesson with early elementary youngsters may be conducted in the following manner:

Scenario: The teacher brings a basket of fruit to class, including bananas, apples, and oranges. The concept of fruit is introduced, along with members of the fruit family.

1. The teacher selects each piece of fruit and shows it to the class, emphasizing the following structures:
   The apple is a fruit.
   The apple is red.
   The apple is round.
   The banana is a fruit.
   The banana is yellow.
   The banana is long.
   The orange is a fruit.
   The orange is round.
   The orange is orange.
   The teacher peels the apple, the banana, and the orange.
   Ms. Pat peeled the apple.
   Ms. Pat peeled the orange.
   Harry peeled the banana.
   Outside, the apple is red.
   Inside, the apple is white.
   Outside, the orange is orange.
   Inside, the orange is orange.
   Outside, the banana is yellow.
   Inside, the banana is white.
   Ms. Pat cut the apple.
   Ms. Pat broke the banana.
   Ms. Pat pulled apart the orange.

2. Check for comprehension by asking the students to point to the basket of fruit, the orange, the apple, and so forth. *Show me the. . . .* Ask the students comprehension questions: *What is round? What is red? What is round and orange?*

3. Identify the noun phrases in the sentences listed previously. They may be labeled as *who* or *what.*

4. Identify the verb phrase: *What did Ms. Pat do with the apple? What did Ms. Pat do with the banana?*

5. Contrast sentence patterns used, writing the pattern for each.

6. Contrast verb phrases used, adverbs, and basic patterns.

Simple sentence transformations may be included as the child's needs indicate and as the experiences relate to the transformational pattern. These patterns are listed in Table 5-7.

The complex level of language development uses the child's competency with the basic sentence patterns and the child's growing need to communicate more complex events and experiences. Basic transformational forms are introduced as the need arises in experiential settings. These structures are conjugation, subordination, and relative clauses. Conjugation includes the joining of simple sentences as well as relational or interdependent structures (e.g., *First we will finish our work, and then we will build a snowman.*) Subordination includes the introduction of adverbial clauses, such as event ordering, time frames, or causality. Relative clauses are embedded phrases that describe or relate to the kernel sentence or to another sentence or to a concept that is not stated. The relative clause is frequently signaled by the *wh* words—for example, *Audrey, who lives next door, feeds my dog ice cream.* The deaf child unfamiliar with the relative clause structure interprets the *wh*-word as indicating a question form (Quigley, Wilbur, Power, Montanelli, and Steinkamp, 1976).

The Rhode Island Curriculum suggests that the syntactic processes of each of the transformations be taught through the identification of the kernel or basic sentence patterns and the position or changes in the pattern in relationship to the transformation. For example,

Table 5-7.   Sentence Transformation in Story Form

Ms. Pat brought a basket of fruit.
An apple is a fruit. An orange is a fruit.
A banana is a fruit, too. Ms. Pat peeled the orange and Harry peeled the banana.
Outside a banana is yellow and inside it is white. Outside an apple is red and inside it is white. An orange is orange inside and outside!

Mary fell down this morning.
Mary hurt her knee.
Mary went to the hospital.
Mary fell down and hurt her knee this morning.
Mary went to the hospital because she fell down and hurt her knee.

More complex structures include complementation, nominalization, and deletion. At this level of tranformational use, sentence diagrams frequently are introduced. Kretschmer and Kretschmer (1978) have questioned the introduction of diagramming into the stages of language development because the student may rely on the surface structure rather than the semantic relationships of the transformations to the kernel sentence structure. However, guidelines within the Rhode Island Curriculum recommend that the transformations be introduced in conjunction with events as they occur. A typical scenario may include the following:

> *Scenario:* A representative from the teen group of MADD (Mothers Against Drunk Driving) will be coming to the class to speak to the students the next day. The students are asked to give their views on drinking and driving. John says:
> *I like beer but I do not like to get drunk.*
> *Beer is alright.*
> *Driving is fun.*
> *Beer and driving are dangerous.*
> *Complementation:* Johnny thinks that mixing beer and driving is dangerous.
>
> MADD is against teenage drinking.
> MADD campaigned against teenage drinking.
> MADD saved many lives.
> *Nominalization:* The campaign against teenage driving by MADD saved many lives.

The Rhode Island Curriculum spans the range of language acquisition from the earliest stages of exposure to language in the environment through complex transformational levels using basic patterns of language as well as transformational diagrams. The teacher, through the basic sentence patterns, is required to interrelate patterns for the purpose of comparing and contrasting structures and semantics within given events. Blackwell and colleagues (1978) stress four basic principles for the acquisition of language with deaf children:

1. The goal for language acquisition should be the development of rules, both grammatical and semantic, that should be kept constant over multiple presentations. Emphasis should be placed on helping the child develop a grammatical strategy.
2. When presenting new linguistic principles, always present them in relation to real-life situations.

3. Errors in production should be accepted, as they reflect an attempt by the child to master linguistic rules. When errors are made, the child should be praised for his or her efforts and provided with a target model from which he or she can gain new information.
4. Linguistic comprehension and production should always be viewed in light of the perceptual-cognitive understanding of the child.

Other Combined and Structured Approaches

Although the Fitzgerald Key (Fitzgerald, 1949), the *Apple Tree* program (Anderson et al., 1980), and the Rhode Island Curriculum (Blackwell et al., 1978) are among the most frequently used combined approaches to teaching language to deaf children, numerous other language materials and curricula have been adopted in programs for the education of deaf children. King (1984) developed an extensive list of materials as a result of her national survey. The majority of the materials and curricula identified have been developed for use with hearing students. A few selected materials and approaches that have been developed specifically for use with deaf children are reviewed here.

The *TSA Syntax Program* (Quigley and Power, 1979) is a set of programmed exercises that provide students with drill and practice in specific syntactic structures. The intent of the program is to reinforce the language experiences and instruction that occur in the classroom through minute sequential steps focusing on a specific linguistic structure. The *TSA Syntax Program* can be used with the *Test of Syntactic Abilities* (Quigley et al., 1978) or with other language assessment methods as determined by the teacher. The program, which focuses on nine of the most frequently used transformational structures in the English language, consists of 20 workbooks divided into nine sets. Each set addresses one of the following linguistic structures: negation, conjunction, determiners, question formation, verb processes, pronominalization, relativization, complementation, and nominalization. Students can proceed through the workbook exercises independently with minimal teacher intervention. The teacher's guides contain explicit descriptions of each of the structures in addition to instructional objectives and activities for the development of language. The *TSA Syntax Program* is supplemental teaching material and should not be considered a curriculum guide or complete system for language development. The materials were developed as remediation programs for children 10 years old and older who were experiencing difficulties with English language structures. Generalization and application of the language structures taught in functional settings remain the responsibility of the teacher.

Lessons in Syntax (McCarr, 1980) was also developed for use with deaf children as a remedial program at the intermediate through post-secondary levels. *Lessons in Syntax*, like the *TSA Syntax Program*, uses a programmed linear approach in the presentation of syntactic structures with drill and practice. The presentation format is available in workbook or on microcomputer disks with accompanying guidelines. Other remedial language materials developed specifically for deaf students include the *Structured Tasks for English Practice* (Costello and Watkins, 1975) aimed at the secondary and postsecondary levels and *Learning Sentence Patterns with Julie and Jack* (Sr. M. Peter, 1984), emphasizing the early elementary grades.

The *Reading Milestones* series (Quigley and King, 1981, 1982, 1983, 1984) applies the combined approach to teaching language through a basal reading series that is the only basal reading program developed for use with deaf students. The reading material introduces syntactic structures and vocabulary in a systematic, reinforcing pattern. Basic sentence patterns are introduced gradually through illustrated stories that are highly motivating to the reader. New sentence patterns and vocabulary are practiced and reinforced in workbooks that accompany the reading series and through teacher activities suggested in the teachers' guides. The basic sentence patterns are reintroduced in sequential order with increasing levels of complexity in story form. *The Reading Milestones* series provides a structure for a whole language approach to reading but is not intended to be the language curriculum.

Other language reading materials include the *Simple Language Fairy Tales* by Newby (1984), which correspond in linguistic structure and vocabulary to the first three levels of *Reading Milestones. Simple English Classic Series* (Di Somma and McTiernan, 1985, 1986) includes a set of literary classics that uses the same basic sentence structures and vocabulary as the first six levels of the *Reading Milestones* series. This type of supportive material, including fairy tales and English classics, provides highly motivating, supplementary reading for deaf students that is not only accessible but fun.

Criticism has been raised (Ewoldt, 1983) regarding the use of linguistically controlled reading materials and text simplification with deaf students. The primary concern is that simplification of text materials will not challenge the student or provide opportunities to develop analytical decoding skills. The proposed alternative includes explicit teaching and repeated intervention in the reading process to assist the students in analyzing and decoding complex linguistic structures that are not understood or may be misunderstood. In addition, Ewoldt (1983) has suggested that the language experience approach "is an excellent way of conveying the message to developing readers or older students with reading problems" (p. 25).

Syntactic Structure series (Outreach, 1985, 1986) is available for high school level deaf students. Each of the books focuses on different types of relative clauses and complex sentence structures. The books attempt to teach the students having difficulty comprehending selected linguistic structures how to analyze or "think through" those structures in the context of a high interest story. This is done through supplemental use of a controlled reading book, teacher activities, filmstrips, and worksheets. The *Syntactic Structure* series does not constitute a curriculum or system of reading skill development; rather, it focuses on a remedial approach, highlighting syntactic structures that are complex or a problem to the student.

INSTRUCTIONAL STRATEGIES

Several fundamental instructional strategies are applicable to the combined or structured approach. Selected models identified by Muma (1971) and Wiig and Semel (1984) are presented in this section as they apply to language programming with deaf children. Each of the instructional models used in the structured or combined method of language development is teacher-initiated, in contrast to those models presented in the natural approach, which generally are child initiated. These models assume that the teacher exhibits competencies in the "nature and structure of language, language learning, and language usage to be able to appreciate dimensions of grammar and principles of linguistic behavior" (Muma, 1971, p. 7).

Correct-Incorrect Model

Teacher: *The girl slipping on the banana peel. Right or wrong*
Child: *No! Wrong!*

The correct-incorrect model requires the student to identify correct grammatical patterns and to determine whether the use of specific structures within the sentence presented are appropriate. This model may be expanded into multiple choice exercises in which students are presented with a set of sentences and asked to identify the correct sentence pattern. The multiple choice format using the correct-incorrect judgment approach is used in the *Test of Syntactic Abilities* (Quigley et al., 1978) to test the student's ability to recognize rules of grammar. It is the primary format for the assessment and instruction of sentence formation rules. It precedes more difficult instructional presentations, such as completion or sentence replacement tasks (Wiig and Semel, 1980).

Completion Model

Teacher: *The boy _____.*
Child: *The boy laughed.*
Teacher: *The boy _____ at the funny clown.*
Child: *The boy laughed at the funny clown.*

The completion model focuses on the presentation of a single element such as a noun, verb, or a sentence pattern with an element missing. The child is required to use the element presented in a phrase or a sentence or to complete the pattern presented. The completion model is used frequently at the preschool level in the presentation of concepts of time and calendar activities. The teacher may present sentence strips with the following phrases:

Yesterday was _____.
Today is _____.
Tomorrow will be _____.

The student may complete the sentence with a noun phrase (e.g., Monday, Tuesday, Wednesday) or with adjectives describing the weather. This model emphasizes the appropriate use of syntactic structures and can be an effective method of practice. The sentence completion model is used frequently for the instruction of morphology and rules for single words and phrases. The teacher may elect to provide the student with a multiple choice format in which the child is given cues for sentence completion, or the difficulty of the task may be increased by allowing the child to fill in the missing segment without choices. The highest level of difficulty would be the presentation of the base word or phrase that is targeted for instruction and asking the child to use the target in a complete sentence following specific rules of grammar.

Replacement Model

Teacher: *The bird is in the tree.*
Child: *The bird is in the nest.*
Teacher: *The baby bird is in the nest.*
Child: *The mommy bird is in the nest.*

The replacement model stresses the presentation of complete sentence patterns. The child is required to replace a single element or phrase of his or her choice. Using the teacher's stimulus pattern just presented, the child could respond appropriately, "The baby bird flew out of the nest." This model is considered a more powerful form of drill and practice than the completion model because it provides the student with a complete syntactic pattern. Students are free to select any element of the pattern they choose to convey an alternative message. In the completion model, the student is required to "fill-in" a predetermined pattern and to match the semantic intent of the teacher's model (Gunter, 1960).

Combination Model

Teacher: *Dad is working.*
Child: *Dad is in the office.*
Teacher: *Dad is busy.*
Child: *Dad is busy working in the office.*

The instructional method of combining sentence patterns into a single transformation pattern has traditionally been used by teachers as an effective method of developing expanded and complex sentence patterns with deaf students. In a peer group learning program, students were given a set of basic sentences and told to combine the sentences into a single sentence. Mellon (1967) reported that the junior high school students participating in the study demonstrated superior writing abilities than students in traditional English grammar classes. Muma (1971) emphasized that the combination model of instruction assumes that the student has an "understanding of phrasestructure and variations on phrase structure (transformations) as well as semantics" (p. 14).

The task of joining two or more related sentences can be introduced in incremental steps through the correct-incorrect, multiple choice, and completion formats. This step-by-step presentation supplies a model for synthesis of basic sentence patterns and provides the student with greater opportunities for success with complex linguistic structures. For example,

Model: *John's shoes are muddy.*
            John put his shoes on the front porch.
Step 1:   **Correct-Incorrect**
            John's shoes on the front porch put muddy.
            John put his muddy shoes on the front porch.
Step 2:   **Multiple Choice**
            John put his muddy shoes on the front porch.
            John's shoes are muddy because put his shoes on the front porch.
            John's put his shoes muddy on the front porch.
            John's shoes put front porch muddy.

Scrambled Sentences

Teacher: *chased   around the room   Garfield   the mouse*
Child 1: *Garfield chased the mouse around the room.*
Child 2: *The mouse chased Garfield around the room.*

Use of scrambled sentences as an instructional method provides the student with practice in ordering words and phrases into basic sentence patterns (Wiig and Semel, 1984). Sister M. Peter (1984) has prepared a number of scrambled sentence exercises using the kernel patterns and simple transformations around the themes of *The Family Circle* and *Jack and Julie* stories. Levels of difficulty are varied by increasing the number of structures the child must manipulate and place into the correct grammatical structure and by increasing the complexity of the structures used.

Revision Model

Teacher: *Teachers work very hard.*
Teachers are dedicated people.
Good teachers have a sense of humor and enthusiasm for their teaching profession.

Student: *The teaching profession requires good teachers who have a sense of humor and enthusiasm for their jobs and who are hard working and dedicated.*

The revision model presents a set of semantically related sentences. The students are required to rearrange and revise the sentences into a single sentence form. The revision method of instruction can be controlled by the teacher to provide exercises in a variety of syntactic patterns and transformations. It can also be controlled by the students through the manipulation and revision of grammatical structures to devise the semantic intent of the patterns presented by the teacher.

No one instructional strategy or method presented provides the ''key'' to language learning with deaf children. Rather, the models provide optional methods for instruction, drill, and practice. The teacher is ultimately responsible for the selection of models of instruction and for providing students with multiple successful practice situations that are highly motivating to ensure acquisition of the rules that govern language.

SUMMARY

The common threads running through the curriculum and practices reviewed include (1) the use of metalinguistic symbols as a guide for the production of appropriate English sentences or to assist the student in evaluating his or her own production in comparison to ''good English form,''(2) repeated exposure through teacher modeling in spoken, signed, and written modalities stressing targeted sentence patterns or grammatical forms, (3) reception and comprehension as demonstrated by the student's ability to classify or categorize sentence patterns precede the child's production of sentence patterns, and (4) language instruction based on the child's experiences, interests, and environmental demands. Each of the curricula varies in the sequence of presentation of basic sentence patterns and in the order of introduction of complex structures. In addition, the metalinguistic symbols used to illustrate the patterns of linguistic structures vary; however, the key symbols, particularly those used in the identification of the verb phrase ========, noun phrase _____ , and adjectives ⌐‾‾‾‾⌐ , appear with some consistency.

The variable elements of each of the systems consist of the degree to which structure is provided to classify or code language into the various structures of the English language. Each of the systems depends on the teacher's ability to provide carefully controlled structures and vocabulary in as natural a setting and manner as possible. As Streng (1958) has stated, ''Grammar is taught by minimizing the number of structures used and introducing each structure in its right place and ideal order. The vocabulary is useful, for it includes those items which the learner can use as quickly as possible, and those which best prepare him for the instruction which follows'' (p. 555).

C H A P T E R 6

Using American Sign Language to Teach English

Peter V. Paul and
Stephen Quigley

In recent years some educators have argued that English should be taught as a second language to deaf students by using techniques found to be effective in bilingual education and second-language learning programs (Barnum, 1984; Quigley and Paul, 1984a; Reagan, 1985). This assertion has been supported mainly by negative data; that is, the overwhelming majority of deaf students have not learned to read and write adequately through the use of existing communication forms that are based on English. There is disagreement, however, on how to improve the English language skills of deaf students. For example, should American Sign Language (ASL) and English be developed concurrently in infancy and early childhood as in a bilingual environment? Or should ASL be taught as a first language to all deaf students, and then English as a second language (ESL)? Finally, should English be taught as a second language only to students who know ASL as a first language or to all deaf students? The major objective of this chapter is to discuss how ASL can be used to teach English literacy skills.

LANGUAGE COMPETENCE OF DEAF STUDENTS

Any discussion of bilingualism and ESL for deaf students should consider the following question: What is the nature of the primary language of the deaf child? This depends on the child's degree of competence in comprehension and production of both the spoken (or signed) and written modes of the language. There are two important aspects of this question: (1) the nature of the language, that is, English or ASL, and (2) the nature of the communication mode, that is, manual or oral. These languages and communication modes may be employed in various combinations and may involve the auditory or visual sense modality, or both (Quigley and Kretschmer, 1982; Quigley and Paul, 1984b). Nearly all educators agree that there are two distinct communication modes and languages, and most agree that vision is used as the primary sense modality for language reception by deaf students, with audition acting in a supplementary fashion. There is little agreement, however, on the nature of the primary language of *most* deaf students (Luetke-Stahlman and Weiner, 1982; Quigley and Paul, 1984b).

It is possible to view the language development of deaf students in relation to the type of input from their parents in early infancy and childhood. Within this perspective, the first language of students in the United States ranges from low to high competency in some form of English because most have English-speaking, hearing parents. It is well documented, however, that most deaf students graduating from high school cannot read or write English at a functional literacy level (Allen, in press; King and Quigley, 1985; Quigley and Paul, 1986). Although care should be exercised in using performance on secondary language assessments as a barometer of primary language skills, it is still safe to conclude that an overwhelming majority of deaf students do not possess an adequate command of English or any other spoken language.

If deaf students come to school knowing a language, this language is most likely to be American Sign Language. This has led to the position that ASL should be the native or first language for *all* deaf students as it can be learned in a normal, interactive manner (Barnum, 1984; Bockmiller, 1981; Charrow and Wilbur, 1975). In essence, this would create a more homogeneous group of students with a well-developed, internal cognitive, and linguistic background, making it easier, theoretically, to acquire a second language later. To discuss how ASL can be used to teach English, it should be made clear how it differs from English and from the English-based signed systems.

AMERICAN SIGN LANGUAGE AND ENGLISH

American Sign Language is a formal language system, socially agreed-on, rule-governed symbol system that is generative in nature (Bellugi and Klima, 1972; Wilbur, 1979). The components of ASL are not phoneme combinations that form words, as in spoken languages, but rather are chereme combinations that form signs. Thus, whereas speech as used in spoken English is an organizational system that is auditory, vocal, and temporal, signs used in ASL are best described as visual, motor, and spatial. American Sign Language is a visual-gestural, rule-governed language (Baker and Cokely, 1980; Lane and Grosjean, 1980; Woodward, 1986). The linguistic units of ASL consist of movements, shapes, and positions of specific body parts, such as hands, arms, eyes, face, and head. ASL, and all other sign languages, is structured to suit the needs and capabilities of the eye. Concepts are executed with manual and other systematic gestural (nonmanual) movements. The native signer develops signs relative to objects in the environment, proceeding from simulated iconic features and movements to more abstract use. Deaf native signers are able to monitor their own signs (and those of others) as well as facial expressions, body movements, and other subtleties. Some aspects of the sign movements have the same function as vocal intonation and other paralinguistic features involved in speech production. The signers learn various subtleties of signs early in childhood and rely on them in communicating, for example, intentions, emotions, and double-meanings.

The scientific study of ASL began with the seminal work of Stokoe (1960); descriptions of its grammar emerged in the late 1970s (Baker and Cokely, 1980; Klima and Bellugi, 1979; Lane and Grosjean, 1980). The acquisition of ASL has been investigated in relation to the various components established for spoken languages: phonology, syntax, semantics, and pragmatics. A number of researchers have reported on certain linguistic aspects, such as markedness (McIntire, 1977), classifiers (Kantor, 1980; Luetke-Stahlman, 1984), and iconicity (Orlansky and Bonvillian, 1984).

American Sign Language differs from English in two important aspects: form and grammar (Baker and Cokely, 1980; Quigley and Paul, 1984a). English is a spoken language in which the primary form is manifested by speech and the secondary form is manifested by a written component. There is some relationship, albeit a complex one, between the primary and secondary forms. American Sign Language is a signed language executed without the accompaniment of speech. The primary form of ASL is sign; there is no corresponding secondary form related to signs. American Sign Language has its own grammar, which is not derived from that of English. American Sign Language, like any other minority language coexisting in a majority-language culture, is influenced somewhat by English, however. This can be seen, for example, in the use of borrowed fingerspelled signs, as in signing NG for *no good* (Battison, 1978). Another example is the execution of adjective signs before noun signs, as in INTELLIGENT WOMAN.

If it is understood how ASL differs from English, it should also be clear that ASL differs from the contrived signed codes that were developed to represent the morphosyntactic structure of English in a manual manner. For example, the various signed codes are executed simultaneously with speech, which provides additional information through the use of intonation and other features. Analogously, ASL, as a sign language, uses nonmanual signals, such as puffed cheeks and pursed lips, to convey important linguistic and paralinguistic information.

Even though the lexicon of ASL forms the basis of most of the signs in the English-based codes, these signs do not retain their original syntactic and semantic properties, as is evident in the context of ASL (Stokoe, 1975). This is the most important, fundamental difference between ASL and the English-based signed codes. Consider the following sentence as an example: *He is looking for his car.* In several English-based signed systems, the phrase *looking for* is expressed as LOOK (usually with initialized *L* shape) plus -ING and FOR (e.g., Bornstein, Saulnier, and Hamilton, 1983; Gustason, Pfetzing, and Zawolkow, 1980). -ING is a contrived sign marker; however, the focus here is on the use of the two ASL-like signs, LOOK and FOR. The sign, *LOOK*, means to watch, see, or look at, and *FOR* means "with a purpose" in the context of ASL (Sternberg, 1981). Thus, as used in the foregoing sentence, it is conceivable that native ASL signers might misunderstand the meaning. In contrast, ASL signers would express the concept *lookingfor* by using signs that mean HUNT or SEARCH.

During the 1970s, the philosophy of total communication (TC) became dominant in educational programs for hearing impaired students (Moores, 1982; Quigley and Kretschmer, 1982). Consequently, most programs use signs, often simultaneously with speech, and usually taken from one or more contrived signed systems (Gallaudet Research Institute, 1985; Jordan, Gustason, and Rosen, 1979). As stated, the primary or native language of some deaf children is ASL. For these children, at least, ASL could be used as an instructional approach to teach English literacy skills in a bilingual or ESL program (Luetke-Stahlman, 1983; Quigley and Paul, 1984a; Reagan, 1985). It appears, however, that many educators of deaf students have not accepted ASL within the philosophy of total communication. Thus, its use in the classroom has not been documented extensively. It may also be that because a grammar of ASL has only recently been published, its role in a bilingual or ESL situation has yet to be explored. Owing to limited data, the instructional methodologies for using ASL to teach English need to be derived mainly from the research on hearing students in bilingual or ESL programs.

SECOND LANGUAGE OR BILINGUAL INSTRUCTION

Research on the effects of exposure to two spoken languages on intelligence, cognition, and educational achievement has resulted in a number of conflicting models and theories. A more detailed description of these positions and their subsequent effects on the development of bilingual education programs and instructional methodologies can be found elsewhere (Cummins, 1984; Paulston, 1980; Quigley and Paul, 1984b). In interpreting the data on level of educational achievement, particularly in the development of the target language, two multifaceted factors should be considered: (1) the characteristics of the students, and (2) the type of education program.

Characteristics of Students

Numerous student characteristics with interrelating linguistic, socio-logical, and psychological perspectives can be considered (e.g., Garcia and Padilla, 1985; Lambert and Tucker, 1972). In light of these, it is possible to differentiate majority-language from minority-language students. This distinction is important because the education programs and objectives for the two groups may need to be different.

Individuals who are educated in a culture in which there are two (main or heritage) languages of nearly equal status can be labeled majority-language students (Bruck, 1985; Genesee, 1983; Swain, 1981). These students usually acquire communication skills in both languages and knowledge of the respective cultures. Majority-language students typically are enrolled in immersion bilingual programs in which the predominant language of instruction in the early grades is that which is not their home or native language. For example, in Quebec (and several other provinces of Canada), students whose native language and culture is English receive most of their early education in French (French immersion). A large number of these programs have been implemented across Canada (Swain and Lapkin, 1982).

Individuals who are educated in a society in which one heritage or majority language is emphasized and whose native language and culture is different from that of the mainstream can be labeled minority-language students. These individuals need to acquire the knowledge of the language and culture of the main society in which they live. In the United States, deaf students whose native or first language is ASL can be considered minority language students.

Type of Program

As might be expected, descriptions of bilingual education programs vary according to the type of student (i.e., majority- or minority-language) as well as to goals and theoretical perspectives. There are programs that range from maximum exposure to the target language to those that espouse the predominant use of the language and culture of the home environment (Navarro, 1985; Otheguy and Otto, 1980; Paulston, 1980). For example, in some programs, the medium of instruction is in L_2 (language of the school), with one component devoted to L_1 (home or native language). As discussed previously, the Canadian early immersion programs are of this type. In some programs, both L_1 and L_2 are used equally as the media of instruction throughout the school day. Finally, there are programs in which L_1 is used predominantly, with one L_2 component. Among these program types, it appears that the primary difference is with the medium of instruction. Variation among programs involves the arrangement and emphasis of the components. The most crucial variables are the sequencing of languages for initial instruction and literacy, the emphasis on L_1 and its culture, and the ethnicity and competency of the instructors. Also of importance is the amount of time allocated to each language for the content areas and other aspects of the curriculum.

Two general bilingual program models can be described: transitional and maintenance. A number of programs in Canada and the United States have followed one or the other of these models or some variation of them (Cummins, 1984; de Kanter and Baker, 1983; Navarro, 1985; Otheguy and Otto, 1980). In transitional programs, the minority language (L_1) typically is employed in the initial stages (first few elementary grades) only to allow the efficient assimilation of curriculum content while the majority language (L_2) is being learned (compare the quick-exit transitional programs described in Cummins, 1984). The L_1 is not seen as functional in minority-language students' academic or cognitive development, and no attempt is made to promote or maintain their competence in that language. Transitional programs typically have ESL instruction, which includes about 50 to 60 minutes daily of structural lessons in the grammar of English. The major aim of the maintenance model, especially developmental maintenance, is to develop a high level of competence in L_1 and L_2. This includes programs involving partial or total immersion in a second language or those in which two languages are employed more or less equally for instructional purposes. Programs following a maintenance model are said to be truly bilingual programs that promote the language and culture of the minority-language students.

The sequencing and amount of emphasis placed on languages and cultures may vary in maintenance bilingual programs. For example, some Canadian immersion programs and some United States Title VII programs have implemented a simultaneous instructional approach (Cohen, 1974; Paulston, 1980). In this approach, the two languages are used more or less equally throughout the school day. This could be considered an alternative immersion program (Cummins, 1984). The salient tenets are as follows:

1. Intensive instruction in all subjects is conducted in one language in the morning and in the other language in the afternoon, or both languages are employed equally to teach all subjects.
2. Reading in both languages is introduced simultaneously in the period in which the oral languages are employed or after proficiency is attained in the oral languages.

In the native language approach, the L_1 of minority-language students is the predominant medium of instruction in the early elementary grades (Baker and de Kanter, 1981; Genesee, 1979). Cummins (1984) refers to this approach as minority-language bilingual immersion. The steps are as follows:

1. Instruction in early grades is in L_1.
2. Reading is introduced in L_1 after oral proficiency is established.
3. Intensive instruction is given in L_2; L_1 may be used to teach L_2; by this time, reading may be established in L_1.
4. Reading in L_2 is introduced after oral proficiency in L_2 is established.

The major question that needs to be answered is which instructional approach leads to the development of literacy skills in the main language(s) of the general society for minority-language students. There is even some debate as to whether bilingual programs are necessary to accomplish this objective (see Quigley and Paul, 1984b).

Synthesis of Research: Minority-Language Hearing Students

A review of the literature reveals that the development of L_2 literacy and educational success for minority-language students are most likely to occur in developmental maintenance bilingual programs (Baker and de Kanter, 1981; Bruck, 1982; Cummins, 1984; Troike, 1978, 1981). In general, students taught through their L_1 for all or part of the school day perform as well as or better than their equivalent counterparts (i.e., majority-language students) in regular programs as determined by standardized scores in language arts, mathematics, and self-concept. When both bilingualism and biculturalism are emphasized, maintenance programs appear to be appropriate for students with a wide range of learning abilities and language skills. Academic achievement in developmental maintenance programs has been reported to be higher than observed in either transitional programs or submersion (sink-or-swim) programs (i.e., English only with little or no attention given to the language or culture of the minority-language student). Success has been noted particularly in alternative immersion (Baker and de Kanter, 1981; Legarreta, 1979) or minority-language immersion programs (Cummins, 1979, 1984; Gamez, 1979). Alternative immersion programs employ some version of the simultaneous instructional approach, whereas minority-language immersion programs espouse the native language instructional approach. It has been argued that the optimal development of L_1 and, subsequently, L_2 for minority-language students is most likely to occur in a bilingual minority-language immersion program (Cummins, 1984).

ASL AND ENGLISH FOR DEAF STUDENTS

The limited research on deaf ASL-signers in bilingual or ESL education programs is described here in relation to three areas: (1) the effects of ASL on the development of English, (2) the performance of bilingual deaf students, and (3) the use of ASL in teaching English as a second language.

Effects of ASL on English

To study the effects of ASL on the development of English, researchers have compared the performances of deaf students of deaf parents (DSDP) with the performances of deaf students of hearing parents (DSHP). Within this paradigm, it was usually assumed that deaf parents were using only ASL with their children. In general, DSDP were found to outperform DSHP significantly in academic achievement, particularly in the reading of English (e.g., Meadow, 1968; Quigley and Frisina, 1961; Stuckless and Birch, 1966). It was concluded that early exposure to manual communication (probably ASL) resulted in higher achievement levels for DSDP.

The assumption that ASL is the only medium of communication for DSDP has been refuted. Some deaf parents may use a signed system based on English, and some may use speech (e.g., Corson, 1973). Furthermore, because a grammar of ASL has only recently been described in detail, it is possible that the communication system of deaf parents may not have been described adequately in the early studies. In addition, the reasons for the superior performance of DSDP have been refined. It has been shown that type of manual communication (as well as parental acceptance and other factors) is important (e.g., Brasel and

Quigley, 1977), especially in the form of an English-based signed system that is not cumbersome (see the discussion in Quigley and Kretschmer, 1982). The point here is that the effects of ASL on the development of English have not been investigated systematically.

Bilingual Deaf Students

A few researchers have assessed the language proficiency of deaf students by using story retelling tasks. For example, Hatfield, Caccamise, and Siple (1978) evaluated competency in ASL and manually coded English (MCE) of students at the National Technical Institute for the Deaf (NTID) in Rochester, New York. The students were divided into three groups according to a sociological scale used to rate levels of competency in ASL. Two videotaped stories, one in ASL and the other in MCE, were administered to the students. The performances of the three groups were found to correspond to their ASL rankings. That is, the High ASL group produced the fewest errors on both the ASL and MCE videotaped versions, followed by the Median group and the Low group. Subjects performing the best on the ASL videotape also made the fewest errors on the MCE videotape. The results seem to suggest that bilingual language competency varies among some deaf students. In addition, it was argued that ASL does not interfere with the development of English language skills. The authors suggested, however, that the high performance on the MCE version by the High ASL group might have been attributable to the inclusion of ASL-like grammatical features in the MCE system that was used.

More recently, Stewart (1985) studied the performances of deaf students in a high school in Vancouver, British Columbia Canada. The signing skills of the students in ASL and signed English (SE) were rated by their teachers and judges selected by the researcher. Videotaped stories in ASL and SE were presented to the students, and they were required to retell the stories. The researcher was interested in exploring the effects of a dominant language, either ASL or SE, in these deaf students. He hypothesized that deaf students would retell stories in their dominant language. It was found that the ASL dominant students preferred to retell stories in ASL. The SE dominant students, however, also preferred to retell stories in ASL. Thus, the hypothesis was tenable for the ASL dominant group only. It should be pointed out that most of the students were labeled ASL dominant as determined by the ratings. Nevertheless, it was concluded that deaf students prefer retelling stories in ASL because it is well suited to the processing capabilities of the eye.

Using ASL to Teach English

The prevailing notion in using ASL to teach English is that most deaf students should learn ASL as a first language in an interactive setting. Theoretically, competency in one language makes it easier to learn a second one. Yet, very little research has been conducted on using ASL to teach English literacy skills.

Crutchfield (1972) compared some count features (e.g., *much, many, few*) of ASL and English. Initially, the students in this study were required to identify incorrect utterances. For example, suppose a student signed: MUCH GIRL LIKE FOOTBALL. For students with competence in ASL, this sentence is not acceptable. After identifying the error, the student was asked to produce an acceptable signed utterance, that is, MANY GIRL LIKE FOOTBALL. Translation into written English should yield: *Many girls like football*. If, however, the written English translation is: *Many girl like football*, the next lesson deals with plurality. The main steps are (1) identify an incorrect utterance in one language, (2) produce an acceptable response, (3) translate the utterance into the other language, and (4) indicate acceptability and unacceptability in both languages.

In a more recent study, Jones (1979) examined the notion of interference between two languages, that is, ASL and English-based signing. He argued that the signing competence and written English productions of deaf students resemble a pidgin form of English because the students neglect to include nonmanual aspects of their ASL utterances. When signing to instructors who do not know ASL, students minimize the use of nonmanual signals (e.g., eyebrow movements, puffed cheeks). Consequently, their written language reflects these omissions, and it is not always comprehensible to the native speaker of English. Because nonmanual signals provide important syntactic and semantic information, the author concluded that deaf students who know ASL need to become aware of the signed information that is absent in their writing. It appears that more attention should be directed to the nonmanual components of ASL as the students are likely to write only the English glosses (i.e., the manual signals) of the ASL signs.

BILINGUAL INSTRUCTIONAL PROGRAM: A MODEL

In this section, a bilingual instructional model is proposed. Insights concerning curriculum, instruction, and evaluation are derived mainly from the research on hearing, minority-language students (e.g., Bowen, Madsen, and Hilferty, 1985; Cummins, 1984) and materials from a few workshops on teaching ASL as a second language or in a bilingual situation in which ASL is the first language (Marbury and Mackinson-Smyth, 1986; Rutherford, 1986; Strong, Burdett, and Woodward, 1986). In this model, both bilingualism and biculturalism are stressed. That is, the emphasis is on developing and maintaining communicative competence in ASL and, eventually, in a form of English-based signing, and on teaching both English literacy and major cultural and educational concepts.

Theoretically and empirically, a minority-language bilingual immersion program is recommended. The major medium of instruction and discussion of activities and subjects in preschool and grades 1 and 2 is ASL. It is important also to establish contact with an accessible community of signers and other members using the language who can reinforce the students' acquisition because they are likely to enter school with wide ranges of communicative competence. Fluent communication with the various participants as well as the classroom teacher might foster the development of cognitive and linguistic abilities. In addition, this might provide a base of real-world knowledge that is necessary for the later development of English literacy (King and Quigley, 1985), which is to be introduced during grade 3. From grade 3 to graduation, both ASL and English are used more or less equally for instructional purposes.

Personnel

In the education of deaf students, one of the major questions that needs to be addressed is; Who should participate in a bilingual program? It is argued that, initially, bilingual programs should be established for those deaf students for whom ASL is the first or native language (Quigley and Paul, 1984a, 1984b). The implementation of such programs is most likely to be acceptable to the students' parents, most of whom are deaf themselves and members of the deaf community. A case can be made also for other profoundly hearing impaired students for whom ASL is not a first language, and who may not have a first or native language (see discussions in Reagan, 1985; Stewart, 1985; and Strong et al., 1986). This should be considered in light of documented improvement on psychoeducational and psychosocial assessments for ASL-using deaf students.

Endless debates can take place regarding the characteristics of competently trained teachers. There is no question that they should possess knowledge of the prevailing thinking and techniques in language-related areas and in other subjects that they teach. What is stressed here is that teachers need to be bilingual, that is, they should be proficient in both ASL and English. It might be of benefit to the students if qualified deaf teachers were employed because they can serve as excellent role models. The deaf teachers can also easily establish a bicultural environment because they are most likely to be members of the deaf community. Another possible situation is to use both deaf and hearing teachers in the same classroom.

Curriculum and Instruction

It should be emphasized that no substantial empirical evidence exists in support of any one specific instructional method for accomplishing the objectives of a bilingual education program (Bowen et al., 1985). Although a wide variety of language-teaching approaches have been promoted, there has been a trend away from a global evaluation of techniques to a focus on *pragmatic eclecticism* or *methodological pluralism* (Bailey, 1983; Krashen, 1982; Krashen and Terrell, 1982, 1983), especially in an interactive educational environment. Consequently, there is a place for the implementation of meaningful structural and natural approaches. (This should sound familiar to teachers of deaf students). In general, instructional approaches are based on descriptive reports of classroom research, broad-based research findings in language-related areas, and common sense and experience (Scovel, 1982).

A comprehensive bilingual program makes provisions for at least the following issues:

1. The educational characteristics (i.e., motivation, learning styles) of individual students.
2. The establishment of a bicultural environment and access to the cultural community.
3. Exposure to and practice in the native and target languages.
4. Realistic, meaningful, and structured lessons.
5. Competently trained teachers and appropriately prepared materials.
6. Evaluation of the program.

In the following paragraphs, these issues are highlighted in relation to specific instructional activities.

ASL as the Medium of Instruction

Primary Development of ASL

A number of resources can be used to enhance the maintenance and development of ASL and the transmission of concepts regarding the deaf culture; for example, videotapes, films, television, computers, speakers, and field trips. The major focus, however, should be on sign production and comprehension. As in any classroom, deaf students should be given numerous opportunities to use their language in spontaneous communicative interaction in structured settings. These activities should further their understanding of the structure and use of ASL and aid them in learning to perform certain cognitive tasks, such as following directions, answering questions, solving problems, and making inferences (Bowen et al., 1985; Crandall and Bruhn, 1981; Rivers and Temperley, 1978).

The following sample of lesson activities serves as an example: *Related Verb-Noun Pairs — The Use of the AGENT Sign* (e.g., teach-teacher).

In ASL, signers differentiate verb signs from noun signs in several ways (Baker and Cokely, 1980; Lane and Grosjean, 1980; Sternberg, 1981): a short, tense, repeated movement, as in SELL and STORE (i.e., SELL SELL); adding the AGENT affix sign to the verb sign, as in LEARN and LEARN AGENT (student); and using an unrelated (in form) sign, as in FISHING (verb) and FISH (noun). The emphasis of the initial activity is on the use of the AGENT sign. This sign typically functions like the English suffixes *-er* and *-or*. The main objectives are to demonstrate the use of the AGENT sign and to develop the concept and related concepts concerning the verb-noun pairs.

Most students should recognize the AGENT sign in some situations; that is, they have an intuitive, not formal, understanding of the concept. For example, they may know the sign concept TEACH plus AGENT meaning teacher. Using this as a starting point, it can be explained that a teacher is a *person* who *teaches*. The intent here is to show the close relationship that exists between the verb sign TEACH and the noun sign TEACH plus AGENT (teacher), which requires the use of a compound sign composed of an abbreviated verb sign and the affix AGENT. It should be emphasized that the teacher is *not* teaching students to recognize the terms *noun* or *verb*, but is dealing with concept development involving the concepts of the AGENT sign, teach, and teacher. The lesson can then proceed with discussions regarding characteristics of teachers, different kinds of teachers (e.g., MUSIC TEACH plus AGENT), and other related concepts.

After a few more examples, a number of variations can be used, possibly in additional lessons. Through storytelling or role playing, the teacher can describe the characteristics of a person by focusing only on a verb sign, such as DANCE. For instance, the teacher can relate to the students that this person loves to dance, practices every day for 2 hours, and so on. The purpose is to lead the students to label the person as, in this case, a DANCE plus AGENT, or dancer. Subsequently, different types of dancers and other related concepts can be presented and discussed. Further discussions and additional variations depend on the interests and sophistication of the students. It may be possible for some exceptional students to conduct the lesson with assistance. Finally, the teacher can encourage students to offer possible examples of other verb-noun sign pairs using the AGENT suffix that have not been discussed in class. In additional lessons, the deaf students can be exposed to the other means by which ASL signers distinguish between verb signs and noun signs. These activities can cover other important—and sometimes difficult — grammatical aspects of ASL, such as questions, pronominalization, classifiers, and pluralization.

Communicative Competence in ASL

To develop communicative competence, deaf students need situations in which they can use ASL to discuss with others topics that are meaningful and interesting to them. Teachers can provide motivation to communicate by suggesting (and sometimes participating in) topics relevant to the students' needs. An infinite number of ideas can be proposed by imaginative teachers and students; for example, (1) Show and Tell, (2) signing your way out of trouble, (3) seeking and giving information, (4) learning to do or make something, (5) sharing hobbies or leisure activities, and (6) problem-solving (Bowen et al., 1985; Crandall and Bruhn, 1981; Rivers and Temperley, 1978).

An expansion of the possibilities for language use with the idea "signing your way out of trouble" is presented as an example. In this activity, simulated or real situations of increasing signing difficulty can be established. Deaf students must figure out what to sign to remove themselves or others from dilemmas. Consider the following situation which the classroom teacher signs to the students.

Situation: Signing Your Way Out of Trouble

On Friday, Mrs. Jones, the teacher, gave her students a homework assignment in math. The assignment was due Monday morning. Mary, one of the students, had plans to visit her grandparents this weekend. She did not want to do any homework. On Saturday and Sunday, Mary visited with her grandparents. She had a lot of fun. She did not do her assignment. On Monday morning, Mrs. Jones asked Mary, "Where is your homework?"

Question

What did Mary say to Mrs. Jones, the teacher?

The students are expected to contrive an answer for Mary that would be "signing her way out of trouble." Other situations that may be of interest are (1) explaining how the flower vase got broken, (2) convincing your mother that there were only four cookies left in the jar, (3) describing how your clothes got dirty, and so on.

Probably one of the best activities for developing linguistic and cognitive skills is problem-solving. In a sense, problem-solving can be a part of all the activities previously discussed or the major part of a particular activity. Depending on the sophistication of the students, problem-solving situations can range from those requiring simple solutions to those requiring more complex ones. The most interesting and beneficial situations are the ones in which answers may vary. It should be mentioned that the presentations can be signed, acted out, or illustrated through the use of visual aids (or all three). The students should, however, initially sign their solutions and later on combine the signing with, for example, role playing.

Consider the following example:

Situation: Problem-Solving

A group of boys is playing baseball in a large field. The field is near a house owned by Mr. Brown. Mr. Brown is away on vacation. One of the boys, John, hits the ball really hard. The ball sails through the air and strikes one of Mr. Brown's windows. The window breaks.

Question

What should John do?

Other activities requiring problem-solving skills that can be used are well-known games such as *Twenty Questions, Who am I?, Who and What?, Animal-Vegetable-Mineral,* and their various derivatives. It is important to remember that these tasks can be constructed in a manner that appeals to young deaf students in the primary grades. It is likely that many students need to build up their real world or background knowledge prior to participating in them. In all of the activities discussed, the teacher can expand on the lesson by engaging the students in cognitive tasks, such as answering different types of questions, making inferences, or drawing conclusions. These are necessary for students to become effective readers and writers.

Literacy-Related Tasks

As discussed previously, reading and writing typically are introduced and established in L_1 after proficiency has been established in the primary form in minority-language bilingual immersion programs. American Sign Language does not, however, have a written language form, although there are ongoing attempts to construct a computerized version (e.g., Hutchins, Poizner, McIntire, and Newkirk, 1986). Given the importance of the relationship between the primary and secondary forms of a language, and the notion that good L_1 readers can develop into good L_2 readers, it appears that this line of research has important implications for ASL-using deaf students attempting to learn written English. In reference to the bilingual model proposed here, there is no way for deaf students to read or create written literature or communicate in print using their native language. Neverthe-less, there are still many literacy-related activities in which students can engage that may facilitate the later acquisition of reading and writing skills in L_2. For example, they can be exposed to reading readiness tasks, some of which are designed to help them learn to differentiate graphic symbols (Gibson, 1965; Mason, 1984); for these tasks, finger-spelling can be used. In addition, the teacher can construct activities aimed at developing a basic vocabulary, particularly in the use of some high-frequency sight words and other related words or concepts.

Reading and writing in L_2 should be limited at this stage to names, labels, or other one- or two-word terms or phrases. Obviously, students are aware of some of these in their environment, that is, from billboards, road signs, and so on. The primacy of using L_1 as much as possible cannot be overstressed. Teachers should use the students' native lan-guage in teaching high-level skills that are necessary for the develop-ment of reading comprehension ability; for example, various aspects of vocabulary knowledge, answering different levels of questions, and making inferences (see the discussion in King and Quigley, 1985). These activities are not presented as ends in themselves but rather as aids in the comprehension of important aspects of the story (either signed or on videotape). A variety of prereading exercises (i.e., prior to reading a story) that have been delineated can be used with some modifica-tions (see the discussions in Johnson and Pearson, 1984, and Pearson and Johnson, 1978).

A number of exercises are available to promote effective means of vocabulary and concept development and thus help students extend the breadth and depth of their word knowledge. Classification activi-ties can be used, such as synonyms, antonyms, semantic aspects, semantic maps, and analogies (Dale and O'Rourke, 1986; Johnson and Pearson, 1984). These activities have the potential to improve compre-hension "by building bridges between the new and known in the minds of learners" (Johnson and Pearson, 1984, p. 37).

The following story is an example for demonstrating how to teach some aspects of vocabulary and other comprehension skills.

Story

It is a beautiful Saturday morning. Joan decided that it is a good day to go fishing. However, she can't make up her mind where to fish. Should she go to the lake? The stream? The river? Well, because it is going to be a hot day, Joan ruled out the lake. She wanted to go barefoot, and the beach would get too hot for her feet. Finally, Joan decided to go to the river. She knew of a perfect spot. In her mind, she could picture this huge tree with branches hanging over a part of the bank of the river. A great place to fish!

As an example, suppose one of the important vocabulary words in the story is *bank*. During the prestory activities the teacher can elicit from students what they know about the sign-concept, *bank*. The word (i.e., label for the concept) can be written on the board, the overhead projector, or a sheet of paper. If students are aware of only one meaning of bank—that is, a place to keep money—it is important to provide opportunities for them to learn another meaning, especially the one that may be necessary for understanding the story to be presented. To bridge the known and unknown, a semantic map or web may be used such as the following, simplified version:

The concept of *bank* should be discussed in the context of *land beside a body of water*. If there is time, other related concepts, such as *shore*, *beach*, and *coast*, can be covered. Again, the lesson is conducted using ASL complemented by pictures, films, or other visual aids, and written labels to represent aspects of the sign-concepts.

Higher-level comprehension skills, such as answering questions, can be handled in a similar manner. Good questions can enhance the comprehension of a story and improve the inferential behaviors of the students (e.g., Hansen, 1981; Raphael, 1984). Students can also use these skills to comprehend new, related stories, especially if the questions aid in extending and enriching their background knowledge. The teacher should also discuss with the students why they are asking questions. A more detailed treatment of this activity in relation to reading comprehension can be found elsewhere (Hansen and Pearson, 1983; Raphael and Pearson, 1982).

The capabilities and interests of the students should be kept in mind. It may be necessary for some students to experience several viewings of the same videotaped stories if they are required to answer questions from memory. As an alternative, the story (especially a long one) can be presented once, and then the students can view it repeatedly while *looking* for the answers to the signed questions. In reference to the previous story, teachers can ask and lead discussions on literal and inferential questions, such as:

1. What day was it?
2. What did Joan decide to do?
3. Where did Joan go fishing? Why?
4. The story says *It is a beautiful Saturday morning.* What does that mean?
5. Where can you find a beach?
6. Where else (i.e., beside bodies of water) can you find a bank?
7. Did Joan like to fish?
8. Do you like to fish?

Some aspects of the last five questions can be discussed during pre-story activities to extend or interact with the background knowledge of the students and prepare them for the story to be presented (see the discussion in Hansen and Hubbard, 1984).

Content Areas

Although the major focus of this chapter is on the teaching of English literacy, it is possible to use activities similar to those discussed in the language arts area to teach other academic subjects, such as social studies and science. Selected topics as specified in the curricula are presented and discussed through the medium of ASL and augmented with talks by guest speakers, films, field experiences, and any other activities relevant to the interests and capabilities of young elementary students. Numerous opportunities should be available for students to develop high-level comprehension skills, such as answering questions and making inferences. As in the previous activities, the use of written English is limited to providing labels for signed or fingerspelled concepts as needed.

Development of English Literacy

Introduction of reading and writing exercises and the use of English-based signing for communication and instruction in English can occur during grade 3. Initially, ASL remains the predominant medium of instruction, and exposure to English-based signing should be gradual, depending on the progress of the students. A bilingual and bicultural environment is still maintained; for example, the two languages eventually are used more or less equally throughout the school day. In addition to the resources discussed previously, textbooks and other printed literature relevant to the academic content areas are used.

As in first-language teaching, there is no one best second-language teaching methodology (e.g., Hyltenstam, 1985; Hyltenstam and Pienemann, 1985). There appear to be as many approaches as there are teaching and learning styles. This is especially true in the education of deaf students, on which limited research has been conducted on the language approaches used to teach English (King, 1984). Thus, as discussed previously, a panorama of natural (e.g., notational-functional) and structural (e.g., grammar-translation) techniques should be implemented. The findings of contrastive and noncontrastive analyses can also be incorporated into the various approaches. Emphasis is placed on the form and function of English in order to develop communicative competency.

English-Based Signing

Typically, both primary (e.g., speech) and secondary (i.e., reading and writing) forms of the target language are used teach both the language and the content of academic courses (Bowen et al., 1985; Cummins, 1984; Raimes, 1983). The selection of a primary form—that is, speech or signing (or both)—with ASL-using deaf students causes a problem. It is clear that the exclusive use of the oral form of English or speech does not have much empirical support (Moores, 1982; Quigley and Kretschmer, 1982; Quigley and Paul, 1984b). Very few profoundly hearing impaired students have been exposed to or have achieved educational success solely through oral English methods. If speech is used at all, it should be in conjunction with some form of English-based signing. However, which English-based signing system should be implemented in a bilingual education program for deaf students is debatable. No signed system is used exclusively in a consistent or systematic manner. Furthermore, no evidence exists that the use of any of the systems results in competency in English in any form.

If the objective is to foster effective communication between teachers and students in a primary form of English (as it is, analogically, in most bilingual programs), a case can be made for the use of Pidgin Sign English (PSE). In general, PSE is described as ASL-like signing in an English word order (Wilbur, 1979; Woodward, 1973). The signs are considered ASL-like because some of their syntactic aspects—for example, the directional elements of verb signs—are eliminated or reduced when executed in the word order of the majority-language—that is, English. It is difficult to define PSE, or any other pidgin, owing to wide variations among its users. Deaf PSE-signers are likely to incorporate more grammatical features of ASL than hearing PSE-signers. Conversely, hearing PSE-signers are likely to use more contrived signs and sign-markers from the other signed systems, none of which are commonly used by members of the deaf community (Bernstein, Maxwell, and Matthews, 1985; Cokely, 1983; Reagan, 1985). Thus, PSE-signing (as executed by members of the deaf community) is recommended because it is a form of English-based signing that is most likely to be understood by native ASL-signers. Additional support for the adoption of this type of signing can be gleaned from studies documenting that the levels of English competency in deaf students exposed to PSE-signing is equal to or better than the levels of competency in students exposed to any other signed system, including those claimed to be most representative of spoken English in the manual form (Babb, 1979; Brasel and Quigley, 1977; see also the review in Quigley and Paul, 1984b).

Sign Communication Development

The development of receptive and expressive sign communication skills in PSE should follow, analogically, those procedures recommended for the development of oral communication skills in ESL or bilingual programs (Bowen et al., 1985; Celce-Murcia and McIntosh, 1979; Pienemann, 1985). Initially, it may be necessary for teachers to alternate between ASL and PSE, then gradually present tasks via PSE augmented by fingerspelling as needed. It is equally important that teachers indicate whether they are using ASL or PSE. As discussed previously, training in communicative competence should emphasize problem-solving tasks. These may include, but not be limited to asking for clarification, requests for directions, engaging in discussions, debates, and rationalizations, and discussing grammatical elements of the target language (i.e., metalinguistic discussions). In general, activities should be constructed so that students' responses proceed from simple to complex.

Signed tasks at the simple end of the continuum require students to respond in a physical manner—that is, sit, stand, jump, and so on (Asher, 1982). Examples include (1) Sit down at your desk, (2) Walk to the window, (3) Please open the door, and (4) Walk around the table. It is important also to use signs or words that help students to understand certain classroom rules and procedures. Examples of more complex listening or watching tasks (especially in the academic content area) are (1) Take out your reading book, (2) Open it to page one, (3) Find the second paragraph, (4) Look at the first line, (5) Find the third word, and (6) Tell (speak or sign) me what it is (adapted from Bowen et al., 1985; Rivers and Temperley, 1978). These commands can be administered and completed one at a time or all at once. Teachers can then proceed to signed activities that require limited sign or speech responses, such as (1) Tell me your name, (2) Do you live in a house?,

(3) Do you live in an apartment?, and (4) Do you live with your family? Teachers can also tell a story and ask questions. To designate this as a listening or watching activity, not a memory one, the questions should be simple. Higher-level questions and those requiring memory should be reserved for reading and the other academic content areas.

Students should engage in a wide variety of expressive activities. These can range from describing a picture or object, to Show and Tell, to engaging in dialogues, interviews, and debates. It is helpful if the tasks reflect meaningful real-life experiences. The deaf students should be encouraged to communicate via PSE but be allowed to alternate between ASL and PSE whenever necessary.

Sign-English Grammar Development

Within the sign communication activities, it is also important to focus on certain grammatical structures of English in which the students are experiencing difficulty (Celce-Murcia and Larsen-Freeman, 1983). Deaf students may need practice in understanding elements such as affixes, inflectional and derivational patterns, determiners, prepositions, phrasal verbs, and question-formations (see Quigley and Paul, 1984b, for details). To provide exposure to these structures, it may be necessary to use fingerspelling or some common, contrived sign-markers that are occasionally used by deaf ASL-signers. For example, suppose that the structure under study is the present progressive, as in the sentence: I *am looking* for a chair. In PSE signing, this may be: I AM SEARCH + ING F-0-R A CHAIR. The students need practice understanding the rule (intuitively) concerning the BE- verb plus *-ing* form in the present tense, as in this case. Thus, in PSE signing, both the BE- verb and the *-ing* form should be emphasized. Additional lessons may cover other aspects of the progressive tense. For contrastive purposes, it may be helpful to show students how this is accomplished in ASL (they may already know this or, at least, should be able to recognize the signs). The main emphasis, however, is on demonstrating clearly the specific aspects of the progressive tense.

To develop Sign-English grammar, students need to be exposed to numerous examples so that they can *internalize* certain grammatical rules. Analogically, activities discussed previously for developing aspects of ASL grammar are applicable here; indeed, other, similar language activities may be found throughout this book. These tasks, in and of themselves, are not crucial. What is crucial is that students receive numerous opportunities to be exposed to the specific aspects and also to use them in PSE. Finally, the sequencing of the grammatical structures should follow developmental patterns that have been documented (e.g., Russell, Quigley, and Power, 1976); that is, new structures should be built up on old, or simple structures should be taught prior to the more complex ones.

Reading and Content Areas

It is well documented that, on graduation from a secondary level program, most deaf students are reading at about the fourth grade level, as determined by standardized reading assessments (Allen, in press; King and Quigley, 1985; Quigley and Paul, 1986). If reading is conceived of as a secondary language form based on the development of primary, aural-oral experiences, then

> Deaf children lack this auditory language and its associated experiential, cognitive and linguistic skills. Thus, for them, learning to read becomes also a process of experience building, cognitive development, and language learning *in English* (words and emphasis added). It should not be surprising, therefore, that most deaf children do not learn to read well. (King and Quigley, 1985, p. xi)

Although the major objective of any reading program is to enable deaf students to read the literature of the general population (Quigley, 1982), relatively little is known regarding the merits of instructional procedures and reading materials used to accomplish this goal (King and Quigley, 1985). In relation to materials, several types have been discussed, such as children's literature, regular or special materials, and the child's or teacher's language in language-experience materials. Debates have ensued regarding the use of materials, regular or special, with deaf students and with students learning English as a second language (Gonzales, 1981; Paul, 1985). Although a variety of materials should be used, it is of benefit to the ASL-using deaf students if the materials present information in a spiraling or cyclical pattern. That is, structures and content are sequenced according to level of difficulty, ranging from simple to complex. In addition, all structures are reinforced (presented) repeatedly throughout the curriculum. This is necessary for beginning readers who do not have adequate control of standard English.

The current view that reading is an interactive process should provide the basis for all instructional strategies. Thus, ASL-using deaf students need to develop bottom-up (e.g., decoding) and top-down (e.g., the use of background knowledge) skills (King and Quigley, 1985). A great deal of emphasis needs to be placed on prereading activities, especially in activating background knowledge, and on teaching vocabulary and comprehension skills (Anderson, 1985; Pearson, 1985). This is true for any academic subject that requires reading. Using ASL (or even PSE) may be helpful in developing certain top-down skills or in explaining difficult aspects of the text; however, it should not or cannot supplant the text. Students may need structured written activities dealing with certain grammatical aspects that cause problems with comprehension, such as vocabulary, syntax, and figurative language. In other words, deaf students need to read (and write) these structures and engage in higher-level comprehension skills (e.g., making inferences) to be able to "crack the code" or "obtain meaning from print."

Written Language

There is evidence that reading and writing are interrelated (Tierney and Leys, 1984; Walmsley, 1983), although it is probably not the case that writing is totally dependent on the complete development of reading. When students perform one skill, they often engage in the other. Thus, reading skills do not have to be at an extremely high level before writing skills can be acquired. Writing most probably develops as a result of, and in conjunction with, the development of reading. It is important to view writing, like reading, as a means to an end, not as an end in itself. Good writers need to develop not only their understanding of the mechanics of grammar but also of higher-level writing skills, such as organization, intent, and purpose.

As might be expected, there is no best approach for teaching writing. Several common approaches have been delineated in the research on hearing students: free writing, paragraph-pattern, grammar-syntax-organization, communication, and process (Hillocks, 1986; Mosenthal, Tamor, and Walmsley, 1983; Raimes, 1983). Most of the recent efforts have centered on the process of writing, not on the written productions. As in language-teaching approaches, it is recommended that teachers be eclectic—that is, that they use a variety of techniques to show "that writing means writing a connected text and not just single sentences, that writers write for a purpose and a reader, and that the process of writing is a valuable learning tool for all" (Raimes, 1983, p. 11). In all lessons, the teacher should provide students with a meaningful purpose for writing: letters, diaries, recipes, short essays, and even signed stories in ASL (Marbury and Mackinson-Smyth, 1986).

The following example of using signed stories in ASL is based on principles presented in a workshop by Marbury and Mackinson-Smyth (1986). They suggested that elementary school-aged deaf students (of deaf parents) view a signed story, and then attempt to translate it into written English. Next, two teachers, (one deaf and the other hearing) and the students discuss the story as a group by asking and answering questions regarding the main characters and events. Using a contrastive approach, the students are led to focus on ASL features in the signed story and incorporate these into their writing. Essentially, this activity is similar to that used by Jones (1979) in discussing the writing of isolated sentences. Finally, teachers and students work together to create a final draft of the story. A number of follow-up activities were also suggested; for example (p. 44):

1. Students rewrite their story based on class discussion.
2. Students edit, rewrite, and illustrate their story.
3. Students create their own comprehension questions and answer key for the story they wrote.
4. Students complete teacher-made worksheets (e.g., Cloze activity).
5. Students role-play the story in ASL.

As discussed previously, noncontrastive approaches can also be used, especially if the deaf students are experiencing problems with specific structures of English.

In general, it is necessary for beginning-level deaf students to receive practice in the mechanics of writing and basic skills (e.g., see the discussion in Bowen et al., 1985). They need to learn, or rather internalize, such aspects as basic spelling patterns of English, rules for capitalization and punctuation, and producing correct phrases and sentences. As with reading, the writing material should be meaningful and presented in a spiraling or cyclical fashion.

As the students' knowledge of English increases, they can generate more complex words, phrases, and sentences. To help students organize their thoughts and express their ideas, teachers should make use of a variety of prewriting and rewriting activities. During the prewriting stage, students are encouraged to generate ideas or topics by participating in activities such as writing, talking to the teacher or other students, drawing, and dramatizing (Hillocks, 1986). Prewriting activities, like prereading ones, are designed to activate the background knowledge of the students and to get them involved in understanding the process and the mechanics of writing. During the rewriting stage, students attempt to revise and refine their ideas and grammar via additional peer and teacher conferences (i.e., discussing their writing with the teacher and other students). At the end of this stage, students produce a final draft of their writing. Consequently, from the beginning to the final stage of the writing process, students have numerous opportunities to participate in low-level (e.g., mechanics) and high-level (e.g., organization) skills of writing.

Evaluation

The importance of evaluation in education programs cannot be overemphasized. As stated by Jones (1984), "A carefully planned assessment program . . . should provide teachers or clinicians with valuable information on students' entry level skills and their progress toward achieving instructional goals and objectives'' (p. 200). Evaluating the effects of ASL on the development of English is related to issues such as determining the appropriate time for beginning instruction via the use of English and assessing the effects of bilingual education on academic achievement. These, in turn, are heavily influenced by an extremely important and complex issue: language proficiency (Cummins, 1984; Mattes and Omark, 1984; Rivera, 1984). Language-proficiency tests vary greatly due to different theoretical perspectives on the nature of language proficiency and the manner in which it should be evaluated. Tests have ranged from those that focus on the acquisition of discrete skills to those that reflect a communicative approach. Nevertheless, a wide variety of informal and formal tests should be used to measure language proficiency in terms of grammatical and communicative competency in the primary and secondary modes. A more detailed treatment of these and other related issues can be found elsewhere (Bowen et al., 1985; Cummins, 1984; Mattes and Omark, 1984).

In essence, the evaluation of a bilingual minority-language immersion program for deaf students should consider, but not be limited to, the following areas:

1. Identification of deaf students for placement in a bilingual program.
2. Assessment of grammar and communicative competency in ASL.
3. Evaluation of achievement in academic subjects presented via ASL.
4. Assessment of grammar and communicative competency in English.
5. Evaluation of achievement in academic subjects presented via English.
6. Evaluation of psychosocial aspects (e.g., attitude, motivation).

The difficulties of constructing tests that are appropriate for deaf students have been well documented (e.g., Allen, in press; Quigley and Paul, 1986). Of importance here, however, is the need for developing an adequate assessment of ASL and of English-based signing (i.e., PSE). This is crucial for evaluating the effects of a bilingual education program, particularly in the areas of language proficiency and academic achievement. At present, in the absence of an adequate linguistic assessment of ASL, sociological scales similar to the one developed by Hatfield and colleagues (1978) can be used to identify deaf students for placement in a bilingual program.

SUMMARY

The major objective of this chapter was to discuss how ASL can be used to teach English literacy skills in a bilingual education program. Among linguists, there is little doubt that ASL is a bona fide language. It is argued that ASL differs from English in form and grammar, and thus, it also differs from the signed codes that were developed to represent the structure of English in a manual manner. From the research on bilingualism and second-language learning, it can be inferred that English should be taught as a second language to those students for whom ASL is the first or native language.

It was reported that the instructional use of ASL in a bilingual or ESL environment is severely limited. Consequently, little research exists on the relationship between ASL and English language development. The present situation may be due, in part, to the general lack of acceptance of ASL within total communication programs. In addition, because a grammar of ASL has only recently been written, its use in a bilingual education program has yet to be examined. In light of this, techniques and methodologies for using ASL to teach deaf students to read and write English have been gleaned from the research on hearing students, particularly minority-language students in bilingual education programs.

The development of literacy in L_2 and educational success for minority-language students have been documented in maintenance bilingual programs, especially in alternative immersion or minority-language immersion programs. In those programs, the home language and culture of the minority students have been promoted and valued, and this has resulted in the later development of the majority language, or L_2. For deaf students, it is argued that the optimal development of ASL, and subsequently English, is most likely to occur in a bilingual minority-language immersion program.

In this minority-language bilingual immersion program, ASL (as L_1) is used as the major medium of instruction during preschool and grades 1 and 2. Because ASL does not have a written component and is a visual-gestural language, educational lessons should be designed to fit the needs and capabilities of the eye. In this vein, a wide range of resources can be used, such as television, videotapes, films, computers, overhead projectors, and field experiences. Fingerspelling is used in a manner similar to the way in which it is employed by ASL-signers. Written English (as L_2) is limited to providing labels for sign-concepts and fingerspelled words as needed.

The major goals of the program during the first few years are to develop and maintain communicative competence in ASL and to teach concepts relating to subjects in the language arts and other content areas. The contents and implementation of the curricula for the areas should be similar to those established for hearing students in regular education programs. Also included are components relating to ASL and the culture of the deaf community. The rate of presentation and the amount of subject matter covered will vary according to the needs and capabilities of the deaf students. Nevertheless, educational activities should be designed not only to present information but also to develop important linguistic and cognitive skills that are necessary for the later development of literacy in L_2—in this case, English.

English literacy activities and English-based signing for communication and instruction are complemented by ASL in the initial stages. As the students' knowledge of English increases, both ASL and English eventually can be used more or less equally (i.e., in separate lessons) throughout the school day. In general, it was argued that English proficiency is dependent, in part, on providing adequate, meaningful, systematic exposure to English in the classroom. Because there is no best language-teaching method, a wide variety of natural and structural approaches should be used. Contrastive and noncontrastive analyses can also be incorporated. The goal is to develop grammatical and communicative competence in English-based signing and in reading and writing English.

It was argued that, to teach the content of academic subjects and to foster effective communication between teacher and students in a primary form of English, a form of English-based signing, namely Pidgin Sign English (PSE), should be used in the classroom. PSE, as used by members of the deaf community, is most likely to be understood by native ASL-signers. A number of activities, ranging from simple to complex, were described for developing receptive and expressive sign communication skills and grammatical proficiency in PSE. If deaf students experience difficulty with certain English structures, such as affixes and inflectional patterns, it was suggested that fingerspelling and some common, contrived sign-markers be incorporated in the lesson activities.

In relation to the teaching of reading and writing, a variety of materials and approaches were recommended. Owing to most deaf students' lack of competency in English, it might be most beneficial if the information in the materials (e.g., vocabulary, syntax) be presented in a spiraling or cyclical fashion, that is, proceeding from simple to complex and reinforced (presented) repeatedly. Deaf students need to participate in numerous activities that focus on developing both low-level (e.g., decoding for reading, mechanics for writing) and high-level (e.g., making inferences) skills. Because reading and writing are interrelated, similar activities can be used with an emphasis on activating and enriching the background knowledge of the students.

Finally, the importance of developing adequate tools for assessing the effects of ASL on the development of English was strongly stressed. It was argued that the evaluation of a bilingual education program depends on an understanding of the notion of language proficiency and the manner in which it should be measured. There is a need for researchers to construct tests for assessing competency in ASL and PSE. In sum, as stated by Quigley and Paul (1984b, p. 197):

> Given the large body of research and practice with minority hearing children to draw from in establishing ASL/ESL programs and the probable willingness of deaf parents to have their deaf children involved in such programs, it should be possible to initiate the programs carefully, evaluate them experimentally, and establish a data base on their effectiveness.

C H A P T E R 7

Specialized Aspects of Language Development

Although the major emphasis regarding language acquisition in deaf children has been on the fundamental aspects of the form and function of English, every professional teacher is acutely aware of the challenges the hearing impaired child faces when confronted with unique or specialized aspects of language. This chapter addresses the acquisition of figurative expressions and of complex semantics, inferencing skills, and written language in deaf children. Each section presents a brief review and implications of relevant research, followed by an emphasis on instructional strategies that have been used in classrooms with hearing impaired children.

FIGURATIVE EXPRESSIONS

Interest in the comprehension of metaphors has led to studies that have attempted to identify developmental levels progressing toward mature comprehension in early adolescence (e.g., Asch and Nerlove, 1960; Winner, Rosenstiel, and Gardner, 1976). Other studies have attempted to show that ability to comprehend metaphors is attached to Piagetian stages of development (e.g., Billow, 1975; Cometa and Eson, 1978), whereas still others have tried to demonstrate that metaphorical uses of language can be understood by children younger than most available studies indicate (e.g, Gentner, 1977; Honeck, Sowry, and Voegtle, 1978). Another approach, such as the one reported by Gentner

(1977), has encouraged the idea that a relationship exists between analogical reasoning and metaphor comprehension. Although the view that metaphors are based on the principles of analogy is a commonly held belief, no empirical evidence exists to support or disprove this hypothesis.

Figurative language occurs in a rich linguistic and physical context, which is a major factor in comprehension (Reynolds and Ortony, 1980). Nevertheless, literature on the comprehension of metaphors and other figurative uses of language continues to report that the figurative language was presented to the subjects with little or no context (e.g., Winner, Rosenstiel, and Gardner, 1976), thus imposing unreasonable and unrealistic demands on children. Reynolds and Ortony (1980) suggested that the available evidence concerning the development of metaphoric comprehension is inconclusive and inconsistent. Some studies (Billow, 1975; Gardner, 1974; Gentner, 1977; Pollio and Pollio, 1979) suggest that very young children, aged 5 years or younger, can use and understand metaphorical language, whereas others (Asch and Nerlove, 1960; Matter and Davis, 1975) suggest that the ability to understand and use metaphorical language does not develop until early adolescence.

Reynolds and Ortony (1980) proposed that one source confounding results of studies is inconsistency in what type of language is considered metaphorical. For example, similes are often considered direct comparison statements, and metaphors, although they are not direct, are based on direct comparisons. Therefore, the statement *John is a turkey* is based on the direct comparison *John is like a turkey*. Reynolds and Ortony (1980) proposed that the simile is also metaphorical because John is not really like a real, live turkey; he is only like a turkey metaphorically. Thus, both statements are metaphorical. The difference between a metaphor and its corresponding simile is not that one is metaphorical and the other is not, but that one is an indirect statement of the other. *John is a turkey* is an indirect way of asserting that *John is like a turkey*, but both are metaphorical. In both statements, understanding the assertion requires relating terms from disparate domains in the appropriate way (Reynolds and Ortony, 1980).

In their investigations, Reynolds and Ortony (1980) found that the variables of indirectness (metaphors being regarded as indirect similes) and specificity of reference had a significant impact on performance. Specificity of reference referred to statements such as the following: In a story about a little boy who was naughty and was sent to his room, the specific referent was *Kenny was a prisoner sent to jail* and the nonspecific referent was *The prisoner was sent to jail*. Similes were found to be understood more easily than corresponding metaphors, and metaphorical language involving specific referents was understood more easily than metaphorical language involving nonspecific referents. Children at grade levels 2 through 6 performed well with metaphors containing a specific referent. The most optimistic interpretation of the data from the nonspecific metaphor condition indicated metaphoric competence around age 9½ years, whereas the specific simile condition showed a high level of performance as early as 7½ years of age.

Emphasis is given here to figurative language because it enters quite early into reading texts. King and Quigley (1985) reported that an analysis of reading series by Houghton-Mifflin, by Ginn, and by Scott, Foresman revealed a great deal of figurative language (especially metaphors, similes, and idioms) used in books at the very beginning levels. Petrie (1979) suggested that readers operate within a four-stage paradigm when attempting to comprehend figurative language. In these stages, the reader (1) recognizes the analogy in the figurative expression, (2) compares the new, unknown material to old, known material, (3) interacts with the new material to create nonlinguistic similarities, and (4) corrects the initial interpretation of the figurative expression. This model requires the reader to use cognitive processing skills, linguistic and nonlinguistic competencies, and existing knowledge schemata to comprehend the figurative language (King and Quigley, 1985).

Research on the comprehension of figurative language has revealed that it develops incrementally. For example, children first recognize correct paraphrases of figurative language (Pollio and Pollio, 1979) and then are able to paraphrase figurative language themselves (Cometa and Eson, 1978); subsequently they are able to explain their paraphrases (Billow, 1975). Arlin (1977) and Billow (1975) have shown that representational metaphors (e.g., *He is a turkey*) are comprehended first, similarity metaphors (e.g., *Life is a bowl of cherries*) are understood next, and proportional metaphors (e.g., *Time was a thief robbing her of youth*) are comprehended last (Giorcelli, 1982). Other factors also affect the comprehension of metaphors, such as frequency of exposure to metaphors and level of usage enjoyed by the metaphor. Children find it easier to understand commonly used metaphors (e.g., *That's the way the cookie crumbles*) than less commonly used metaphors (e.g., *Any port in a storm*) (Cometa and Eson, 1978; Pollio and Pollio, 1979).

Figurative Language and Deaf Children

Most teachers of deaf children know well the problems presented to their students by extensive exposure to figurative language, particularly in the early stages of reading. Many forms of figurative language emerge consistently in daily communicative interaction and in reading materials, the most common being metaphors, similes, and idioms. Ability to comprehend and use figurative language is essential to communication in English and presents great difficulty for deaf students learning English (Giorcelli, 1982).

Few research studies have dealt with deaf children's comprehension of figurative language. Conley (1976) compared comprehension of idiomatic expressions by hearing and deaf children and found significant differences in favor of the hearing students for reading levels above 3.0. Wilbur, Fraser, and Fruchter (1981) showed unexpectedly high levels of comprehension of idiomatic expressions and speculated that at least some idioms might be memorized or learned as a whole so that vocabulary and syntax might not present confounding problems. Page (1981) and Houck (1982) concluded that deaf children are not impaired in their comprehension of idioms when there is sufficient contextual information in the written material and when "extraneous factors" are controlled. Giorcelli (1982) assessed 10 aspects of figurative language and found that the performance for the deaf students improved with the addition of context but was still well below the performance of the hearing students. The 18-year-old deaf subjects did not perform as well as the 9-year-old hearing subjects, and their performance did not improve much beyond 13 and 14 years of age, which is similar to their plateaus in reading (DiFrancesca, 1972).

Payne (1982) investigated deaf and hearing students' comprehension of verb particle combinations in English. These combinations are referred to by Pugh (1955) as double-verbs. Verb particle combinations may have a literal meaning (e.g., *I looked over the paper this morning and saw a mouse on the windowsill*) or an idiomatic interpretation (e.g., *I looked over the paper this morning while I had a cup of coffee,* meaning "skimmed"). Payne found that, on all tasks, the hearing subjects performed significantly better than the deaf subjects.

Iran-Nejad, Ortony, and Rittenhouse (1981) investigated metaphorical comprehension by deaf children and found that the children, although able to understand metaphorical uses of language, seldom did so spontaneously. They suggested that failure to respond appropriately may be due largely to strong inclinations to respond literally. Presumably, had there been a way to suggest to the deaf subjects that they consider metaphorical interpretations, they would have done considerably better. The results suggested that deaf children are capable of comprehending metaphorical language and probably do not have a cognitive deficiency precluding their use of figurative language.

Rittenhouse, Morreau, and Iran-Nejad (1981) conducted a study in which deaf and hard of hearing children, ages 11 to 17 years old, were presented with conservation of liquid and weight problems and with metaphor items. The data revealed that the skills required to interpret metaphors were related to those needed to solve conservation problems. The study also demonstrated that hearing impaired children can, with alternative instructional procedures, successfully interpret metaphorical language. The authors concluded that there is a need for teachers to provide deaf children with cognitive experiences of an analogical nature and to expose them to figurative uses of language, particularly metaphor and simile.

Figurative Language: Classroom Practice

Very few empirical data are available that verify the effectiveness of specific teaching strategies, and the area of figurative language comprehension is no exception. Recently, however, research findings have begun to provide teachers with guidelines for a developmental sequence in the comprehension of figurative language, although even that information is relatively sparse. What can be gleaned from research findings suggests sequences based on levels of difficulty of various forms of figurative language and a brief order of intervention strategies. A suggested sequence, based on increasing difficulty, for the order of presentation to hearing children is (1) analogy, (2) simile, (3) metaphors with specific referents, and (4) metaphors with nonspecific referents (Reynolds and Ortony, 1980). In the more specific area of metaphorical language, the order of increasing difficulty seems to be (1) representational metaphors, (2) similarity metaphors, and (3) proportional metaphors (Arlin, 1977; Billow, 1975). In intervention strategies, children are first able to recognize a paraphrase of figurative language (Pollio and Pollio, 1979) before they can paraphrase figurative language independently (Cometa and Eson, 1978), and subsequently they are able to explain their paraphrases (Billow, 1975).

Putting the research findings into practice requires considerable "gap filling"; for example, idioms are not mentioned in the order of difficulty of various forms of figurative language. The next section provides suggested guidelines for classroom practices that will, perhaps, improve the opportunities for deaf childen to develop skills with which to comprehend figurative language. The guidelines are based, in part, on research findings, and in part on the extensive classroom experiences of the authors. As with all complex skills, the abilities needed to comprehend figurative language cannot be developed within a single short unit of work, nor can they be initiated at the intermediate level (grades 5 and 6), when deaf students are often expected to be able to handle idioms, similes, and metaphors. Rather, a logical base of foundation skills necessary to build more advanced skills is probably the language and reading readiness activities presented in many preschool classrooms.

Most forms of figurative language are based on comparison, which requires the ability to ascertain similarities and differences of various attributes in varying degrees. Therefore, activities aimed at recognizing similarities and differences may be one of the first steps toward understanding complex forms of figurative language. The next section is not intended to be a complete curriculum for skill development for comprehending figurative language. It is a suggested guideline of sample activities from preschool through intermediate levels. It is expected that for each sample activity, many additional activities similar in format and difficulty will be developed by the teacher and used for additional teaching, reinforcement, and practice.

Classroom Activities for the *Preschool Level* (4 and 5 years old)

GOAL: The children will develop skills for making comparisons.

OBJECTIVE: The children will identify similarities and differences among various objects, pictures, and configurations.

ACTIVITY 1: The children will identify similarities and differences of objects on the basis of size, shape, and texture each time. The teacher will reinforce what is similar and what is different.

ACTIVITY 2: The children will identify similarities and differences among pictures of objects on the basis of size, shape, and color. The children will begin to communicate what is the same and what is different. The children will match pictures containing increasing amounts of detail and decreasing differences. The children will explain how the pictures are similar and how they are different.

ACTIVITY 3: From a series of four objects or pictures, the children will discard or cross out the one that is different. The differences should become finer and more difficult to discriminate, as is illustrated in Figure 7-1. The children will explain why they made their particular choices.

ACTIVITY 4: After being exposed to different nursery stories (and repeated tellings of each one), the children will discuss how stories are similar and how they are different.

How are the stories the same?
- They all have animal groups of three (Goldilocks and the 3 Bears, The 3 Little Kittens, The 3 Little Pigs, The 3 Billy Goats Gruff).
- The stories all have animals.
- The animals in the stories all talk.
- The stories are all pretend.

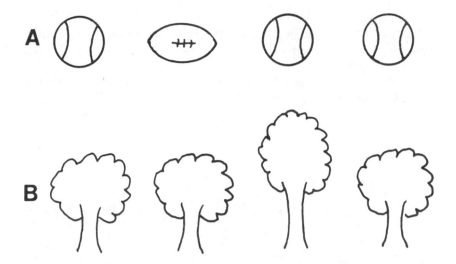

FIGURE 7-1. *Object discrimination. (**A**) Objects in the same class representing different percepts. (**B**) Two closely related percepts.*

How are the stories different?
- One story has a little girl.
- One story has a wolf.
- Each story has different animals.

Classroom Activities for the *Primary Level* (6, 7, and 8 years old)

The teacher should continue to reinforce the skills developed at the preschool level and build on them.

GOALS: The children will continue to develop skills for making comparisons. The children will begin to develop analogical reasoning skills. The children will begin to understand and use idiomatic language and similes.

OBJECTIVES: The children will match similar numbers, letters, and words. The children will complete analogical comparisons. The children will paraphrase idiomatic language when it is presented in context.

ACTIVITY 1: The children will match similar numbers, series of numbers, letters, and words.

ACTIVITY 2: The children will discuss how all the stories in a reading unit are similar and how they are different.

ACTIVITY 3: The children will begin to develop analogical reasoning skills by completing analogical statements. Examples:

1. *Multiple choice*
   foot and leg
   hand and _____ (nose, head, arm)
2. *Recall*
   finger and hand
   toe and _____
3. After experience with analogies, leave the blank in different positions.
   - dog and _____
     cat and kitten
   - _____ and cow
     lion and tiger
   - eye and see
     _____ and smell

ACTIVITY 4: The children will read a short, one-paragraph story containing an idiom, identify the correct picture, and recognize the correct paraphrase. Example:

> Kenny was in the house.
> He wanted to go outside and play.
> He looked out the window and said, "I can't go outside. *It is raining cats and dogs.*"

- The teacher points to and rereads the idiom. Then she asks, "What does that mean?" and shows two pictures. One picture portrays the literal meaning showing dogs and cats falling from the sky and the other portrays the figurative meaning showing a downpour of rain. The children and teacher discuss the pictures and the children determine which is correct.
- Next, the teacher shows the pictures with the paraphrases (*Cats and dogs are falling from the sky* and *It is raining very hard*), and the children choose the correct paraphrase with the picture cue.
- The teacher presents similar examples and deletes the picture cues in the last step.
- The teacher presents similar examples but encourages the children to paraphrase the idiomatic language.
- The teacher uses and encourages the children to use the idioms (previously discussed) in conversational language whenever appropriate.

ACTIVITY 5: The teacher presents verb particles in a similar format.

ACTIVITY 6: The teacher presents a short, one-paragraph story containing a simile that is underlined. The children read the story and choose the appropriate paraphrase. Example:

> Mother is cooking Thanksgiving dinner. She fixed the turkey, mashed the potatoes, made the salad, and baked two pumpkin pies. *She is as busy as a bee.*

• After reading and discussing the story, the children choose the appropriate paraphrase.

> *"She is as busy as a bee"* means:
> Mother is lazy.
> Mother is a bee.
> Mother is working hard.

• The teacher presents similar examples and, when ready, the children paraphrase the idiomatic language.
• The teacher presents examples containing similes using *like* (*She runs like a deer*) and follows a similar format.
• The teacher uses and encourages the children to use the similes (previously discussed) in conversational language whenever appropriate.

Classroom Activities for the *Upper Primary Level* (9 and 10 years old)

The teacher should continue to reinforce the skills developed at the primary level and build on them.

GOALS: The children will continue to develop skills for making comparisons. The children will continue to develop analogical reasoning skills. The children will continue to develop skills necessary to understand and use idiomatic language and similes. The children will begin to understand metaphorical comparisons in language.

OBJECTIVES: The children will compare and contrast different concepts in science and social studies. The children will complete more complex analogical comparisons. The children will paraphrase idiomatic language and similes when encountered in their reading text and use these structures in conversational language. The children will paraphrase metaphors with specific referents when written as direct statements and as indirect assertions.

ACTIVITY 1: The children continue work with similes using a format similar to that used at the primary level. The simile should not be underlined in the story; the children should be able to identify it and then provide the paraphrase.

ACTIVITY 2: The teacher presents a short story containing a metaphor with a specific referent. The children read and discuss the story. The teacher presents three choices of metaphors with specific referents; the children pick the one that best fits the story and discuss why it is appropriate. Initially, the teacher will probably have to explain the comparison, but later he or she should encourage the children to explain it. Example:

> John plays football. He is very big and strong. He runs fast.
> a. John is like a horse.
> b. John is like a football.
> c. John is like a robin.

• After several stories have been presented, the teacher presents a story in the same format.

• After several stories have been presented using a similar format, the teacher presents more stories, but the metaphors do not contain the word *like*. (The previous stories may be used with the word *like* deleted. The teacher explains to the children that the statements still mean the same.) Example:

> Susie wants a new dress. She does not have enough money. She puts $5.00 in her bank every week. Soon she can buy the new dress.
> a. Susie is a squirrel burying nuts.
> b. Susie is an old shoe.
> c. Susie is a bird flying south.

• The teacher should reinforce metaphorical comparisons when they are encountered in the reading text.

Classroom Activities for the *Intermediate Level* (10, 11, and 12 years old)

The teacher should continue to reinforce the skills developed at the upper primary level and build on them.

GOAL: The students will understand metaphorical comparisons when presented in context.

OBJECTIVES: The students will identify metaphors with specific referents and paraphrase them. The students will select the appropriate metaphor with nonspecific referent to fit a story. The student will identify metaphors with nonspecific referents and paraphrase them.

ACTIVITY 1: The students read a story containing a metaphor with a specific referent, select the appropriate paraphrase, and explain the comparison. Example:

> Aunt Lori lives in New York City and has a good job. She lives by herself so she has a lot of money. She spends most of her money buying clothes. When she visits us, she changes her clothes three times a day. She wants us to see all her beautiful new clothes. Mother says, ''Aunt Lori is a peacock spreading its tail!''
> a. Aunt Lori is showing off and is strutting around.
> b. Aunt Lori is fat and waddles when she walks.
> c. Aunt Lori is not very smart.

ACTIVITY 2: The students read a story, select a metaphor with a nonspecific referent that best fits the story, and explain the comparison. Example:

> Ken grew up in Minnesota. He loved the cold winters. He got a new job and moved to Southern California. He became homesick and missed the snow and ice.
> a. The Arctic polar bear was in the Miami zoo.
> b. The horse was in the barn.
> c. The TV was broken.

ACTIVITY 3: The students read a story containing a metaphor with a nonspecific referent, identify the metaphor, paraphrase it, and explain the comparison.

ACTIVITY 4: The teacher and students read selected poems, identify metaphors in them, and explain the comparisons.

These guidelines should be helpful in planning language programs that include the development of skills needed to comprehend figurative language. Rittenhouse (1981) has produced a book, *An Anthology of Metaphor Stories for Hearing Impaired Children*, which includes metaphorical stories that can be used in the classroom. It should be noted that the language structures and vocabulary used in the sample stories were purposefully kept at a relatively simple reading level. Thus, the students do not have to expend energy trying to understand the story but can turn their full attention to the comprehension of figurative language.

INFERENCING SKILLS

Understanding language development necessitates an understanding of the role that inference plays in the communication process. The term inference is defined as "a relationship noted between one event and another that is not directly stated" (Santrock, 1986, p. 284). In the absence of inferencing, the world around us would appear to be a complex of lists, events, and unrelated things with little sense of order. Inferencing develops as a result of internalizing interactions and experiences with the environment. Infants lack a set of world knowledge and the ability to infer, but as a result of experiencing events in the world around them, their abilities improve as they mature (Yussen, 1982). During the early developmental years, children's inferential style tends to be static, rigid, and restrictive (Paris and Lindauer, 1976; Wimmer, 1980). This may be attributed to the limited language and experience that children bring to a specific event. For example, a 6-year-old deciphered a poster that read, "Lord, don't let nothing get ahold of me that you and me can't lick." The child thought for a moment and insightfully replied, "Oh, I know, the dog wants to lick anything." Comprehension of language, whether it is spoken, signed, or read, is dependent on an individual's world knowledge—that is, what the person already knows, a knowledge of linguistic forms, and the ability to integrate information.

Inferencing may be described as two specific structures: (1) script, and (2) semantic networks. Script is the cultural or social behaviors that are known to most people (Santrock, 1986). For example, when planning a vacation, it is a cultural expectation that an individual will request approval from the supervisor for the time off from work. This is an unwritten rule that was never explicitly taught in any academic course, nor is it found in any textbook; rather a person learns the rule through life experiences. However, those who have never participated in planning a vacation and have had no opportunity to interact with others in the process may be unfamiliar with the general sequence of events that should occur in the situation. Because of limited experiences with the societal events and language to convey those events, deaf children may have difficulty in developing inferencing skills. The second event, semantic network, "is a set of concepts that are related in a variety of ways. The more scripts available to interpret an event or the richer the semantic networks available, the more inferences will be drawn" (Santrock, 1986, p. 286).

Inferencing, as it relates to reading and written language production, is subdivided into four hierarchical levels of classification (Anderson, 1981). The first level is lexical—that is, the knowledge that comes from words and the interrelationship among words and phrases. The second level incorporates the connections made from one sentence to the next, tying the text into a meaningful unit of information and communication. Level three couples the schemata of the reader with the information presented in the text to depict a complete picture or event. The fourth level integrates the schemata and the text into a singular and, perhaps, a new framework. To a teacher of deaf children, each of these levels is critical to the understanding of language.

Related Research

Research regarding the development of inferencing skills in deaf children is extremely limited. Suppes (1974) and Waldron and Rose (1983) suggest that the ability to infer is unrelated to auditory or language skills. If a child falls down and cuts his knee, his mother puts a bandage on his knee. On seeing another individual with a bandage, the child may infer that the person fell down. Neither symbolic linguistic codes nor audition is required for the use of inferencing skills in this example. However, language and auditory input shape our knowledge of the world and develop the schemata. Rose (1975) investigated the social inferencing skills of deaf adolescents using the *Test of Social Inference Skills* (Edmonson, de Jung, Leland, and Leach, 1974). Each student was shown a situational picture and asked to describe what happened. Students with mental retardation typically responded to the pictures by identifying objects within the picture but were able to relate objects to one another. Deaf students were very capable of producing inferences based on the people and actions implied by the photographs; however, the deaf students' inferences were different from those provided by hearing students.

Fischgrund (1978) studied the syntactic complexity of mathematical word problems with 12- to 14-year-old hearing impaired students. Word problems that included the use of inference statements (e.g., if...then) were the most difficult for the students to interpret. Fischgrund (1978) found that, after students were taught to identify the process and the data prior to solving the word problems, they increased their comprehension of the problem. However, he concluded that "what is not apparent is a teaching strategy that adequately facilitates the movement of inferential thinking" (p. 145). In response to Fischgrund's dilemma, Martin (1984) is attempting to restructure the mental schemata, including inferencing skills, with hearing impaired adolescents. Using mediated learning experiences developed by Feuerstein (1979), Martin provides students with explicit instruction on the process of thinking through problems using paper and pencil tasks and teacher intervention strategies. As the students develop mediated learning strategies, the strategies are applied to explicit, real-life situations. Students receiving this instruction demonstrated improved reading comprehension scores over the scores of hearing impaired students not receiving instruction.

LOGO, a software microcomputer language developed by Papert (1980), has been used with hearing impaired children for the purpose of problem-solving (Stone, 1983). LOGO is a language code that depends on mathematical relationships that produce graphic images. Inferences are inherent in the process as the students acquire LOGO programming skills for the development of various forms, shapes, and images on the computer screen. The relationship of the students' development of inferencing skills using LOGO and the application of these skills to reading, writing, or daily living is not known.

Classroom Application

Games such as checkers, chess, *Monopoly*, *Othello*, and treasure hunts are just a few highly accessible activities that require inferencing skills with minimal English language requirements. Perhaps the most critical means of enhancing the inferencing skills of deaf children is to provide students with qualitative and quantitative experiences for the purpose of increasing the world knowledge they bring to reading and writing tasks. A second fundamental intervention strategy is the development of syntactic structures. Wiig and Semel (1984, p. 257) suggested activities to help students with adequate knowledge of the world and syntactic skills learn to recognize inferential information:

Detecting Inconsistencies and Absurdities

He hit the baseball with a racket.
• Was anything wrong with this statement?
• What was wrong?

Mr. Adams lived 30 miles from his work. After 4 years, he decided to buy a new bicycle to get there faster and to save money.
• Was anything wrong with this statement?
• What was wrong?
It was raining so hard yesterday that Phil took off his shirt to get a suntan.
• Was anything wrong with this statement?
• What was wrong?

It was a beautiful summer day and Laura decided to go swimming. She put on her bathing suit and dived into the warm water of the lake. After half an hour of swimming, she dried herself off on the shore and lay in the hot summer sun. Then she looked at the water and said, ''Gee, I think I'll go ice skating. The ice is perfect today.''
• What was wrong in this story?

Correcting Inconsistencies and Absurdities

Charlie drank the hamburger.
* What word would you change?

Brian liked the book so much he burned it.
* What word would you change?

Ted was going to Europe. He didn't know whether to go by boat or bus.
* What word would you change?

Predicting Outcomes and Inferring Causes

Sue was hanging a picture on the wall. She tried to use a thumb tack. The thumb tack bent against the wall. She thought and thought about what she could do. Finally, she. . . .
* Can you finish the story? What could she do? (use tape? give up? find another tack?)

Durkin (1983) offers another set of activities for the explicit development of inference skills related to reading and written language. She suggests assembling a set of related pictures, such as a child eating breakfast, eating lunch, and eating dinner. The pictures can be inserted into a scrapbook. A short description of each picture is written on a card. The children can read the description and place it below the picture.

Another exercise in inferred information includes the preparation of two sets of sentence strips. One set contains direct information, such as *Ms. Pat is a wonderful teacher; The Green Bay Packers are the champions of the NFL.* After the students read the sentences, the teacher questions the student regarding the interpretation of the sentences. The teacher then presents related sentence strips containing implied information such as, *All of the students in Ms. Pat's class were on the honor roll; The outstanding defense of the Green Bay Packers was the key to their winning season* (Durkin, 1983). The related sentences are placed under the sentences containing the direct information. A similar activity is giving students sentences or a short paragraph that describes a person or an event. For example,

Mr. Brown's office is very interesting. He has many awards and trophies. The children liked the zebra skin and the tiger's head. Tommy liked Mr. Brown's trophy for the Pike's Peak Marathon.

The children are questioned about what kind of things Mr. Brown does and where he has been that are not mentioned in the paragraph. Newspaper ads also provide students with a variety of inferential experiences. Students can review ads and identify explicit and implicit information. High school students enjoy responding to advertisements that include "free" promotions such as a "free checking account."

As reading material is presented to hearing impaired children, the teacher must be aware that most language materials require inferencing. It is important to note whether the child has sufficient world knowledge to comprehend the information presented in the material as well as the structure of language for the interpretation of the symbolic forms. Prereading questions presented by the teacher can assist the children in becoming aware of what is important in the reading materials and can help set the scene for the information given. Carefully planned postreading questioning can highlight not only the facts presented in the passage but also the inferences that are included in the writing (Durkin, 1983).

QAR Techniques

A major consideration when teaching language to deaf children is the development of comprehension skills and strategies for acquiring these skills. Although research on language comprehension and instructional effectiveness with deaf children has been scant, Raphael (1982) has conducted a series of studies focused on the development of language comprehension strategies with hearing children. By explicitly teaching students the relationships between the type of question asked and the process used for locating the answer, Raphael was able to demonstrate that students in the upper elementary grades significantly improved in their ability to respond to comprehension questions during reading instruction. The question-answer-relationship, or QAR technique, as developed by Raphael and Wonnacott (1981), identifies three types of questions: (1) text explicit: the answer is *right there* in the text, (2) text implicit: the question requires the student to *think and search* through the text, and (3) script implicit: The answer requires the student to use known information in his or her head or *on my own*. The type of answers required in the third category could not be located in the text alone (Mason and Au, 1986).

Raphael (1982) devised a training protocol for the development of QAR skills that was used specifically with early elementary school students and less intensively with fifth and sixth grade students. The protocol uses four basic strategies, "Give immediate feedback, progress from shorter to longer texts, build independence by guiding students from group to independent activities, and provide transition from the easier task of recognizing an answer to the more difficult task of creating a response from more than one source of information" (Raphael, 1982, p. 187). In the initial stages of training, students were introduced to the concept of QAR through illustration with key terms *right there, think and search*, and *on my own*. The teachers modeled the process of reading a passage, looking at the question, and determining if the response was *right there* in the text, located somewhere in the text that required a *think and search* process, or required the students to answer *on their own*. As the students mastered the labels and identified this strategy used by the teacher, they were given a short passage to read, with a set of questions and answers. The students practiced the QAR technique by identifying the type of QAR used in answering the question correctly. For example:

> Minnesota is in the northern part of the United States. It is called "the land of ten thousand lakes," but there are really double that number of lakes in the state.

Question: Where is Minnesota located?
Answer: In the northern part of the United States. (*Right there*)
Question: How many lakes are there in Minnesota?
Answer: There are about 20,000 lakes in Minnesota. (*Think and search*)
Question: What kind of weather do they have in the State of Minnesota?
Answer: It is very cold, sunny, and snowy in the winter time and warm and sunny in the summer time. (*On my own*)

As the students demonstrate their competencies in the identification of strategies used to identify the correct answers, additional short passages with questions are given to the students. When students locate the correct answers, the class discusses which QAR strategy was used. As the training progresses, the passages increase gradually in length and the question types become more complex. During the training phase, teachers are encouraged to assist students in locating the correct answers through discussion and prior to recording their answers on paper. Although the QAR technique has not been assessed in terms of its effectiveness with deaf children, it may be a worthwhile instructional strategy for increasing language comprehension skills.

SEMANTIC MAPPING

Teachers emphasize vocabulary development for deaf children throughout the school years because an extensive and accurate vocabulary is essential for skilled reading. Beginning at the preschool level, teachers begin to develop vocabulary concepts through experiences and storytelling and, at the upper levels, many teachers present vocabulary units to enable students to have a better command of words. Some teachers, when preparing for a reading lesson, "preteach" the new words in the reading story so students will be able to read more fluently. (Discussion of vocabulary development has been covered in previous chapters.) These practices are all good, but semantic development includes more than just acquiring isolated vocabulary words, and successful reading requires more than understanding only single words. The language user and successful reader must understand the relations among and between words in spoken or signed language and in written language. They also must understand the ideas represented by those words and the relationships and connections among many ideas of different levels of importance. Developing semantic relationships or the interrelated meanings of words, sentences, and ideas cannot be accomplished by teaching the concepts of single words; different intervention strategies are needed.

A reading comprehension strategy called *mapping* provides an innovative model for the development of comprehension skills and, subsequently, for improved reading. It does not focus on individual word meanings; it focuses on conceptual relationships. Mapping involves a synthesis of the students' syntactic, lexical, and world knowledge as they read and interact with written text.

Six conceptual relationships form the basis of the mapping technique: characteristics, definitions, consequences, examples, sequence, and comparisons and contrasts. Studies conducted with hearing college students (Dansereau et al., 1979) and with hearing impaired college students (Long and Aldersley, 1982; Long and Conklin, 1979) generally have been supportive of teaching semantic mapping strategies to older students to obtain improved comprehension in reading. No studies have investigated the effects of mapping on younger children, and the results of the investigations with college students should not be generalized to children who are at earlier stages of reading development. However, suggestions for teachers who teach reading to younger children may be drawn from the mapping model. One requirement of successful reading is interaction between the reader and the text. Successful readers are active information processors and their goals include constructing a model of what the text means (Anderson, 1981). Training students to use semantic mapping to comprehend text provides those students with strategies that lead to greater interaction between reader and text.

Long and Aldersley (1982) state that mapping is an analytical tool that can teach students to identify concepts within a text, specify the relative importance of ideas, and diagram the information from the text into a "map" that makes the ideas and their relationships visible. Mapping training in Long and Aldersley's study consisted of "discussions and exercises centered on (1) analyzing the paragraph to discover main ideas and the relationship of subordinate ideas to the main idea, (2) placing the resulting ideas into a network (node-link diagram), and (3) writing two-sentence summaries of the same paragraph from the network" (pp. 817–818). As the students applied mapping strategies to the reading task, they became more actively involved in information processing. Through mapping the students may have been led to more manipulation and involvement with the material and, thus, to better comprehension. An example of a paragraph is presented next and a semantic mapping diagram is shown in Figure 7–2. Clearly, the thought and synthesis needed to build the map would require the student to become actively involved with the text.

Although there are many breeds of horses, Susie was not interested in a particular breed. She wanted a horse she could show. She had been looking for a horse for several weeks and had narrowed her choices to two, a Quarter horse and an Arabian. Both breeds can make good show horses, although there are noticeable differences in their physical appearance. A Quarter horse has large muscles that are well defined and a broad chest. It is a versatile animal and can be shown in many classes. An Arabian horse is not usually as muscular and has a narrower chest. It is also a versatile animal. Susie decided to buy the Quarter horse because she liked the muscular build of that animal.

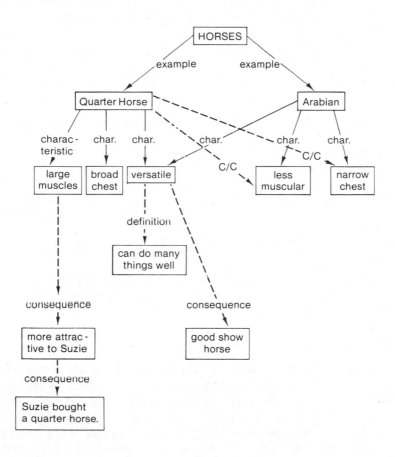

FIGURE 7–2.   *Semantic mapping diagram.*

Implications for teaching younger children may be derived from the semantic mapping model and the research results, which generally indicated that comprehension was improved when older students were taught to use mapping strategies. If one factor of successful reading is reader-text interaction, and if mapping does, in fact, facilitate reader-text interaction, teachers of younger children perhaps should focus more on activities that will promote reader involvement with the text. Some of the basic strategies in the mapping model can be modified and adapted for students in intermediate grades, junior high, and high school. Some of the basic skills necessary for mapping may be developed at the primary level and, in fact, are already a part of the primary curriculum in most programs for hearing impaired students. For example, the development of such skills as comparing and contrasting (identifying likenesses and differences), sequencing, noting characteristics (describing), and giving examples are all skills that are prerequisites to mapping and are initially developed as early as the primary level. Another requirement for mapping is identifying main and supporting ideas, and work on these comprehension skills is usually begun at the upper primary level. Thus, skill development that will lead to the ability to do mapping begins at the primary level and includes activities focused in the following skill areas:

Primary
- Identifying likenesses and differences in objects, pictures, events
- Sequencing
- Describing objects, pictures, events
- Classifying or categorizing

Upper Primary
- Continuing skill development from the primary level, gradually increasing the difficulty
- Identifying main and supporting ideas

Intermediate
- Continuing skill development from previous levels, gradually increasing the difficulty
- Defining terms
- Drawing conclusions
- Summarizing

At the upper intermediate level, the students might begin a modified version of mapping. Often, during reading lessons, teachers ask questions that focus on the same relationships that form the basis of the mapping model. However, the results of Long and Conklin's study (1979) suggested that comprehension was better when mapping was written out on paper. Using the same sample paragraph presented earlier in this chapter, the teacher could begin developing networking strategies as a group project. The teacher should ask questions that focus on the six basic conceptual relationships, and, as students provide answers, the mapping diagram can be developed on the chalkboard. Each student might duplicate the diagram on paper if it seems to aid comprehension and recall. The questions and modified mapping diagram are shown in Figure 7–3.

The results of Long and Aldersley's study (1982) indicated that after the subjects (college students) had been trained in mapping techniques and could diagram independently, they were able to summarize the information in a passage better than they could prior to training. They also could successfully summarize information in a passage they had studied but had not mapped. Thus, teachers at the intermediate and junior high school levels might gradually fade their guidance and work toward enabling the students to perform independently.

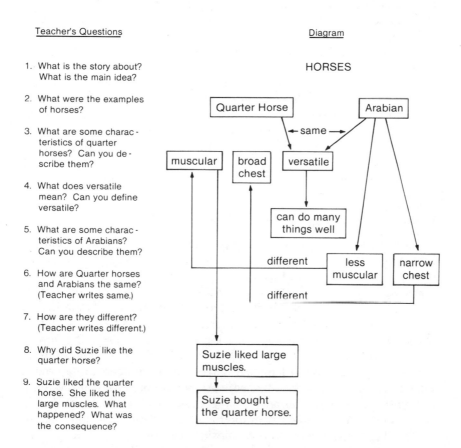

FIGURE 7–3.   *Modified semantic mapping diagram.*

In summary, semantic mapping appears to be a productive strategy for improving reading comprehension skills in older students. It may be helpful for students at younger levels, although before attempting the actual diagramming, students should have previously developed the basic skills necessary to perform the more complex tasks required in mapping. It must be remembered that this is only one of many reading comprehension strategies, and the development of mapping should not preclude the development of an array of comprehension strategies, which students must possess and use if they are to be successful readers.

WRITTEN LANGUAGE

Writing is a fundamental skill that is assumed in the term "literacy" to be a counterpart to reading; however, the definition of writing has several interpretations. Writing can be viewed as a mechanical process, that is, the act of reproducing shapes and forms on paper. Writing is also the product of composition that incorporates a series of steps, including planning, notations, evaluation, rewriting, and editing (Graves, 1984). The following information highlights written expression, that is, the symbolic production frequently referred to as composition that communicates information to another person (Klein, 1985). As a mode of communication, writing is a secondary form of expression dependent on primary systems, such as speech or sign language, as the foundation for development. Writing, like spoken or signed language, is a means of expressing what an individual already knows (Kretschmer and Kretschmer, 1978).

Written Language Development in Hearing Children

Research regarding the development and use of written language is far too extensive for a complete discussion within this book. A select set of findings is addressed as it relates to the development of written language skills in deaf children. Loban (1976) studied the oral and written language development of children in kindergarten through grade 12. His data support those of numerous other researchers using the analytical approach to describe language development (Hunt, 1965; O'Donnell, Griffin, and Norris, 1967; O'Hare, 1973). In comparison to the linear trend of oral language, written language growth patterns tend to be erratic. Growth spurts in written language were noted specifically at the ninth and tenth grade levels. LaBrant (1933) reported that the number and complexity of clauses increased with the hearing student's age. Ten-year-old children began using connectors as transitions to concepts, including terms such as *although, even if, and nonetheless*. By 12 years of age, students were using nouns modified by a participle, the gerund phrase, the adverbial infinitive, and the compound predicate (Loban, 1976).

Recently, the study of written language among hearing children has changed in emphasis from the analysis of linguistic structures to processes used in the development of composition. The term "composition" has been defined broadly, not simply as an end product, but rather as the act of composing, of recording a person's ideas into symbolic form (Moffett and Wagner, 1983). Composition in its beginning expressive forms may include illustration, scribbles, pantomime, and storytelling. The written form of composition is the most complex. Researchers, such as Graves (1984), Perron (1978), Petty (1978), and others, have established a foundation for understanding the variables that influence the process of written composition. Klein (1985) proposed a set of principles based on the research of Graves (1984) and others that can be translated into practice by teachers and clinicians.

1. Children in the primary grades produce more and higher-quality writing when operating in an informal learning environment that permits considerable freedom in choosing topics and defining their own strategies for completing the writing assignment.
2. Children in the primary grades turn inward for the content of their writing. Personal experiences and immediate family and friends are critical root sources of their writing.
3. Learners should see composition as consisting of three important phases—prewriting, writing, and revision. These three phases need to be incorporated throughout the instructional program, including grades 1 through 8.
4. Writing serves different purposes—to inform, to describe, to explain, to persuade or argue, to entertain—none of which is age-specific. Beginning writers, older children, and adult writers all employ writing for these purposes. It is only the degree of sophistication that differs, not the range or general character of the purposes.
5. Writing occurs in many different forms—stories, poems, essays, journals, notes, letters, reports, and scripts for plays. These forms incorporate a more limited number of discourse modes—exposition, narration, argumentation, and fiction.
6. The writer writes for different audiences. During the intermediate school years, students need to develop necessary skills in adapting written structure and content to context and audience.
7. Students should write often. (Klein, 1985, pp. 78–81)

Written Language Development in Deaf Children

The study of reading and written language has been the most frequent means of describing language development in deaf children, with the majority of studies paralleling the research conducted with hearing children. The primary focus has been on the structure or form of the product of written language. Yoshinaga-Itano and Snyder (1985) summarized the five basic types of analysis conducted by numerous researchers in the field of education of deaf children as a means of describing written language. The types of analysis include (1) quantity of sentence and composition length, (2) complexity of syntactic forms used in sentence and composition development, (3) analysis and categorization of errors made in compositions; (4) quantitative use of various parts of speech, and (5) quantitative analysis of various types of transformational grammatical structures used.

Comprehensive discussion and summary of studies conducted with deaf children can be found in *Language and Deafness* (Quigley and Paul, 1984b) and *Language Development and Intervention with the Hearing Impaired* (Kretschmer and Kretschmer, 1978). A summary of the years of research on the written language of deaf children indicates that there are notable delays and substantial differences in the development of written language forms (Heider and Heider, 1940; Ivimey and Lachterman, 1980; Kretschmer and Kretschmer, 1986; Quigley et al., 1976; Stuckless and Marks, 1966). Deaf children tend to use greater numbers of basic syntactic structures, including the nouns, verbs, and determiners, and demonstrate less frequent use of adverbs, auxiliaries. and conjunctions than hearing children. Syntactic and semantic growth patterns in written language development in hearing impaired children were reported by Yoshinaga (1983) and Yoshinaga-Itano and Snyder (1985). These findings were similar to those of Marshall and Quigley (1970). Like hearing children, deaf children's written syntactic language growth patterns tend to accelerate between 10 and 15 years of age. Yoshinaga (1983) noted that semantic complexity peaks in hearing children at 13 years of age, whereas the hearing impaired child tends to peak at age 12 years. However, a significant number of deaf children demonstrated continued growth in complex semantic units across the age range of 10 to 18 years. Unfortunately, there are no established relationships between the oral or signed productions of deaf children and their written language productions.

Although the most recent studies in the language development of hearing children focused on the processes used in composing and recording "inner language," there is a dearth of information regarding the processes of writing with deaf children (Kretschmer and Kretschmer, 1986). The data regarding the written language of deaf children have primarily illustrated the deficiencies in the product rather than identifying the process used. Critics generally attribute these characteristics to the methods of teaching used in the classroom. Ewoldt (1985) proposes that the use of the natural approach to language development could alleviate the stilted and underdeveloped characteristics of written language produced by deaf children. According to the critics, application of a more pragmatic approach to instruction, focusing on written language as a process of connected discourse, has the potential for development of increased literacy in both reading and writing.

This proposition has not been substantiated. Bunch (1979) studied the internalized use of grammatical rules by 75 deaf children between the ages of 9 and 16 years. His results indicated that there were no differences in the deaf students' abilities to use grammatical rules and written language structures relating to the method of teaching (the natural method versus the formal method). Ewoldt (1985) described the use of process, or the composition approach, to the development of reading and writing skills with nine hearing impaired children over a 3-year period. Following the model used by Harste, Burke, and Woodward (1983) with hearing children, a framework was established using demonstration modeling similar to the language experience approach, followed by frequent free writing experiences and an environment that encouraged the child to "risk" composing. The results of Ewoldt's work are generally inconclusive at this time.

Story writing abilities of hearing impaired children using various types of stimuli are described by Truax (1985). The three stimuli provided to the students were (1) write a story; (2) given three sets of characters, select one set of characters and write a story; and (3) given three sets of opening lines to a story, select one set and write a story. Analysis of the stories focused on the composition of a setting, a problem or a goal, and episodes leading to the resolution of the story. Truax reported that a majority of the students across all ages were able to develop a story line. Younger children in the primary and intermediate grades frequently used personal experiences as the basis for their storytelling. At the secondary level, students demonstrated the ability to use the essential components of storytelling in written form.

Implications of Research

Written language as a form of communication presents a particular challenge to deaf children and their teachers. The process of writing, unlike speech or signing, is produced in the absence of external expressive stimuli, such as facial expressions, artifacts or objects of reference, intonations, speed of delivery, or emphasis. Written language depends on the child's ability to represent internal personal thoughts in symbolic form using the rules of English to convey intent in the absence of other expressive features (Rivers and Temperley, 1978). The natural approach to teaching language assumes that the child can access the rules of spoken language, which in turn can be applied to the rules of reading and writing. On the other hand, application of the structured approach to teaching written language creates a format for the production of written language forms rather than composition. Although instructional dilemma has not been resolved, it appears that a balance in teaching strategies using the natural and structured approaches to written language development may provide the maximum advantage.

Written language is a process rather than a static activity. Thus, teachers are encouraged to use the abilities of the deaf child in the development of that process using illustrations, drama, storytelling, and interactions as the foundation for writing experiences. No one can be expected to write a perfect product at the first sitting. Rather, students learn by doing and by being actively involved in both the planning and prewriting process and the editing and reediting stages. Students will require assistance and practice in writing linguistic forms, in spelling, and in writing for various purposes. A variety of strategies that are applicable to the teaching of written language are presented in previous chapters. The following section provides a sampling of additional strategies that have been applied to classroom settings with deaf children.

Classroom Applications

Truax (1985) used a writing workshop format with primary and high school level hearing impaired students. Primary students were exposed to the writing process through the teacher modeling prewriting activities. The teacher began by telling of a personal event that had occurred recently. Students were encouraged to ask questions and request clarification of the teacher's experience. Each student was then given the opportunity to tell about something that had happened to him or her. In like manner, the teacher questioned the student, asked for clarification, and restated and expanded on the child's production. The next phase included a recording of the story in picture form. The teacher, and then the students, drew pictures recording the main events, characters, and setting of the story. Using the drawings made by the teacher and each of the students, the stories were retold. The students then retold their stories once again while the teacher recorded the dictation in writing. The stories were read and edited. The final products—drawings and edited stories— were bound into a book that remained in the library, where the children and their peers could read and reread their products.

The process used with high school hearing impaired students followed much the same format as applied in the primary grades. The writing workshop began with the teacher's modeling of prewriting or planning skills. The teacher and students used a brainstorming approach to identify various topics that they would like to write about. The teacher recorded the various ideas as they were suggested by the students. After agreeing on a specific topic, the teacher jotted down comments, words, ideas, and events related to the topic. In the next writing session, the teacher and the students identified a sequence of events and then described the setting in which the story would take place. The teacher then began to write, modeling the composition process for the students. The first draft was read by the class. The students were encouraged to ask questions about the story. Editing occurred as the discussion proceeded, adding information, crossing out redundancies and known quantities, cutting and pasting, and rearranging and rephrasing. Final writing occurred only after a series of edits. The final stage was the students' preparation of their own lists of interests and conferencing with the teacher regarding various ideas and editing.

Winkelman (1971) used a modified structured approach for the writing of news stories with deaf students. Using a triangular diagram, storytelling or literary works generally begin with the introduction or "setting the stage" at the apex, the building of the story at the center of the triangle, and the climax at the base of the figure. In teaching newswriting, Winkelman presented the inverted triangle as the format for writing. The most important facts were related first, followed by the body of the story and then the less important information. Planning for the writing of the news story began with the identification of the five W's: Who? What? Where? When? Why? A five-pointed star was used for the identification of the facts. The star outline provided the lead-in for the storyline. The body of the news story included additional facts that related to the five W's. Additional information could be appended to the story as students elected to do so. Students edited their draft copies in conference with the teacher; the Fitzgerald Key was used as a format for structural edits. Final products were published in the student newspaper and were distributed throughout the school.

Comic strips have long been a favorite form of stimulus for written language instruction. Hoover (1972) favored the comic strip *Henry* for the development of story line, sequencing of events, and the use of idiomatic language and vocabulary. Sister M. Peter (1981, 1984) used the *Family Circle* and *Jack and Julie* as characters for written language development. Through the use of cartoons, pictures, objects, and dramatization, students engaged in the process of composing, that is, prewriting and planning for writing.

"Good writing implies a knowledge of the conventions of the written code" (Rivers and Temperley, 1978, p. 264). Unfortunately, the written code depends on the knowledge of the auditory and spoken code of language, to which deaf children do not have direct access. The dilemma for the teacher of the hearing impaired child frequently is how much grammatical or syntactic editing or correction should be done in assisting the child to develop a final written product? There is no simple answer. A rule of thumb is generally to focus on a single rule or element for correction rather than addressing all of the composition deficiencies. The identification of a specific objective for improvement and noting that objective in the editing process eliminates the frustration of the teacher and the child, and, at the same time, provides the basis for the development of that skill.

From the work of Graves (1984), Judy and Judy (1983) identified six phases in the writing process:

1. Set up a "work in progress" file.
2. Contract with students for the preparation of final written products. The students are then free to select and elect to write within a broad time span rather than within the 20-minute specified writing period.
3. Create a writing sequence—that is, use one written product as a link to another product.
4. Allow students to experiment with writing, drawing, and using words for different sizes, shapes, and colors. Students may elect to write for a variety of purposes and with different audiences.
5. Allow for cooperative learning and interactions during the writing process. Students may seek help from each other or they may request assistance from the teacher or from other resources in the classroom. Cooperative learning (Johnson, 1986) can begin with two students writing a joint composition.
6. Written products should be purposeful. Post students' works on boards where others can review them, have a writing fair, collect and bind final written products into a book, and make the book available for others to read. Publish the students' work in booklets for distribution to the school and home.

The classroom microcomputer has become a valuable tool in the writing process. Writing and editing programs such as the *Bank Street Writer* (Smith, 1984) provide the students with an easy-to-use tool for jotting down notes, reviewing, and editing without fear of the "red marks syndrome." Files can be developed for work in progress and reviewed as needed by the teacher and the student. Rose, Waldron, and Yanoff (1984) developed microcomputer software for use by deaf children, incorporating illustrations of family members, including mother, father, sister, brother, grandmother, and grandfather. Through the use of cartoon bubbles, students or the teacher can write their own personalized dialogue for each of the characters. The dialogue scripts can be saved in separate files. Students review each others scripts and guess "Who said what to whom" by pointing to the picture of mother, father, or another member on the screen. Photography and composition were used by Sheie (in press) to develop writing skills in hearing impaired students. Using photographs produced by the students as well as microcomputer graphics and text displays, Sheie focused on relaying factual content. Students produced newspapers that could be shared in print with their peers or sent through the computer modem to students in other school buildings.

TDDs may also provide an excellent tool for the production and improvement of written language skills in deaf children. Coupling the graphic display with the written dialogue is extremely helpful in the development of language forms. Interactive microcomputers—that is, linkages between computers—allow students to share their written products with each other. The teacher can review a student's work and provide comment or questioning as the writing is in process. Peyton and Batson (1986) discussed the numerous possibilities and advancements that may occur as a result of using networking or interactive microcomputers to simulate natural language development in written form with deaf students. ENFI (English Natural Language Form Instruction), developed at Gallaudet University (Peyton and Batson, 1986), uses interactive microcomputers for written social communication. Each student and the teacher type a message on his or her personal computer. By pressing a key, the user can send a message to all members in the class immediately. Messages sent among the students and the teacher emulate social conversation in written form. Although these technology advancements may provide teachers with more efficient tools than the traditional paper and pencil or overhead projector format, teaching of writing skills still fundamentally depends on the teacher's knowledge of the English language and the ability to translate that knowledge into the identification and application of linguistic principles for the development of language in deaf children.

SUMMARY

The specialized metalinguistic aspects of language development highlight the student's need for knowledge of basic linguistic structures, experience, and understanding of concepts. Language development in areas such as composition, use of figurative language, and linguistic inferencing skills is accomplished through practice, modeling, and natural interactions with hearing children. Every parent of an adolescent is frequently bewildered by their child's use of figurative language and the manner of manipulation of various language forms. By virtue of interactions with others, children, adolescents, and adults alike implicitly provide new and unique definitions of figurative language, networking, inferencing, and composition.

Deaf children do not acquire these specialized aspects of language in the same manner or at the same rate as hearing children. Rather, explicit experiences and instructional strategies must be included in the curriculum to allow for the development of metaphors, idioms, and inferencing embedded in language and composition through writing. Approaches that appear to have potential for use in classrooms with deaf children include semantic networking, the question-answer-relationship (QAR) approach, emphasis on writing with the explicit intent of composing, and various types of technology. The common thread that runs through all of the explicit teaching strategies used or suggested is the application of a visual-graphic form or function for the development and use of specialized aspects of language. Each of the strategies assumes the deaf student has had sufficient experience with and knowledge of the concepts being used in the development of these specialized aspects of language. As stated in previous chapters, much of the deaf student's development will depend on the teacher's careful planning, instruction, and knowledge of language development principles.

CHAPTER 8

A Brief Synthesis

Normal development of language seems to depend, above all else, on fluent and intelligible communicative interaction between a child and a competent user of the language that is to be acquired. This means the child must have such interaction from birth through a communication system that allows easy reception and easy expression and that functions as an automatic integrated system without any need for conscious control of the system or any of its parts by the child. Verbal language acquisition typically is based on auditory-vocal mechanisms. In this system, which Fairbanks (1954) described as a servosystem, hearing is the controlling element. Hearing allows the constant intake of auditory events, including speech, the storage of internal representations of the auditory events, and automatic control of the vocal mechanism to reproduce the events. The child does not have to control the system consciously, concentrating on forming the lips, tongue, teeth, and other parts of the speech mechanism to produce particular speech sounds. The whole process is controlled automatically by hearing, and when the system is functioning smoothly and interacting with a competent adult language model, the child will develop, during a period of only a few years, a rich and complex language with little apparent effort and no formal instruction. Hearing is the key to the system and, when hearing is damaged or destroyed, the system is disrupted; it can no longer function as a system with fluent and automatic control of its own operation.

Although from few statements the acquisition of language would seem to be a simple matter, which indeed it is for the typical hearing child, many events can disrupt the process, and the greater the extent of the disruption and the earlier in life it occurs, the greater will be its effects on language development. For example, if the child has an intact communication system, but little stimulation or communicative interaction is provided by the adults in the child's environment, the type of language deficits found in children in Head Start programs can result, and the severity of these deficits usually is related to the severity and duration of the environmental deprivation. Disruptions in the communication system itself will likewise produce deficits in language development, and deafness certainly represents a massive disruption. There is ample evidence that even modest degrees of hearing impairment will produce language deficits and consequently educational deficits and that the degree of deficit appears to be at least roughly linked to degree of impairment (Davis, 1977). Of greater interest and relevance here is the evidence (Conrad, 1979; Ling, 1976) that somewhere along the decibel continuum of Hearing Threshold Level (HTL) hearing ceases to be the major communication channel and is replaced by vision; the child becomes linked to the world of communication by eye rather than by ear. This is the point at which a child can be considered to be deaf rather than hard of hearing. The impairment shifts from being a difference in degree to being a difference in kind, assuming that the eye receives and processes information differently from the ear.

If an automatic, self-controlling communication system is essential for normal development of language, and if the auditory-vocal mechanisms provide that system for hearing people, there appear to be three ways to provide a system for deaf children. The first way would be to repair the defective auditory component to the extent that the auditory-vocal mechanisms would be a functional communication system. The second would be to substitute other physiological mechanisms for the auditoryvocal mechanisms, such as vision for audition and manual for vocal. This would result in a communication system based on visual-manual mechanisms. The third way would be to use the auditory-vocal mechanisms as much as possible and to supplement them with the visual-manual mechanisms. Each of these three ways is the basis for a major approach to educating deaf children with the main objective for all being to produce as normal and adequate development of language as is possible.

Oral-aural approaches, whether multisensory or unisensory (emphasis on audition), strive, by means of educational practices and technological devices, to use the auditory-vocal mechanisms as the basic communication system for the deaf child. The child is expected, with appropriate training, to use residual hearing, to perceive and understand the speech of others visually (i.e., speechreading) and to monitor his or her own speech by whatever auditory feedback is available and by the use of proprioceptive and kinesthetic feedbacks, which supply to the central nervous system information about the placement and movement of various organs involved in speech production. But all of these input and feedback mechanisms can only partially replace the lost hearing. The main effect is that this communication system is labored and only semi-intelligible rather than fluent and fully intelligible, as is required for normal development of language. It follows that language development by this means is likely to be a labored process. For example, if information relayed to a deaf child is not understood, the teacher can convey it again one word at a time or, if he or she is striving for more natural input, can keep repeating the information in different language and in different contexts until the child comprehends. Either way, this is a labored rather than a fluent process. Similarly, a speech response from the child is usually labored. Without the automatic, servosystem type of control whereby hearing can produce speech without conscious attention by the child on how it is produced, the deaf child has to rely on some slight auditory feedback and the relatively crude proprioceptive and kinesthetic feedbacks to monitor and control speech output. This child has to think not only of *what* to say but *how* to say it, without knowing how to do either very well.

In spite of these problems, the oral-aural approaches have been successful with some deaf children. Ogden (1979), Quigley, Jenne, and Phillips (1969), and others have documented the language, educational, and occupational successes of substantial numbers of students from incontestably oral schools. The oral-aural approaches have the advantages that they use the same communication system used by hearing children to establish language, they seek to establish a similar internalized verbal language, and they can use that primary internalized language as a basis for developing the secondary language forms of reading and writing in ways similar to those used with hearing children. There is evidence that such an internalized verbal language might be essential in the development of reading and writing (see the discussion in Quigley and Paul, 1984b, pp. 44–50), but the oral-aural approaches seem to require special students and special conditions for success. During the past two decades, most day programs for deaf children, which previously used oral-aural approaches almost exclusively, have changed to the simultaneous method of combined oral and manual communication now known as total communication (discussed later as the third approach).

The second way to provide the deaf child with a communication system for the development of language is to substitute other physiological mechanisms for the auditory-vocal mechanisms. This usually is done by using the visual-manual mechanisms to develop American Sign Language (ASL) as the primary language of the child. (Although the various forms of manually coded English, including fingerspelling, can be used in a visual-manual communication system, these usually are used in synchronization with speech and are discussed later as the third approach to a communication system for deaf children.) Proponents of the ASL approach cite several major advantages. The one of interest here is the contention that ASL and the visual-manual mechanisms through which it is transmitted offer the same fluency and intelligibility as do spoken languages transmitted by means of the auditory-vocal mechanisms (e.g., English, Spanish). As stated at the beginning of this chapter, these are primary requirements for normal development of language.

Although ASL does seem to offer easy visual receptive communication in that most signs involve large movements that are readily intelligible visually, and relatively easy expressive communication in that most signs involve gross muscular movements that are within the manual capabilities of young children, the communication system does not seem to have quite the automaticity of control that is a major feature of the oral-aural system with intact auditory-vocal mechanisms. The sense of hearing monitors, adjusts, and controls the speech output of the hearing child without conscious direction by the child. It is not clear how this automaticity of output is achieved in a visual-manual system. Furthermore, hearing is nondirectional in that sound, including speech, can enter the ear from any direction, and the normal ear cannot be closed against sound other than artificially, so auditory input is almost constant in the typical young hearing child's waking environment. Any visual communication input, such as ASL, is apparent to deaf children only when they are looking at the source of the communication, and the children can always eliminate the source simply by closing their eyes or looking away. Thus, the amount of language input a deaf child receives from ASL is likely to be much less than the amount of auditory language input to a typical hearing child. The importance of this will be pointed out later in discussing some problems of purely "natural" ways of developing language in deaf children.

Even if for the deaf child ASL can function by means of a visual-manual communication link as fluently, intelligibly, and effectively as oral language for the hearing child, certain questions about its use as the primary language for deaf children remain. First, can ASL perform the same cognitive and conceptual functions as spoken language?

Granted that it functions adequately for most conversational and other basic transactional purposes, does it have the vocabulary, the structure, the nuances, the rigor for transmission of a lecture on the physiology of the eye or on symbolism in Dylan Thomas' poetry? Some proponents would answer "yes," and perhaps they are right; others would claim that, given a history of repression of the language, it might not at present be able to perform these functions, but it has the same capability for expansion as spoken languages and can be expanded to perform these functions; perhaps they, too, are right. But convincing evidence is lacking, and the question remains legitimate.

A second question concerns how English, or any other spoken language, can be developed if ASL is the primary language. Chapter 6 provides information on this problem and presents some of the proposals for its resolution. All of these seem to involve using techniques of bilingual teaching to move from ASL to English by means of various forms of manually coded English (MCE). Notably lacking in these proposals is any detailed plan for moving to oral English, yet there is evidence (see the detailed discussion in Quigley and Paul, 1984b, pp. 44–50) that an internalized speech or verbal code is important to the development of reading. If this is so, how does a deaf child, who has acquired ASL as a primary language and some form of manually coded English as a second language, learn to read text that is based on and derived from a spoken language? This question has not yet received a satisfactory answer.

The third approach to establishing a communication system for deaf children is the combination of auditory-vocal mechanisms and visual-manual mechanisms to produce simultaneous speech and manually coded English, which was formerly called the simultaneous method and is now known as total communication. This, in some form, is at present the most widely used approach in the United States. The recent forms of manually coded English have been developed on the grounds that they provide deaf children with visually intelligible and fluent forms of linguistic input and that they conform to the syntactic (including morphologic) structure of English. The major systems are Seeing Essential English (SEE I) and Signing Exact English (SEE II), which attempt, each in its own way, to use ASL signs and contrived signs to make sign language conform to English structure. Some studies (Marmor and Pettito, 1979; Reich and Bick, 1977) have indicated that these systems are cumbersome to use exactly as prescribed and often evolve in the hands of practitioners into forms of Pidgin Sign English (PSE).

Practitioners of aggressively oral programs have wondered, knowing how difficult oral-aural approaches alone are, how it is possible to combine them with visual-manual approaches without degrading or neglecting one or both types of approaches. And investigators of ASL have argued that the signed codes, being visual-manual in nature, cannot adequately represent English, which is auditory-vocal in nature (Baker and Cokely, 1980; Kluwin, 1981). Some support for this contention is found in the work of Lichtenstein (1983) and others, which indicates that the syntax of English is heavily dependent on possession of a speech code. *The problem seems to lie, not only in lack of capacity on the part of visual-manual mechanisms to transmit English structure, but also in the inability of deaf children to extract that structure from the visual input they are receiving.* Deaf children seem to be able to look at manually coded English for years and still respond with non-English manual output, just as deaf students can look at appropriate English structure in books for 20 years in school and still write with non-English structure. In neither case do the students seem to be able to extract English structure from the visual input and internalize it.

The last point is one of three that need to be considered in selecting among communication approaches and among language development practices for use with deaf children. These three points are (1) none of the communication systems described can replace the automatic servosystem operation of the auditory-vocal mechanisms in developing English or any other auditory-based language; (2) none of these systems can provide the same amount of input in English or any other auditory-based language as does the auditory-vocal system; and (3) if deaf children are defined as those who must process information primarily by eye rather than by ear, it should be recognized that the eye seems to be a relatively inefficient processor of spoken languages, especially of the structures of those languages that depend heavily on temporal-sequential input and suprasegmental aspects of speech for correct interpretation. The eye seems to be more efficiently adapted to processing the spatial and motion features that are basic to ASL. If these points are accepted, some conclusions can be made about the use of various communication systems for language development.

First, oral-aural approaches are difficult to use and seem to require special conditions for success, conditions that cannot easily be met in the public school system. Some of these conditions are as follows: students with above-average intelligence; literate and highly motivated parents; school administrators and staff totally convinced of the value of oral methods and highly trained in using them; complete control of staff, curriculum, and methodology to ensure consistent use of oral English by staff and students at all times; and acceptance by parents, staff, and administrators that years of painstaking effort are required for success (Quigley and Kretschmer, 1982, p. 27). In spite of these conditions and the obvious enormity of the task, oral-aural approaches appeal to parents who accept their goal of preparing deaf children along the same educational paths as hearing children and equipping them to cope with the general society. Private oral schools are thriving and will continue to thrive, and some day programs provide separate oral-aural programs for deaf children whose parents request them. Perhaps as many as 30 percent of deaf children in the United States are in such programs.

The ASL-ESL approach (American Sign Language as a first language and English as a second language) is relatively new, although ASL is not. Only in recent years have investigators suggested that English be considered a second language and that the techniques and research in bilingualism and second-language learning be applied with deaf children. Some of the problems with this approach have been discussed—the adequacy of ASL as language, how the reading and writing of English can be based on ASL—but several positive factors are worthy of comment. First, although the visual-manual mechanisms by means of which ASL is conveyed might not have the same automaticity as the auditory-vocal mechanisms of spoken languages, they are closer to it than the other two communication approaches, oralaural and simultaneous. Thus, the fluency and intelligibility of communication in both reception and expression that are necessary for normal development of language are probably present in greater degree in this approach than in the other two. Second, although ASL does not provide English input (it is a different language), it perhaps provides the same amount of input of information in its own referential symbols and its own structure as do spoken languages. Third, ASL is perhaps adapted to the processing requirements of the eye rather than the ear. These are convincing enough points to justify serious exploration of the ASL-ESL approach with deaf children. Quigley and Paul (1984b, p. 195) have proposed that careful experimental studies be conducted with deaf children of ASL-using deaf parents who are willing to enroll their children in programs specially designed to test the ASL-ESL approach.

The third approach, now known as total communication, will probably continue in some form as the major approach for perhaps 70 percent of deaf children in the United States. A major question is, which form? Residential schools used a simultaneous approach with older deaf children for many decades, in which speaking was combined with signs used in English word order but without the other aspects of English structure, such as the inflectional system. This manner of using signs, and variations of it incorporating some aspects of ASL structure, has had various names but currently is known as Pidgin Sign English (PSE).

When day programs became convinced that their use of oral-aural approaches were not succeeding in developing English in deaf students, many of them adopted the simultaneous use of speech and signs but used sign systems, first SEE I and later SEE II, which had been constructed to use signs (natural and contrived) in conformity with English structure. The belief was that communicative interaction between parents and children and teachers and children in simultaneous spoken and signed English would establish English as the deaf child's basic internalized language. Unfortunately, it seems not to have worked that way.

Quigley and Paul (1984b, pp. 115–117) reviewed the reading performances and educational achievement levels of deaf students from about 1916–1983 and found no educationally significant improvements. It is possible, of course, that significant improvements in some individual schools were obscured in the largescale studies reviewed, but this seems unlikely. It is also possible that total communication has not been in use long enough for its effects to become apparent, but this too seems unlikely. The approach has been in widespread use in the United States for almost 20 years. That is long enough for a whole generation of deaf students to have been exposed to it.

The problem might lie in the point made earlier, that *the eye is an inefficient processor of spoken languages, particularly the important suprasegmental aspects, and that deaf children do not seem to be able to extract the structure of English from purely visual presentations of it.* As stated, almost every deaf child reads (or at least looks at) books in English for 10 to 20 years in school without much of the vocabulary or structure being acquired (internalized). It might be argued that books provide only passive exposure, whereas interactive exposure is needed. Leaving aside the fact that reading should be an active process wherein a reader interacts with an author by means of a text, the use of MCE in interactive communication between parent and child and teacher and child apparently provides no greater command of English for the deaf child. There must be something very basic missing in the process. What is missing, of course, is hearing in the deaf child, coupled with the fact that much of the meaning in spoken language, especially hierarchical structure, is conveyed by intonation, pause, and other suprasegmental aspects of speech, which MCE has no means for conveying. ASL does have means for conveying such information through its own suprasegmental features; oral-aural approaches employ the same means used by hearing children.

All of this would seem to argue for use of the ASL-ESL or oral-aural approaches, but the present limitations of these approaches have been discussed. Total communication is likely to continue for considerable time as the major communication approach with deaf children. It is likely, however, that this approach could be greatly simplified by the use of spoken English along with ASL signs presented in English word order but without the other features of English structure. This would be much less cumbersome for children, parents, and teachers to learn and use than the fully developed MCE systems. If, despite the arguments made, teachers prefer to use the MCE systems, they might bear in mind that what the deaf child is perceiving is at least as important as what the teacher is transmitting, and the child, lacking information on suprasegmental aspects of the input, is likely perceiving only the surface features of the language input, and thus is perceiving PSE even though the teacher is transmitting fully developed MCE.

For what was to be a synthesis of language development practices with deaf children, this chapter has dealt so far almost exclusively with communication approaches. It was stated in the first two sentences, however, that normal development of language depends, above all else, on fluent and intelligible communicative interaction between a child and a competent user of the language to be acquired. And apparently (with the exception of the as yet to be tested ASL-ESL approach) none of the communication systems available to the deaf child provides this fluency and intelligibility. It would seem to follow from this that language cannot be expected to unfold for the typical deaf child in the seemingly effortless way in which it unfolds for the hearing child. A competent teacher of deaf children needs to have a good deal of knowledge about the course and process of language development in hearing and in deaf children and skill in the various communication systems and language practices useful with deaf children.

A combination of natural and more structured language development practices, as presented in Chapters 4 and 5, would seem at present to hold the most promise for success. As in communication approaches, the field in theory, although perhaps not in practice, keeps swinging from one approach to the other, from natural to structured and back again. This alone is usually a strong indication that each approach holds only part of the answer.

The natural approach offers a logical framework for the development of language and is in keeping with the ways in which hearing children acquire language. Anyone who works with young hearing children is fully aware that children do not acquire language by stringing words together into sentences or by being taught relative clauses and complement structures formally. Children do not learn sounds, words, and sentences and then find meanings for the forms; instead, children learn about objects and events based on their interests and experiences and imaginative teaching and then learn how to code these objects and events.

They do not learn about eating lunch because their mother says *It's time for lunch*. Rather, they already know that their daily routine contains such an activity and, at some point, they realize that mother's statement refers to that familiar experience. The principles and practices detailed in Chapters 1 and 4 provide the basic information on use of the natural approach.

But the natural approach will not suffice for language development in many deaf children. It requires, in the typical hearing child, great amounts of linguistic input for appropriate associations to be made between symbols and objects, codes and events. This is particularly true for much of linguistic structure, which requires induction of rules from input. For the typical hearing child this works smoothly, without any formal planning or teaching of structure by parent or teacher. Things do not work that smoothly for the typical deaf child, however. The points discussed previously prevent this. First, the input of language to the deaf child is much less than to the typical hearing child because of the limitations of visual input. Second, the visual input does not contain the same information as auditory input—for example, all of the suprasegmental information that is important to acquisition of many hierarchical structures of English, such as embedded relative clauses. Important language structures such as *either. . .or, neither. . .nor, if x . . .then y, more than, less than*, and myriad others simply will not occur frequently enough in natural language input for the deaf child to understand them inductively. It is not that the *concepts* are more difficult for deaf children than for hearing children. Furth (1966) showed how to develop some of these nonverbally, and some of them can be readily developed by means of ASL. However, acquiring the English code for these and many, many other concepts is very difficult for most deaf children if natural language practices are relied on as the sole means of development.

Many verbal concepts in English and much—perhaps most—of its structure require that the teacher have detailed knowledge of the language to be acquired, its syntax, its morphology, and its semantics, in order to structure language learning within natural situations. Learning inductively requires far more input of language and far more intelligible input of English than deaf children receive; thus, the input has to be controlled and structured so the deaf child is receiving intensive input on English language phenomena, which might occur infrequently in the normal course of events. Until viable alternatives are available, it seems that natural and structured approaches need to be combined to meet the language acquisition needs of deaf children.

References

Allen, T. (in press). *Academic achievement among hearing impaired students: 1974–1983.* In A. Schildroth and M. Karchmer (Eds.), *Children in America* (pp. 161–206). San Diego: Little, Brown and Company.

Anderson, M., Boren, N., Caniglia, J., Howard, W., and Krohn, E. (1980). *Apple Tree.* Beaverton, OR: Dormac.

Anderson, R. (1981). *A proposal to continue a center for the study of reading* (Tech. Proposal, 4 vols.). Urbana: University of Illinois, Center for the Study of Reading.

Anderson, R. (1985). Role of the reader's schema in comprehension, learning, and memory. In H. Singer and R. Ruddell (Eds.), *Theoretical models and processes of reading* (3rd ed.) (pp. 372–384). Newark, DE: International Reading Association.

Anglin, J. (1977). *Word, object, and conceptual development.* New York: Norton.

Arlin, P. (1977). *The function of Piagetian operational levels in the preference and production of metaphors.* Paper presented to the Society for Research in Child Development, New Orleans, LA.

Asch, S.E., and Nerlove, H. (1960). The development of double-function terms in children. In B. Kaplan and S. Wapner (Eds.), *Perspectives in psychological theory.* New York: International Universities Press.

Asher, J. (1982). *Learning another language through actions: The complete teacher's guidebook* (2nd ed.). Los Gatos, CA: Sky Oaks Productions.

Babb, R. (1979). *A study of the academic achievement and language acquisition levels of deaf children of hearing parents in an educational environment using Signing Exact English as the primary mode of manual communication.* Unpublished doctoral dissertation, University of Illinois, Urbana-Champaign.

Bailey, K. (1983). Competitiveness and anxiety in adult second language learning: Looking AT and THROUGH the diary studies. In H. Seliger and M. Long (Eds.), *Classroom-oriented research in second language acquisition* (pp. 67–103). Rowley, MA: Newbury House.

Baker, C. (1980). Sentences in American sign language. In C. Baker and R. Battison (Eds.),

Sign language and the deaf community. Silver Spring, MD: National Association of the Deaf.

Baker, C., and Cokely, D. (1980). *American Sign Language: A teacher's resource on grammer and culture.* Silver Spring, MD: T.J. Publishers.

Baker, K., and de Kanter, A. (1981). *Effectiveness of bilingual education: A review of the literature.* Washington, DC: U.S. Department of Education, Office of Planning and Budget.

Baldwin, K. (1925). *Progress in the methods adopted in the German States for the teaching of language to the deaf and dumb from the time of Frederick Moritz Hill to the present day.* London: William H. Taylor & Sons.

Barnard, F. (1836). *Analytical grammer with symbolic illustrations.* New York: E. French Company.

Barnum, M. (1984). In support of bilingual/bicultural education for deaf children. *American Annals of the Deaf, 129,* 404–408.

Baron, M., and Kaiser, A. (1975). Semantic components in children's errors with pronouns. *Journal of Psycholinguistic Research, 4,* 303–317.

Barry, K.E. (1899). *The five-slate system. A system of objective language teaching.* Philadelphia: Sherman and Co., Printers.

Bartlett, E.J. (1977). The acquisition of the meaning of color terms: A study of lexical development. In R. Campbell and P. Smith (Eds.), *Recent advances in the psychology of language* (Vol. 4a, pp. 89–108). New York: Plenum Press.

Bates, E. (1976a). Pragmatics and sociolinguistics in child language. In D. Morehead and A. Morehead (Eds.), *Normal and deficient child language* (pp. 411–463). Baltimore: University Park Press.

Bates, E. (1976b). *Language and context: The acquisition of pragmatics.* New York: Academic Press.

Bates, E. (1979). *The emergence of symbols: Cognition and communication in infancy.* New York: Academic Press.

Bates, E., and Snyder, L. (in press). The cognitive hypothesis in language development. In I. Uzgiris and J.M. Hunt (Eds.), *Research with scales of psychological development in infancy.* Urbana: University of Illinois Press.

Bates, E., Benigni, L., Camaioni, L., and Volterra, V. (1977). From gesture to the first word: On cognitive and social prerequisites. In M. Lewis and L. Rosenblum (Eds.), *Interaction, conversation and the development of language* (pp. 247–307). New York: Wiley.

Bates, E., Camaioni, L., and Volterra, V. (1975). The acquisition of performatives prior to speech. *Merrill-Palmer Quarterly, 21,* 205–226.

Battison, R. (1978). *Lexical borrowing in American Sign Language.* Silver Spring, MD: Linstok.

Beckwith, L. (1977). Relationships between infants' vocalizations and their mothers' behaviors. *Merrill-Palmer Quarterly, 17,* 211–226.

Bell, A.G. (1883). Upon a method of teaching language to a very young congenitally deaf child. *American Annals for the Deaf, 28,* 124–139.

Bellugi, U. (1967). *The acquisition of negation.* Unpublished doctoral dissertation, Harvard University, Cambridge, MA.

Bellugi, U. (1980). How signs express complex meanings. In C. Baker and R. Battison (Eds.), *Sign language and the deaf community.* Silver Spring, MD: National Association of the Deaf.

Bellugi, U., and Klima, E. (1972). The roots of sign language in the sign talk of the deaf. *Psychology Today, 76,* 61–64.

Bender, R.E. (1960). *The conquest of deafness.* Cleveland: The Press of Western Reserve University.

Benedict, H. (1977). Early lexical development: Comprehension and production. *Journal of Child Language, 6,* 183–200.

Berko, J. (1958). The child's learning of English morphology. *Word, 14,* 150–177.

Berliner, D.C. (1984). *Effective classroom teaching: Conditions for developing exemplary schools.*

Paper presented at the Association for College Educators for the Hearing Impaired, Tucson, AZ.

Bernstein, D.K., and Tiegerman, E. (1985). *Language and communication disorders in children.* Columbus, OH: Charles E. Merrill.

Bernstein, M., Maxwell, M., and Matthews, K. (1985). Bimodal or bilingual communication. *Sign Language Studies, 47,* 127–140.

Bever, T.G. (1970). The cognitive basis for linguistic structure. In J.R. Hayes (Ed.), *Cognition and the development of language* (pp. 279–362). New York: Wiley.

Bever, T., Fodor, J., and Weksel, W. (1965). On the acquisition of syntax: A critique of "contextual generalization." *Psychological Review, 72,* 467–482.

Billow, R.M. (1975). A cognitive developmental study of metaphor comprehension. *Developmental Psychology, 11,* 415–423.

Blackwell, P.M., Engen, E., Fischgrund, J.E., and Zarcadoolas, C. (1978). *Sentences and other systems: A language learning curriculum for hearing-impaired children.* Washington, DC: A.G. Bell Association for the Deaf.

Blank, M., and Solomon, F. (1968). A tutorial language program to develop abstract thinking in socially disadvantaged preschool children. *Child Development, 39,* 379–390.

Blanton, R.L. (1968). Language learning and performance in the deaf. In S. Rosenberg and J.H. Koplin (Eds.), *Developments in Applied Psycholinguistics Research.* New York: Macmillan.

Bloom, L. (1970). *Language development: Form and function in emerging grammars.* Cambridge, MA: MIT Press.

Bloom, L. (1973). *One word at a time.* The Hague, Netherlands: Mouton.

Bloom, L., and Lahey, M. (1978). *Language development and language disorders.* New York: John Wiley & Sons.

Bloom, L., Lahey, J., Hood, L., Lifter, K., and Fiess, K. (1980). Complex sentences: Acquisition of syntactic connectives and the semantic relations they encode. *Journal of Child Language, 7,* 235–261.

Bloom, L., Hood, L., and Lightbown, P. (1974). Imitation in language development: If, when, and why. *Cognitive Psychology, 6,* 380–420.

Bloom, L., Lifter, K., and Hafitz, J. (1980). Semantics of verbs and the development of verb inflection in child language. *Language, 56,* 386–412.

Bloom, L., Lightbown, P., and Hood, L. (1975). Structure and variation in child language. *Monographs of the Society for Research in Child Development, 40*(2), 1–97.

Bloom, L., Miller, P., and Hood, L. (1975). Variation and reduction as aspects of competence in language. In A. Pick (Ed.), *Minnesota symposium on child psychology.* Minneapolis: University of Minnesota Press, *9,* 3–55.

Bochner, J.H. (1982). English in the deaf population. In D.G. Sims, G. Walter, and R.L. Whitehead (Eds.), *Deafness and communication: Assessment and training* (pp. 107–123). Baltimore: Williams & Wilkens

Bockmiller, P. (1981). Hearing impaired children: Learning to read a second language. *American Annals of the Deaf, 126,* 810–813.

Bohannon, J.N., and Warren-Leubecker, A. (1985). Theoretical approaches to language acquisition. In J.B. Gleason (Ed.), *The development of language* (pp. 173–226). Columbus, OH: Charles E. Merrill.

Bondurant, J. (1977). *An analysis of mothers' speech provided to children with normal language as compared to mothers' speech provided to children with delayed language.* Unpublished doctoral dissertation, University of Cincinnati, Cincinnati, OH.

Bonvillian, J., Nelson, K.E., and Charrow, V. (1976). Languages and language-related skills in deaf and hearing children. *Sign Language Studies, 12,* 211–250.

Bornstein, H., Saulnier, K., and Hamilton, L. (1980). Signed English: A first evaluation. *American Annals of the Deaf, 125,* 467–481.

Bornstein, H., Saulnier, K. and Hamilton, L. (1983). *The comprehensive Signed English dictionary.* Washington, DC: Gallaudet College Press.

Bowen, J.D., Madsen, H., and Hilferty, A. (1985). *TESOL: Techniques and procedures.* Rowley, MA: Newbury House.

Bowerman, M.F. (1973). Structural relationships in children's utterances: Syntactic or semantic? In T.E. Moores (Ed.), *Cognitive development and the acquisition of language* (pp. 197–213). New York: Academic Press.

Bowerman, M. (1975). Commentary on L. Bloom, P. Lightbown, and L. Hood (Eds.), Structure and variation in child language. *Monograph of the Society on Research in Child Development, 38,* 80–90.

Bowerman, M. (1978). Systematizing semantic knowledge: Changes over time in the child's organization of word meaning. *Child Development, 49,* 977–987.

Brasel, K., and Quigley, S. (1977). The influence of certain language and communication environments in early childhood on the development of language in deaf individuals. *Journal of Speech and Hearing Research, 20,* 95–107.

Brennan, M. (1975). Can deaf children acquire language? *American Annals of the Deaf, 120,* 463–479.

Brock, M.S. (1868). A better method of instructing a class of beginners. *American Annals of the Deaf, 13,* 209.

Brown, R. (1970). Derivational complexity and order of acquisition in child speech. In R. Brown, *Psycholinguistics.* New York: Free Press.

Brown, R. (1973). *A first language: The early stages.* Cambridge, MA: Harvard University Press.

Brown, R. (1975). *Social psychology.* New York: Free Press.

Brown, R., and Bellugi, U. (1964). Three processes in the child's acquisition of syntax. In E.H. Lenneberg (Ed.), *New directions in the study of language* (pp. 131–151). Cambridge, MA: MIT Press.

Brown, R., and Hanlon, C. (1970). Derivational complexity and order of acquisition. In J.R. Hayes (Ed.), *Cognition and the development of language* (pp. 11–53). New York: Wiley.

Bruck, M. (1982). Language disabled children's performance in an additive bilingual education program. *Applied Psycholinguistics, 3,* 45–60.

Bruck, M. (1985). Consequences of transfer out of early French immersion programs. *Applied Linguistics, 6,* 101–120.

Bruner, J.S. (1975). The ontogenesis of speech acts. *Journal of Child Language, 2,* 1–19.

Bryen, D.N. (n.d.). *Inquiries into child language.* Boston: Allyn and Bacon.

Buckler, M.S., Sr. (1968). Expanding language through patterning. *Volta Review, 70,* 89–96.

Buell, E.M. (1931). *A companion of the Barry five slate system and the Fitzgerald Key.* Washington, DC: The Volta Bureau.

Buium, N.J., Rynders, J., and Turnure, J. (1974). Early maternal linguistic environment of normal and Down's syndrome language-learning children. *American Journal of Mental Deficiency, 29,* 52–58.

Bunch, G.O. (1979). Degree and manner of acquisition of written English language rules by the deaf. *American Annals of the Deaf, 124,* 10–15.

Caniglia, J., Cole, N.J., Howard, W., Krohn, E., and Rice, M. (1975). *Apple Tree.* Beaverton, OR: Dormac.

Carey, S., and Bartlett, E. (1978, August). Acquiring a single new word. *Papers and Reports on Child Language Development, 15,* 17–29.

Carr, M. (1971). *Communicative behavior of three and four year old deaf children.* Unpublished doctoral dissertation, Teachers College, Columbia University, New York.

Caselli, M. (1983). Communication to language: Deaf children's and hearing children's development compared. *Sign Language Studies, 38,* 1–23.

Cazden, C.B. (1965). *Environmental assistance to the child's acquisition of grammar.* Doctoral dissertation, Harvard University, Cambridge, MA.

Cazden, C. (1970). The situation: A neglected source of social class differences in language use. *Journal of Social Issues, 26,* 35–60.

Celce-Murcia, M., and Larsen-Freeman, D. (1983). *The grammar book: An ESL/EFL teacher's course.* Rowley, MA: Newbury House.

Celce-Murcia, M., and McIntosch, L. (Eds.). (1979). *Teaching English as a second or foreign language.* Rowley, MA: Newbury House.

Champie, S. (1981). Language development in our preschool deaf child. *American Annals of the Deaf, 126,* 43–48.

Chang, H., and Trehub, S. (1977). Auditory processing of relational information by young infants. *Journal of Experimental Child Psychology, 24,* 324–331.

Charrow, V., and Wilbur, R. (1975). The deaf child as a linguistic minority. *Theory into Practice, 14,* 353–359.

Cheskin, A. (1982). The use of language by hearing mothers of deaf children. *Journal of Communication Disorders, 15,* 145–153.

Chipman, H.H., and deDardel, C. (1974). Developmental study of the comprehension and production of the pronoun "it." *Journal of Psycholinguistic Research, 3,* 91–99.

Chomsky, N. (1957). *Syntactic structures.* The Hague, Netherlands: Mouton.

Chomsky, N. (1965). *Aspects of the theory of syntax.* Cambridge, MA: MIT Press.

Chomsky, N. (1968). *Language and mind.* New York: Harcourt, Brace, & World.

Clark, E. (1973). What's in a word? On the child's acquisition of semantics in his first language. In T. Moore, (Ed.), *Cognitive development and the acquisition of language* (pp. 65–110). New York: Academic Press.

Clark, E. (1974). Some aspects of the conceptual basis for first language acquisition. In R. Schiefelbusch and L. Lloyd (Eds.), *Language perspectives—acquisition, retardation, and intervention* (pp. 105–128). Baltimore: University Park Press.

Clarke-Stewart, K.A. (1973). Interactions between mothers and their young children: Characteristics and consequences. *Monographs of the Society for Research in Child Development, 38,* (Serial No. 153), 1–109.

Clifton, C., and Odom, P. (1966). Similarity relations among certain English sentence constructions. *Psychological Monographs, 80,* 1–35.

Cohen, A. (1974). The Culver City Spanish immersion program: The first two years. *Modern Language Journal, 58,* 95–103.

Cokely, D. (1983). When is a pidgin not a pidgin? An alternate analysis of the ASL-English contact situation. *Sign Language Studies, 38,* 1–24.

Cole, N.J. (1979). *Apple Tree story books.* Beaverton, OR: Dormac.

Collins-Ahlgren, M. (1975). Teaching English as a second language to young deaf children: A case study. *Journal of Speech and Hearing Disorders, 39,* 486–500.

Cometa, M.S., and Eson, M.E. (1978). Logical operations and metaphor interpretation: A Piagetian model. *Child Development, 49,* 649–659.

Conley, J. (1976). Role of idiomatic expressions in the reading of deaf children. *American Annals of the Deaf, 121,* 381–385.

Conrad, R. (1979). *The deaf school child.* London: Harper and Row.

Cooper, R. (1967). The ability of deaf and hearing children to apply morphological rules. *Journal of Speech and Hearing Research, 10,* 77–86.

Cooper, R., and Rosenstein, J. (1966). Language acquisition of deaf children. *Volta Review, 68,* 58–67.

Cornell, E. (1978). Learning to find things: A reinterpretation of object permanence studies. In L. Siegel and C. Brainerd (Eds.), *Alternatives to Piaget.* New York: Academic Press.

Corson, H. (1973). *Comparing deaf children of oral parents and deaf parents using manual communication with deaf children of hearing parents on academic, social, and communication functioning.* Unpublished doctoral dissertation, University of Cincinnati, Cincinnati, OH.

Costello, E., and Watkins, T. (1975). *Structured tasks for English practice.* Washington, DC: Gallaudet College, Division of Public Services.

Course of Study. (1918). Minnesota School for the Deaf: A brief exposition of the Wing's symbols. (Prepared by the Teacher's Association).

Crandall, J., and Bruhn, T. (1981). Developing an effective language teaching curriculum. In F. Caccamise, M. Garretson, and U. Bellugi (Eds.), *Teaching American Sign Language as a second/foreign language: Proceedings of the third national symposium on sign language research and teaching* (pp. 72–85). Silver Spring, MD: National Association of the Deaf.

Crandall, K.E., and Albertini, J.A. (1980). An investigation of variables of instruction and their relation to rate of English language learning. *American Annals of the Deaf, 125,* 427–434.

Croker, G.W., Jones, M.K., and Pratt, M.E. (1920, 1922, 1928). *Language stories and drills, Books I, II, III, IV Manuals.* Brattleboro, VT: The Vermont Printing Co.

Cross, T.G. (1977). Mother' speech adjustments: The contributions of selected child listener variables. In C. Ferguson and C. Snow (Eds.), *Talking to children: Language input and acquisition* (pp. 151–187). Cambridge, England: Cambridge University Press.

Crutchfield, P. (1972). Prospects for teaching English Det + N structures to deaf students. *Sign Language Studies, 1,* 8–14.

Cruttenden, A. (1979). *Language in infancy and childhood: A introduction to language acquisition.* New York: St. Martin's Press.

Crystal, D. (1973). Non-segmental phonology in language acquisition: A review of the issues. *Lingua, 32,* 1–45.

Cummins, J. (1979). Linguistic interdependence and the educational development of bilingual children. *Review of Educational Research, 49,* 222–251.

Cummins, J. (1984). *Bilingualism and special education: Issues in assessment and pedagogy.* San Diego: College-Hill Press.

Curtiss, S. (1981). Dissociations between language and cognition: Cases and implications. *Journal of Autism and Developmental Disorders, 11,* 15–30.

d'Arc, J., Sr. (1958). The development of connected language skills with emphasis on a particular methodology. *Volta Review, 60,* 58–65.

Dale, P.S. (1976). *Language development: Structure and function.* New York: Holt, Rinehart, and Winston.

Dale, E., and O'Rourke, J. (1986). *Vocabulary building: A process approach* (2nd ed.). Columbus, OH: Zaner-Bloser.

Dansereau, D.F., Collins, K.W., McDonald, B. A., Holley, C.D., Garland, J., Diekhoff, G., and Evans, S.H. (1979). Development and evaluation of a learning strategy training program. *Journal of Educational Psychology, 71,* 64–73.

Davis, J. (1977). Our forgotten children: Hard-of-hearing pupils in the schools. Minneapolis: University of Minnesota.

de Kanter, A., and Baker, K. (1983). *Bilingual education: A reappraisal of federal policy.* Lexington, MA: Lexington Books.

de Land, F. (1931). *The story of lipreading. Its genesis and development.* Washington, DC: The Volta Bureau.

de Villiers, J.G., and de Villiers, P.A. (1973). A cross-sectional study of the acquisition of grammatical morphemes in child speech. *Journal of Psycholinguistic Research, 2,* 267–278.

de Villiers, J.G., Tager-Flusberg, H., and Hakuta, K. (1976). *The roots of coordination in child speech.* Paper presented at the First Annual Boston University Conference on Language Development, Boston, MA.

de Villiers, J.G., Tager-Flusberg, H., Hakuta, K., and Cohen, M. (1979). Children's comprehension of relative clauses. *Journal of Psycholinguistic Research, 8,* 499–518.

de Villiers, P., and de Villiers, J. (1972). Early judgments of semantic and syntactic acceptability by children. *Journal of Psycholinguistic Research, 1,* 299–310.

DiFrancesca, S. (1972). *Academic achievement test results of a national testing program for hearing-impaired students—United States,* Spring 1971 (Series D, No. 9). Washington, DC: Gallaudet College, Office of Demographic Studies.

Di Somma, E.V., and McTiernan, M.L. (1985, 1986). *Simple English classic series.* Beaverton, OR: Dormac.

Dore, J. (1974). A pragmatic description of early language development. *Journal of Psycholinguistic Research, 3,* 343–350.

Dunn, L.M. (1965). *Peabody Picture Vocabulary Test.* Minneapolis: American Guidance Service.

Durkin, D. (1983). *Teaching them to read* (4th ed.). Boston: Allyn and Bacon.

Edmonson, B., de Jung, J., Leland, H., and Leach E.M. (1974). *The test of social inference.* Baldwin, NY: Educational Activities, Inc.

Ervin-Tripp, S. (1970). Discourse agreement: How children answer questions. In J.R. Hayes (Ed.), *Cognition and the development of language* (pp. 79–107). New York: Wiley.

Ervin-Tripp, S., and Mitchell-Kernan, C. (Eds.). (1977). *Child discourse.* New York: Academic Press.

Ewoldt, C. (1983). Text simplification: A solution with many problems. *Perspectives, 1,* 23–25.

Ewoldt, C. (1985). A descriptive study of the developing literacy of young hearing-impaired children. *Volta Review, 87,* 109–126.

Fairbanks, G. (1954). Systematic research in experimental phonetics: A theory of the speech mechanism as a servosystem. *Journal of Speech and Hearing Disorders, 19,* 133–139.

Fay, E.A. (1867). The methods of Prendergast and Marcel. *American Annals of the Deaf, 14,* 193–204.

Feldman, H. (1975). *The development of a lexicon by deaf children of hearing parents or, there's more to language than meets the ear.* Unpublished doctoral dissertation, University of Pennsylvania, College Park.

Ferguson, C.A. (1964). Baby talk in six languages. *American Anthropologist, 66,* 103–114.

Feuerstein, R. (1979). *The dynamic assessment of retarded performers: The learning potential assessment device theory, instruments, and techniques.* Baltimore, MD: University Park Press.

Fey, M.E. (1986). *Language intervention with young children.* San Diego: College-Hill Press.

Fischgrund, J.E. (1978). *Mixing apples and oranges: Syntactic complexity and math word problems.* Paper presented at the MSSD Research Conference on The Nature of English Acquisition Process of Deaf Adolescents, Washington, DC, Gallaudet College.

Fitzgerald, E. (1929). *Straight language for the deaf.* Staunton, VA: The McClure Company.

Fitzgerald, E. (1949). *Straight language for the deaf: A system of instruction for deaf children.* Washington, DC: The Volta Bureau.

Fokes, J. (1982). *Fokes written language program.* Hingham, MA: Teaching Resources.

Forman, J.D., and Spector, P.B. (1980). A multidisciplinary approach to teaching English. *American Annals of the Deaf, 125,* 400–405.

Foss, D.J., and Hakes, D.T. (1978). *Psycholinguistics: An introduction to the psychology of language.* Englewood Cliffs, NJ: Prentice-Hall.

Francis, H. (1972). Toward an explanation of the syntagmatic-paradigmatic shift. *Child Development, 43,* 949–958.

Fruchter, A., Wilbur, R., and Fraser, J. (1984). Comprehension of idioms by hearing impaired students. *Volta Review, 86,* 7–17.

Furth, H. (1966). *Thinking without language.* New York: Free Press.

Gallaudet Research Institute. (1985). *Gallaudet Research Institute Newsletter* (J. Harkins, Ed.). Washington, DC: Gallaudet College.

Gamez, G. (1979). Reading in a second language: Native language approach vs. direct method. *Reading Teacher, 32,* 665–670.

Garcia, E., and Padilla, R. (Eds.). (1985). *Advances in bilingual education research.* Tucson: University of Arizona.

Gardner, H. (1974). Metaphors and modalities: How children project polar adjectives onto diverse domains. *Child Development, 45,* 84–91.

Gardner, J., and Zorfass, J. (1983). From sign to speech: The language development of a hearing impaired child. *American Annals of the Deaf, 129,* 20–24.

Garnica, O. (1977). Some prosodic and paralinguistic features of speech to young children. In C. Snow and C. Ferguson (Eds.), *Talking to children* (pp. 63–88). New York: Cambridge University Press.

Geffner, D., and Freeman, L. (1980). Assessment of language comprehension of six-year-old deaf children. *Journal of Communication Disorders, 4,* 98–110.

Genesee, F. (1979). Acquisition of reading skills in immersion programs. *Foreign Language Annals, 12,* 71–77.

Genesee, F. (1983). Bilingual education of majority-language children: The immersion experiments in review. *Applied Psycholinguistics, 4,* 1–46.

Gentner, D. (1977). On the development of metaphoric processing. *Child Development, 48,* 1034–1039.

Gibson, E. (1965). Learning to read. *Science, 148,* 1066–1072.

Gilman, L., and Raffin, M. (1975). *Acquisition of common morphemes by hearing impaired children exposed to the Seeing Essential English sign system.* Paper presented at the Annual Meeting of the American Speech and Hearing Association, Washington, DC.

Giorcelli, L. (1982). *The comprehension of some aspects of figurative language by deaf and hearing subjects.* Unpublished doctoral dissertation, University of Illinois, Urbana.

Gleason, J.B. (1985). *The development of language.* Columbus, OH: Charles E. Merrill.

Gleitman, L., and Wanner, E. (1982). Language acquisition: The state of the state of the art. In E. Wanner and L. Gleitman (Eds.), *Language acquisition: The state of the art.* Cambridge, England: Cambridge University Press.

Goldin-Meadow, S., and Feldman, H. (1975, April). *The creation of communication system: A study of deaf children of hearing parents.* Paper presented to the Society for Research in Child Development, Denver, CO.

Gonzales, P. (1981). Beginning English reading for ESL students. *The Reading Teacher, 35,* 154–162.

Goodluck, H., and Tavakolian, S. (1982). Competence and processing in children's grammar of relative clauses. *Cognition, 11,* 1–27.

Gough, P. (1965). Grammatical transformations and speed of understanding. *Journal of Verbal Learning and Verbal Behavior, 4,* 107–111.

Grant, J. and Semmes, P. (1983). A rationale for LOGO for hearing-impaired preschoolers. *American Annals of the Deaf, 128,* 564–569.

Graves, D.H. (1984). *Writing: Teachers and children at work.* Portsmouth, NH: Heinemann Educational Books.

Green, W., and Shephard, D. (1975). The semantic structure in deaf children. *Journal of Communication Disorders, 8,* 357–365.

Greenberger, D. (1879). The natural method. *American Annals of the Deaf, 24,* 33–38.

Greenfield, P., and Smith, J. (1976). *The structure of communication in early language development.* New York: Academic Press.

Greenstein, J.M., Bush, B., McConville, K., and Stellini, L. (1977). *Mother-infant communication and language acquisition in deaf infants.* New York: Lexington School for the Deaf.

Grewel, F. (1963). Remarks on the acquisition of language in deaf children. *Language and Speech, 6,* 37–45.

Groht, M.A. (1933). Language as taught in the Lexington School. *American Annals of the Deaf, 78,* 280–281.

Groht, M.A. (1958). *Natural language for deaf children.* Washington, DC: The Volta Bureau.

Gross, R.N. (1970). Language used by mothers of deaf children and mothers of hearing children. *American Annals of the Deaf, 115,* 93–96.

Gunter, R. (1960). Proportional drill as a technique for teaching grammar. *Language Learning, 10,* 123–134.

Gustason, G., Pfetzing, D., and Zawolkow, E. (1980). *Signing exact English.* Los Alamitos, CA: Modern Signs.

Hakuta, K., de Villiers, J.G., and Tager-Flusberg, H. (1982). Sentence coordination in Japanese and English. *Journal of Child Language, 9,* 193–207.

Hamburger, H., and Crain, S. (1982). Relative acquisition. In S.A. Kuczaj (Ed.), *Language development: Vol. 1.* Syntax and semantics. Hillsdale, NJ: Erlbaum.

Hansen, J. (1981). The effects of inference training and practice on young children's reading comprehension. *Reading Research Quarterly, 16,* 391–417.

Hansen, J., and Hubbard, R. (1984). Poor readers can draw inferences. *The Reading Teacher, 37,* 586–589.

Hansen, J., and Pearson, P.D. (1983). An instructional study: Improving the inferential comprehension of fourth grade good and poor readers. *Journal of Educational Psychology, 75,* 821–829.

Harste, J., Burke, C., and Woodward, V. (1983). *The young child as writer-reader, and informant* (Final report No. NIE-G-80-0121). Indiana University, Bloomington.

Hart, B. (1981). Pragmatics: How language is used. *Analysis and Intervention in Developmental Disabilities, 1,* 299–313.

Hart, B., and Rogers-Warren, A. (1978). The milieu approach to teaching language. In R. Scheifelbusch (Ed.), *Language intervention strategies.* Baltimore: University Park Press.

Hatfield, N., Caccamise, F., and Siple, P. (1978). Deaf students' language competency: A bilingual perspective. *American Annals of the Deaf, 123,* 847–851.

Heider, F., and Heider, G. (1940). A comparison of sentence structure of deaf and hearing children. *Psychological Monographs, 52,* 42–103.

Heider, F., Heider, G., and Stykes, J. (1941). A study of the spontaneous vocalizations of fourteen deaf children. *Volta Review, 43,* 10–14.

Heidinger, V. (1984). *Analyzing syntax and semantics.* Washington, DC: Gallaudet College Press.

Hess, L. (1972). *The development of transformational structures in a deaf child and a normally hearing child over a period of five months.* Unpublished master's thesis, University of Cincinnati, Cincinnati, OH.

Hillocks, G., Jr. (1986). *Research on written composition: New directions for teaching.* Urbana, IL: National Conference on Research in English.

Hoffmeister, R., and Moores, D. (1973). *The acquisition of specific referents in a deaf child of deaf parents.* Report No. 53, Research Development and Demonstration Center in Education of the Handicapped, University of Minnesota, Minneapolis.

Hoffmeister, R., and Wilbur, R. (1980). The acquisition of sign language. In H. Lane and F. Grosjean (Eds.), *Recent perspectives on American Sign Language.* Hillsdale, NJ: Erlbaum.

Honeck, R.P., Sowry B.M., and Voegtle, K. (1978). Proverbial understanding in a pictorial context. *Child Development, 49,* 327–331.

Hoover, R.C. (1972). Language for the deaf according to Henry. *American Annals of the Deaf, 117,* 590–594.

Houck, J. (1982). *The effects of idioms on reading comprehension of hearing impaired students.*

Unpublished doctoral dissertation, University of Northern Colorado, Greeley, CO (Abstract).

Hudson, P.L. (1979). Recommitment to the Fitzgerald Key. *American Annals of the Deaf,* 124, 397–399.

Hughes, R. (1966). Verbal conceptualization in the deaf and hearing children. *Exceptional Children,* 27, 21–25.

Hunt, K.W. (1965). A synopsis of clause-to-sentence length factors. *English Journal,* 54, 300–309.

Hutchins, S., Poizner, H., McIntire, M., and Newkirk, D. (1986, April). *Language acquisition implications of a computerized written form of ASL.* Paper presented at the American Sign Language Research and Teaching Conference, Newark, CA.

Hyltenstam, K. (1985). L2 learners' variable output and language teaching. In K. Hyltenstam and M. Pienemann (Eds.), *Modelling and assessing second language acquisition* (pp. 113–136). Clevedon, England: Multilingual Matters, Ltd.

Hyltenstam, K., and Pienemann, M. (1985). Introduction. In K. Hyltenstam and M. Pienemann (Eds.), *Modelling and assessing second language acquisition* (pp. 3–22). Clevedon, England: Multilingual Matters, Ltd.

Iran-Nejad, A., Ortony, A., and Rittenhouse, R. (1981). The comprehension of metaphorical uses of English by deaf children. *Journal of Speech and Hearing Research,* 24, 551–556.

Ivimey, G., and Lachterman, D. (1980). The written language of deaf children. *Language and Speech,* 23, 351–377.

Jacobs, J.A. (1858). A synopis or exposition of primary lessons for the deaf and dumb. *Proceedings of the fifth Convention of American Instructors of the Deaf.* Alton, IL: Courier Steam Job Printing House.

Jaffe, J., Stern, D., and Perry, C. (1973). Conversational coupling of gaze behavior in prelinguistic human development. *Journal of Psycholinguistic Research,* 2, 321–330.

Johnson, D.W. (1986). *Reaching out: Interpersonal effectiveness and self-actualization* (3rd ed.). Englewood Cliffs, NJ: Prentice-Hall.

Johnson, D., and Pearson, P.D. (1984). *Teaching reading vocabulary* (2nd ed.). New York: Holt, Rinehart, and Winston.

Jones, B. (1984). Assessment and language instruction. In S. Quigley and P. Paul, *Language and deafness* (pp. 199–227). San Diego: College-Hill Press.

Jones, P. (1979). Negative interference of signed language in written English. *Sign Language Studies,* 24, 273–279.

Jordan, I., Gustason, G., and Rosen, R. (1979). An update on communication trends at programs for the deaf. *American Annals of the Deaf,* 124, 350–357.

Judy, S.N., and Judy, S.J. (1983). *The English teacher's handbook.* Boston: Little, Brown and Company.

Kantor, R. (1980). The acquisition of classifiers in American Sign Language. *Sign Language Studies,* 28, 193–208.

Kearsley, R. (1973). The newborn's response to auditory stimulation: A demonstration of orienting and defensive behavior. *Child Development,* 44, 582–590.

Kemp, J.C., and Dale, P.S. (1973, March). *Spontaneous imitation and free speech: A grammatical comparison.* Paper presented to the Society for Research in Child Development, Philadelphia.

Kessen, W., Levine, J., and Hendrich, K. (1979). The imitation of pitch in infants. *Infant Behavior and Development,* 2, 93–100.

King, C. (1983). *Survey of language methods and materials used with hearing impaired students in the United States*. Paper presented at the Entre Amis '83 Convention of the Association of Canadian Educators of the Hearing Impaired, Convention of the American Instructors of the Deaf, and the Convention of Executives for American Schools for the Deaf, Winnipeg, Manitoba, Canada.

King, C.M. (1984). National survey of language methods used with hearing-impaired students in the United States. *American Annals of the Deaf, 129,* 311–316.

King, C.M., and Quigley, S.P. (1985). *Reading and deafness*. San Diego: College-Hill Press.

Klein, M.L. (1985). *The development of writing in children: Pre-K through grade 8*. Englewood Cliffs, NJ: Prentice-Hall.

Klima, E., and Bellugi, U. (1966). Syntactic regularities in the speech of children. In J. Lyons and R. Wales (Eds.), *Psycholinguistic Papers* (pp. 183–208). Edinburgh: Edinburgh University Press.

Klima, E., and Bellugi, U. (1979). *The signs of language*. Cambridge, MA: Harvard University.

Kluwin, T. (1981). The grammaticality of manual representations of English in classroom settings. *American Annals of the Deaf, 126,* 417–421.

Kluwin, T. (1982). Deaf adolescents' comprehension of English prepositions. *American Annals of the Deaf, 127,* 852–859.

Koplin, J.H., Odom, P.B., Blanton, R.L., and Nunnally, J.C. (1967). Word association test performance of deaf students. *Journal of Speech and Hearing Research, 10,* 126–132.

Krashen, S. (1982). *Principles and practice in second language acquisition*. Oxford, England: Pergamon.

Krashen, S., and Terrell, T. (1982). *The natural approach: Language acquisition in the classroom*. Elmsford, NY: Pergamon.

Krashen, S., and Terrell, T. (1983). *The natural approach*. San Francisco: Alemany.

Kretschmer, R.R., Jr., and Kretschmer, L.W. (1978). *Language development and intervention with the hearing impaired*. Baltimore: University Park Press.

Kretschmer, R.R., Jr., and Kretschmer, L.W. (1986). Language in perspective. In D.M. Luterman, (Ed.), *Deafness in Perspective* (pp. 131–166). San Diego: College-Hill Press.

Kuczaj, S. (1979). Evidence for a language learning strategy: On the relative ease of acquisition of prefixes and suffixes. *Child Development, 50,* 1–13.

LaBrant, L. (1933). A study of certain language developments of children in grades four to twelve, inclusive. *Genetic Psychology Monographs, 14,* 387–491.

Lambert, W., and Tucker, G. (1972). *Bilingual education of children: The St. Lambert experiment*. Rowley, MA: Newbury House.

Lane, H., and Grosjean, F. (Eds.). (1980). *Recent perspectives on American Sign Language*. Hillsdale, NJ: Erlbaum.

LaSasso, C. (1985, June). *1984 National survey of materials and procedures used to teach reading to hearing impaired students: Preliminary results*. Paper presented at the Conference on Reading Instruction for the Hearing Impaired. South Carolina State Department of Education: The Office of Programs for the Handicapped.

Layton, T., Holmes, D., and Bradley, P. (1979). A description of a pedagogically imposed signed semantic-syntactic relationship in deaf children. *Sign Language Studies, 35,* 127–152.

Legarreta, D. (1979). The effects of program models on language acquisition by Spanish speaking children. *TESOL Quarterly, 13,* 521–534.

Lenneberg, E. (1966). *Biological foundations of language*. New York: Wiley.

Lewis, M., and Freedle, R. (1973). Mother-infant dyad: The cradle of meaning. In P. Pliner, L. Krames, and T. Alloway (Eds.), *Communication and affect, language and thought* (pp. 127–155). New York: Academic Press.

Lewis, M.M. (1959). *How children learn to speak*. New York: Basic Books.

Liberman, A.M. (1974). Language processing: State-of-the-art report. In R. E. Stark (Ed.), *Sensory capabilities of hearing impaired children*. Baltimore: University Park Press.

Lichtenstein, E. (1983). *The relationship between reading processes and English skills of deaf students*. Rochester, NY: National Technical Institute for the Deaf.

Ling, D. (1976). *Speech and the hearing impaired child: Theory and practice*. Washington, DC: A.G. Bell Association for the Deaf.

Loban, W. (1976). *Language development: Kindergarten through grade twelve*. Urbana, IL: National Council of Teachers of English. (No. 18 in a series of research reports sponsored by the NCTE Committee on Research).

Long, G.L., and Aldersley, S. (1982). Evaluation of a technique to enhance reading comprehension. *American Annals of the Deaf, 127*, 816–820.

Long, G., and Conklin, D. (1979). The implementation and evaluation of a technique for improving the prose comprehension of deaf college students. In G. Propp (Ed.), *1980's schools...Portals to century 21*. Selected papers (pp. 158–170). Silver Spring, MD: Convention of American Instructors of the Deaf.

Looney, P., and Rose, S. (1979). The acquisition of inflectional suffixes by deaf youngsters using written and fingerspelled modes. *American Annals of the Deaf, 124*, 765–769.

Lowenbraun, S., Appelman, K.I., and Callahan, J.L. (1980). *Teaching the hearing impaired*. Columbus, OH: Charles E. Merrill.

Lucas, E. (1980). *Semantic and pragmatic language disorders: Assessment and remediation*. Rockville, MD: Aspen Systems.

Luetke-Stahlman, B. (1983). Using bilingual instructional models in teaching hearing-impaired students. *American Annals of the Deaf, 128*, 873–877.

Luetke-Stahlman, B. (1984). Classifier recognition by hearing-impaired children in residential and public schools. *Sign Language Studies, 42*, 39–44.

Luetke-Stahlman, B., and Weiner, F. (1982). Assessing language and/or system preferences of Spanish-deaf preschoolers. *American Annals of the Deaf, 127*, 789–796.

MacGinitie, W. (1964). Ability of deaf children to use different word classes. *Journal of Speech and Hearing Research, 7*, 141–150.

MacNamara, J. (1972). Cognitive bases of language learning in infants. *Psychological Review, 79*, 1–13.

Maratsos, M. (1983). Some current issues in the study of the acquisition of grammar. In P. Mussen (Ed.), *Handbook of child psychology* (pp. 705–786). New York: Academic Press.

Maratsos, M., Kuczaj, S.A., Fox, D.E.C., and Chalkley, M.A. (1979). Some empirical studies in the acquisition of transformational relations: Passives, negatives and the past tense. In W.A. Collins (Ed.), *Children's language and communication*. Hillsdale, NJ: Erlbaum.

Marbury, N., and Mackinson-Smyth, J. (1986, April). *ASL and English: A partnership*. Paper presented at the American Sign Language Research and Teaching Conference, Newark, CA.

Marmor, G., and Pettito, L. (1979). Simultaneous communication in the classroom: How well is English grammer represented? *Sign Language Studies, 23*, 99–136.

Marshall, W. (1970). Contextual constraint on deaf and hearing children. *American Annals of the Deaf, 115*, 682–689.

Marshall, W., and Quigley, S.P. (1970). *Quantitative and qualitative analysis of syntactic structures of written language of deaf students*. Urbana, IL: Institute of Research on Exceptional Children.

Martin, D. (1984). Cognitive modification for the hearing impaired adolescent: The promise. *Exceptional Children, 51*, 235–242.

Martin, J. (1972). Rhythmic (hierarchical) versus serial structure in speech and other behavior. *Psychological Review, 79*, 487–509.

Mason, J. (1984). Early reading from a developmental perspective. In P.D. Pearson (Ed.), *Handbook of reading research* (pp. 505–543), New York: Longman.

Mason, J.M., and Au, K.H. (1986). *Reading instruction for today.* Glenview, IL: Scott, Foresman and Co.

Matter, G.A., and Davis, L.A. (1975). A reply to metaphor and linguistic theory. *Quarterly Journal of Speech, 61,* 322–327.

Mattes, L., and Omark, D. (1984). *Speech and language assessment for the bilingual handicapped.* San Diego: College-Hill Press.

McCarr, J.E. (1980). *Lessons in syntax.* Beaverton, OR: Dormac.

McDonald, J. D. (1982). Communication strategies for language intervention. In D.P. McClowry, A.M. Guilford, and S.O. Richardson (Eds.), *Infant communication: Development, assessment and intervention.* New York: Grune & Stratton.

McDonald, J.D., and Nickols, M. (1974). *The environmental language inventory.* Columbus: Nisonger Center, Ohio State University.

McGill-Franzen, A., and Gormley, K. (1980). The influence of context on deaf readers' understanding of passive sentences. *American Annals of the Deaf, 125,* 937–942.

McIntire, M. (1977). The acquisition of American Sign Language hand configurations. *Sign Language Studies, 16,* 247–266.

McLean, J., and Snyder-McLean, L. (1978). A transactional approach to early language training. Columbus, OH: Charles E. Merrill.

McNeill, D. (1966a). A study of word association. *Journal of Verbal Learning and Verbal Behavior, 5,* 548–557.

McNeill, D. (1966b). Developmental Psycholinguistics. In F. Smith and G. Miller (Eds.), *The genesis of language.* Cambridge, MA: MIT Press.

McNeill, D. (1970). *The acquisition of language: The study of developmental psycholinguistics.* New York: Harper and Row.

Meadow, K. (1980). *Deafness and child development.* Los Angeles: University of California Press.

Meadow, K. (1968). Early manual communication in relation to the deaf child's intellectual, social, and communicative functioning. *American Annals of the Deaf, 113,* 29–41.

Meadow, K., Greenberg, M., Erting, C. and Carmichael, H. (1981). Interactions of deaf mothers and deaf preschool children: Comparisons with three other groups of deaf and hearing dyads. *American Annals of the Deaf, 126,* 454–468.

Mellon, J. (1967). Transformational sentence-combining: A method for enhancing the development of syntactic fluency in English composition. *Harvard Research and Development Center,* Report No. 1.

Menyuk, P. (1963). Syntactic structures in the language of children. *Child Development, 34,* 407–422.

Menyuk, P. (1971). *The acquisition and development of language.* Englewood Cliffs, NJ: Prentice Hall.

Menyuk, P. (1977). *Language and maturation.* Cambridge, MA: MIT Press.

Mervis, C.B., and Mervis, C.A. (1982). Leopards are kitty-cats: Object labelling by mothers for their thirteen-month-olds. *Child Development, 53,* 267–273.

Mey, J. (1979). *Pragmalinguistics: Theory and practice.* The Hague, Netherlands: Mouton.

Miller, J.F. (1981). *Assessing language production in children: Experimental procedures.* Baltimore: University Park Press.

Miller, J.F., and Chapman, R.S. (1981). The relation between age and mean length of utterance in morphemes. *Journal of Speech and Hearing Research, 24,* 154–161.

Moerk, E. (1972). Principles of interaction in language and learning. *Merrill-Palmer Quarterly, 18,* 229–257.

Moerk, E.L. (1977). *Pragmatic and semantic aspects of early language development.* Baltimore: University Park Press.

Moffett, J., and Wagner, B.J. (1983). *Student-centered language arts and reading, K-13: A handbook for teachers.* Boston: Houghton Mifflin.

Moog, J.S. (1970). Approaches to teaching preprimary hearing-impaired children. *AOEHI Bulletin, 1*, 52–59.

Moog, J., and Geers, A. (1985). EPIC: A program to accelerate academic progress in profoundly hearing-impaired children. *Volta Review, 87*(6), 259–277.

Moore, M. (1973). The genesis of object permanence. Paper presented at meeting of Society for Research in Child Development. Cited in D.K. Bernstein, and E. Tiegerman. (1985). *Language and communication disorders in children.* Columbus, OH: Charles E. Merrill.

Moorehead, D.M., and Ingram, D. (1973). The development of base syntax in normal and linguistically deviant children. *Journal of Speech and Hearing Research, 16*, 330–352.

Moores, D. (1978). *Educating the deaf: Psychology, principles and practice.* Boston: Houghton Mifflin.

Moores, D.F. (1982). *Educating the deaf: Psychology, principles and practices,* (2nd ed.). Boston: Houghton Mifflin.

Morkovin, B. (1960). Experiment in teaching deaf preschool children in the Soviet Union. *Volta Review, 62,* 260–268.

Morse, P. (1972). The discrimination of speech and non-speech stimuli in early infancy. *Journal of Exceptional Child Psychology, 14,* 477–492.

Morse, P.A. (1974). Infant speech perception: A preliminary model and review of the literature. In R.L. Schiefelbusch and L.L. Lloyd (Eds.), *Language perspective—acquisition, retardation, and intervention* (pp. 19–53). Baltimore: University Park Press.

Mosenthal, P., Tamor, L., and Walmsley, S. (Eds.) (1983). *Research on writing: Principles and methods.* New York: Longman.

Muma, J.R. (1971). Language intervention: Ten techniques. *Language speech and hearing services in schools #5* (pp. 7–17). Washington, DC: American Speech and Hearing Association.

Myklebust, H. (1954). *Auditory disorders in children.* New York: Grune and Stratton.

Navarro, R. (1985). The problems of language, education, and society: Who decides. In E. Garcia and R. Padilla (Eds.), *Advances in bilinual education research* (pp. 289–313). Tucson: University of Arizona.

Nelson, K. (1973). Structure and strategy in learning to talk. *Monograph of the Society on Research in Child Development, 38,* (1–2).

Nelson, K., Benedict, H., Gruendel, J., and Rescorla, L. (1977). *Lessons from early lexicons.* Paper presented at the meeting of the Society for Research in Child Development, New Orleans, LA.

Nelson, M.S. (1947). A tabulation of schools for the deaf, *American Annals of the Deaf, 92,* 8–28.

Nelson, M.S. (1949). The evolutionary process of methods of teaching language to the deaf with a survey of the methods now employed. *American Annals of the Deaf, 94,* Part I, 230–294; Part II, 354–396; Part III, 491–499.

Newby, R.F. (1984). *Simple language fairy tales.* Beaverton, OR: Dormac.

Newport, E.L. (1975). *Motherese: The speech of mothers to young children* (Technical Report No. 52). San Diego: University of California, Center for Human Information Processing.

Niemoeller, A.F. (1978). Hearing aids. In H. Davis and S.R. Silverman (Eds.), *Hearing and deafness* (pp. 280-317). New York: Holt, Rinehart, and Winston.

Nunnally, J.C., and Blanton, R.L. (1966). Patterns of word association in the deaf. *Psychological Reports, 18,* 87–92.

Odom, P., Blanton, R., and Nunnally, J. (1967). Some 'cloze' technique studies of language capability in the deaf. *Journal of Speech and Hearing Research, 10,* 816–827.

O'Donnell, R.C., Griffin, W.J., and Norris, R.C. (1967). *Syntax of kindergarten and elementary school children: A transformational analysis.* Research Report No. 8. Urbana, IL: National

Council of Teachers of English.

Ogden, P. (1979). *Experiences and attitudes of oral deaf adults regarding oralism*. Unpublished doctoral dissertation, University of Illinois, Urbana.

O'Hare, F. (1973). *Sentence combining: Improving student writing without formal grammar instruction*. Research Report No. 15. Urbana, IL: National Council of Teachers of English.

Orlansky, M., and Bonvillian, J. (1984). The role of iconicity in early sign language acquisition. *Journal of Speech and Hearing Disorders, 49,* 287–292.

Otheguy, R., and Otto, R. (1980). The myth of static maintenance in bilingual education. *Modern Language Journal, 64,* 350–356.

Outreach. (1985, 1986). *Syntactic structure series*. Washington, DC: Gallaudet College Press.

$\mathbf{P}$age, S. (1981). *The effect of idiomatic language in passages on the reading comprehension of deaf and hearing students*. Unpublished doctoral dissertation. Muncie, IN: Ball State University, (Abstract). Muncie, IN

PAL: Programmed Assisted Learning. (1986). Ballston Lake, NY: Instructional Industries.

Palermo, D.S., and Molfese, D. (1972). Language acquisition from age five onward. *Psychological Bulletin, 6,* 429–432.

Papert, S. (1980). *Mindstorms: Children, computers and powerful ideas*. New York: Basic Books.

Paris, S., and Lindauer, B. (1976). The role of inference in children's comprehension and memory. *Cognitive Psychology, 8,* 217–227.

Paul, P.V. (1985). Reading and other language-variant populations. In C. King and S. Quigley, *Reading and deafness* (pp. 251–289). San Diego: College-Hill Press.

Paulston, C. (1980). *Bilingual education: Theories and issues*. Rowley, MA: Newbury House.

Payne, J.A. (1982). *A study of the comprehension of verb-particle combinations among deaf and hearing subjects*. Unpublished doctoral dissertation. University of Illinois at Urbana-Champaign.

Pearson, P.D. (1985). *The comprehension revolution: A twenty-year history of process and practice related to reading comprehension* (Reading Education Report No. 57). Champaign: University of Illinois, Center for the Study of Reading.

Pearson, P.D., and Johnson, D. (1978). *Teaching reading comprehension*. New York: Holt, Rinehart, and Winston.

Peet, H. (1851). Memoir on the origin and early history of the art of teaching the deaf and dumb. *American Annals of the Deaf, 3,* 200–211.

Peet, H.P. (1869). *The order of the first lesson in language for a class of deaf mutes*. Proceedings of the Sixth Convention of American Instructors of the Deaf (pp. 19–26). Washington, DC: U.S. Government Printing Office.

Perron, J. (1978). *Changing the question: Psycholinguistics and writing*. Paper presented at the Conference on English Education, Minneapolis, MN.

Peter, M., Sr. (1981). *The family circus for developing sentence comprehension*. Jefferson, WI: St. Coletta School.

Peter, M., Sr. (1984). *Learning sentence patterns with Julie and Jack*. Jefferson, WI: St. Coletta School.

Petrie, H. (1979). Metaphor and learning. In A. Ortony (Ed.), *Metaphor and thought* (pp. 438–461). Cambridge, England: Cambridge University Press.

Petty, W. (1978). The writing of young children. In C. Cooper and L. Odell (Eds.), *Research on composing: Points of departure*. Urbana, IL: National Council of Teachers of English.

Peyton, J.K., and Batson, T. (1986). Computer networking: Making connections between speech and writing. *ERIC Clearinghouse on Languages and Linguistics News Bulletin, 10,* 1–6.

Pfau, G.S. (1974). Project LIFE a decade later: Some reflections and projections. *American Annals of the Deaf, 119,* 549–553.

Phillips, J.R. (1973). Syntax and vocabulary of mothers' speech to young children: Age and sex comparisons. *Child Development, 44,* 182–185.

Piaget, J. (1954). *The construction of reality in the child* (M. Cook, trans.). New York: Basic Books (originally published 1937).

Piaget, J. (1955). *The language and thought of the child*. New York: Meridian Books.

Piaget, J. (1971). *Biology and knowledge: An essay on the relations and cognitive processes* (B. Walsh, trans.). Chicago, IL: University of Chicago Press (originally published 1967).

Pienemann, M. (1985). Learnability and syllabus construction. In K. Hyltenstam and M. Pienemann (Eds.), *Modelling and assessing second language acquisition* (pp. 23–75). Clevedon, England: Multilingual Matters, Ltd.

Pollio, M., and Pollio, H. (1979). A test of metaphoric comprehension and some preliminary developmental data. *Journal of Child Language, 6,* 111–120.

Porter, S. (1868). *Professor Porter's paper on grammar.* Proceedings of the Sixth Convention of American Instructors of the Deaf. Washington, DC: U.S. Government Printing Office, pp. 144–145.

Porter, S.S. (1869). The instruction of the deaf and dumb in grammar. *American Annals of the Deaf, 14,* 30–43.

Power, D., and Quigley, S. (1973). Deaf children's acquisition of the passive voice. *Journal of Speech and Hearing Research, 16,* 5–11.

Prinz, P., and Nelson, K.E. (1985). A child-computer-teacher interactive method of teaching reading to young deaf children. In D.S. Martin (Ed.), *Cognition, education and deafness: Directions for research and instruction* (pp. 124–127). Washington, DC: Gallaudet College Press.

Prutting, C.A., and Kirchner, D.M. (1983). Applied pragmatics. In T.M. Gallagher and C.A. Prutting (Eds.), *Pragmatic assessment and intervention issues in language.* San Diego: College-Hill Press.

Pugh, B.L. (1955). *Steps in language development for the deaf: Illustrated in the Fitzgerald Key.* Washington, DC: The Volta Bureau.

Quigley, S. (1982). Reading achievement and special reading materials. *Volta Review, 84*(5), 95–106.

Quigley, S., and Frisina, R. (1961). Institutionalization and psychoeducational development of deaf children. *CEC Research Monograph.* Washington, DC: Council on Exceptional Children.

Quigley, S., Jenne, W., and Phillips, S. (1969). *Deaf students in colleges and universities.* Washington, DC: A.G. Bell Association for the Deaf.

Quigley, S., and King, C. (Eds.) (1981, 1982, 1983, 1984). *Reading milestones.* Beaverton, OR: Dormac.

Quigley, S., and Kretschmer, R.E. (1982). *The education of deaf children: Issues, theory, and practice.* Baltimore: University Park Press.

Quigley, S., and Paul, P. (1984a). ASL and ESL? *Topics in Early Childhood Special Education, 3*(4), 17–26.

Quigley, S.P., and Paul, P.V. (1984b). *Language and deafness.* San Diego: College-Hill Press.

Quigley, S., and Paul, P. (1986). A perspective on academic achievement. In D. Luterman (Ed.), *Deafness in perspective* (pp. 55–86). San Diego: College-Hill Press.

Quigley, S.P., and Power, D.J. (Eds.). (1979). *TSA Syntax program.* Beaverton, OR: Dormac.

Quigley, S., Montanelli, D., and Wilbur, R. (1976). Auxilliary verbs in the language of deaf students. *Journal of Speech and Hearing Research, 19,* 536–550.

Quigley, S., Power, D., and Steinkamp, M. (1977). The language structure of deaf children. *Volta Review, 79,* 73–83.

Quigley, S., Smith, N., and Wilbur, R. (1974). Comprehension of relativized sentences by deaf students. *Journal of Speech and Hearing Research, 17,* 325–341.

Quigley, S.P., Steinkamp, M.W., Power, D.J., and Jones, B.J. (1978). *Test of syntactic abilities.* Beaverton, OR: Dormac.

Quigley, S., Wilbur, R., and Montelli, D. (1975). *Complement structures in the language of deaf children.* Unpublished manuscript, Institute for Research on Exceptional Children, University of Illinois, Urbana.

Quigley, S., Wilbur, R., and Montanelli, D. (1974). Question formation in the language of deaf students. *Journal of Speech and Hearing Research, 17,* 69–713.

Quigley, S., Wilbur, R., Power, D., Montanelli, D., and Steinkamp, M. (1976). *Syntactic structures in the language of deaf children.* Urbana: University of Illinois, Institute for Child Behavior and Development.

Raffin, M., Davis, J., and Gilman, L. (1978). Comprehension of inflectional morphemes by deaf children exposed to a visual English sign system. *Journal of Speech and Hearing Research, 21,* 387–400.

Raimes, A. (1983). *Techniques in teaching writing.* New York: Oxford University.

Raphael, T. (1984). Teaching learners about sources of information for answering comprehension questions. *Journal of Reading, 27,* 303–311.

Raphael, T.E. (1982). Question-answering strategies for children. *Reading Teacher, 36,* 186–190.

Raphael, T., and Pearson, P.D. (1982). *The effect of metacognitive training on children's question-answering behavior.* Urbana: University of Illinois, Center for the Study of Reading. (ERIC Document Reproduction Service No. ED 215 315).

Raphael, T.E., and Wonnacott, C. (1981). *The effect of type of response and type of post-test on understanding of and memory for text.* Paper presented at the National Reading Conference, Dallas, TX. (ERIC Document Reproduction Service No. ED 212 998).

Reagan, T. (1985). The deaf as a linguistic minority: Educational considerations. *Harvard Educational Review, 55,* 265–277.

Reich, P., and Bick, M. (1977). How visible is visible English? *Sign Language Studies, 14,* 59–72.

Reynolds, R.E., and Ortony, A. (1980). Some issues in the measurement of children's comprehension of metaphorical language. *Child Development, 51,* 1110–1119.

Rice, M.L. (1980). *Cognition to language: Categories, word meanings, and training.* Baltimore: University Park Press.

Richardson, J.E. (1981). Computer assisted instruction for the hearing impaired. *Volta Review, 83,* 328–335.

Rittenhouse, R.K. (1981). *An anthology of metaphor stories for hearing impaired children: An instructional program.* Normal, IL: Illinois Associates.

Rittenhouse, R.K., Morreau, L.E., and Iran-Nejad, A. (1981). Metaphor and conservation in deaf and hard-of-hearing children. *American Annals of the Deaf, 126,* 450–453.

Rivers, W., and Temperley, M. (1978). *A practical guide to the teaching of English as a second or foreign language.* New York: Oxford University.

Roe, K.V., McClure, A., and Roe, A. (1982). Vocal interaction at 3 months and cognitive skills at 12 years. *Developmental Psychology, 18,* 15–16.

Rosch, E., and Mervis, C.B. (1975). Family resemblances: Studies in the internal structure of categories. *Cognitive Psychology, 7,* 382–439.

Rose, S. (1975). *Adaptation of the Test of Social Inference with deaf adolescents.* Unpublished doctoral dissertation. Columbus: The Ohio State University.

Rose, S., and Waldron, M. (1984). Use of microcomputers in educational programs for the hearing impaired. *American Annals of the Deaf, 129,* 338–342.

Rose, S., Waldron, M., and Yanoff, J. (1984). Training of preservice teachers of the hearing impaired in microcomputer and computer graphic techniques. *Conference Proceedings: 6th Annual National Educational Computing Conference.* Dayton, OH: NECC, 295–297.

Rosenshine, B. (1979). The third cycle of research on teacher effects: Content covered, academic engaged time, and direct instruction. In P.L. Peterson and H.J. Walberg (Eds.),

Research on teaching: Concepts, findings and implications. Berkeley, CA: McCutchan.

Ruke-Dravina, V. (1977). Modifications of speech addressed to young children in Latvian. In C. Snow and C. Ferguson (Eds.), *Talking to children.* New York: Cambridge University Press.

Russell, K., Quigley, S., and Power, D. (1976). *Linguistics and deaf children: Transformational syntax and its applications.* Washington, DC: A.G. Bell Association for the Deaf.

Rutherford, S. (1986, April). *Second culture acquisition for the second language learner of ASL: Classroom and curriculum strategies.* A paper presented at the American Sign Language Research and Teaching Conference, Newark, CA.

Sachs, J. (1977). The adaptive significance of linguistic input to prelinguistic infants. In C. Snow and C. A. Ferguson (Eds.), *Talking to children.* New York: Cambridge University Press.

Sachs, J., and Johnson, M. (1972). *Language development in a hearing child of deaf parents.* Paper presented at the International Symposium on First Language Acquisition, Florence, Italy.

Santrock, J.W. (1986). *Life-span development* (2nd ed.). Dubuque, IA: Wm. C. Brown.

Savin, H., and Perchonock, E. (1965). Grammatical structure and immediate recall of English sentences. *Journal of Verbal Learning and Verbal Behavior, 4,* 348–353.

Schafer, D., and Lynch, J. (1980). Emergent language of six prelingually deaf children. *Teachers of the Deaf, 5,* 94–111.

Schlesinger, I. (1982). *Steps to language: Toward a theory of native language acquisition.* Hillsdale, NJ: Erlbaum.

Schlesinger, H., and Meadow, K. (1972). *Sound and sign: Childhood deafness and mental health.* Berkley: University of California Press.

Schmitt, P. (1966). Language instruction for the deaf. *Volta Review, 68,* 85–105.

Scovel, T. (1982). Questions concerning the application of neurolinguistic research to second language learning/teaching. *TESOL Quarterly, 16,* 323–331.

Scoville, R. (1983). Development of the intention to communicate: The eye of the beholder. In L. Feagans, C. Garvey, and R. Golinkoff (Eds.), *The origins and growth of communication.* Norwood, NJ: Ablex.

Searle, J. (1969). *Speech acts.* Cambridge: Harvard University Press.

Shatz, M., and Gelman, R. (1973). The development of communication skills: Modifications in the speech of young children as a function of the listener. *Monographs of the Society for Research in Child Development, 38*(152).

Sheie, T.P. (in press). The "new" in newsroom: Software and language arts. *American Annals for the Deaf*

Shipley, E.F., Smith, C.S., and Gleitman, L.R. (1969). A study in the acquisition of language: Free responses to commands. *Language, 45,* 322–342.

Sinclair, H. (1973). Language acquisition and cognitive development. In T. Moore (Ed.), *Cognitive development and the acquisition of language* (pp. 9–25). New York: Academic Press.

Siple, P. (Ed.). (1978). *Understanding language through sign language research.* New York: Academic Press.

Simmons, A. (1962). A comparison of the type-token ratio of spoken and written language of deaf children. *Volta Review, 64,* 417–421.

Skarakis, E., and Prutting, C.A. (1977). Early communication: Semantic functions and communicative intentions in the communication of the preschool child with impaired hearing. *American Annals of the Deaf, 122,* 382–391.

Skinner, B.F. (1957). *Verbal behavior.* Englewood Cliffs, NJ: Prentice-Hall.

Slobin, D. (1966). The acquisition of Russian as a native language. In F. Smith and C.A. Miller (Eds.), *The genesis of language: A psycholinguistic approach* (pp. 129–248). Cambridge, MA: MIT Press.

Slobin, D.I. (1973). Cognitive prerequisites for the development of grammar. In D.I. Slobin and C. Ferguson (Eds.), *Studies of child language development* (pp. 175–208). New York: Holt, Rinehart and Winston.

Slobin, D. (1982). Universal and particular in the acquisition of language. In E. Wanner and L. Gleitman (Eds.), *Language acquisition: The state of the art* (pp. 128–170). Cambridge, England: Cambridge University Press.

Smith, C. (1972). *Residual hearing and speech production in deaf children.* Unpublished doctoral dissertation: City University of New York.

Smith, F. (1975). *Comprehension and learning.* New York: Holt, Rinehart, and Winston.

Smith, F.E. (1984). *Bank street writer.* San Rafael, CA: Broderbund Software, Inc.

Smith, F., and Miller, G.A. (1966). *Genesis of language: A Psycholinguistic approach.* Cambridge, MA: MIT Press.

Smith, M.E. (1926). *An investigation of the development of the sentence and the extent of vocabulary in young children* (Studies in Child Welfare, Vol. 3, No. 5). Iowa City: University of Iowa.

Snow, C.E. (1972). Mothers' speech to children learning language. *Child Development, 43,* 549–565.

Snow, C. (1977). The development of conversation between mothers and babies. *Journal of Child Language, 4,* 1–22.

Snow, C.E. (1984). Parent-child interaction and the development of communicative ability. In R. Schiefelbusch and J. Pickar (Eds.), *The acquisition of communicative competence.* Baltimore: University Park Press.

Springer, S., and Deutsch, G. (1981). *Left brain, right brain.* San Francisco: W.H. Freeman.

Stark, R.E., and Levitt, H. (1974). Prosodic feature perception and production in deaf children. *Journal of the Acoustical Society of America, 55,* S63(A).

Stepp, R.E. (1981). Educational media and technology for the hearing impaired learner: An historical overview. *Volta Review, 83,* 265–274.

Stern, D.N., and Wasserman, G.A. (1979). *Maternal language to infants.* Paper presented at a meeting of the Society for Research in Child Development. Cited in J.B. Gleason (1985), *The development of language.* Columbus, OH: Charles E. Merrill.

Sternberg, M. (1981). *American Sign Language: A comprehensive dictionary.* New York: Harper and Row.

Stewart, D. (1985). Language dominance in deaf students. *Sign Language Studies, 49,* 375–385.

Stokoe, W., Jr. (1960). Sign language structure: An outline of the visual communication system of the American deaf. *Studies in Linguistics,* Occasional Paper No. 8.

Stokoe, W., Jr. (1975). The use of sign language in teaching English. *American Annals of the Deaf, 120,* 417–421.

Stoloff, L., and Dennis, Z. (1982). Matthew. *American Annals of the Deaf, 123,* 452–459.

Stone, P.S. (1983). LOGO: A powerful learning environment for hearing impaired children. *American Annals of the Deaf, 128,* 648–652.

Storrs, R.S. (1880). Methods of deaf-mute teaching II. *American Annals of the Deaf, 24,* 233–250.

Streng, A. (1958, May). *On improving the teaching of language.* Paper presented at the Spring Meeting of the Teachers of the Deaf, Oshkosh, WI.

Streng, A.H. (1972). *Syntax, speech and hearing: Applied linguistics for teachers of children with language and hearing disabilities.* New York: Grune and Stratton.

Strong, M., Burdett, J., and Woodward, J. (1986, April). *A bilingual syllabus for deaf children.* Paper presented at the American Sign Language Resarch and Teaching Conference, Newark, CA.

Stuckless, E.R. (1981). Real-time graphic display and language development for the hearing impaired. *Volta Review, 83,* 291–300.

Stuckless, E.R. (1983). Real-time transliteration of speech into print for hearing impaired students in regular classes. *American Annals of the Deaf, 128,* 619–624.

Stuckless, E.R., and Birch, J. (1966). The influence of early manual communication on the linguistic development of deaf children. *American Annals of the Deaf, 111,* 452–460, 499–504.

Stuckless, E.R., and Marks, C. (1966). *Assessment of the written language of deaf students.* Pittsburgh: University of Pittsburgh, School of Education.

Sugarman, S. (1978). A description of communicative development in the prelanguage child. In I. Markova (Ed.), *The social context of language.* New York: Wiley.

Sugarman, S. (1984). The development of preverbal communication. In R.L. Schiefelbusch and J. Pickar (Eds.), *The acquisition of communicative competence.* Baltimore: University Park Press.

Suppes, P. (1974). Cognition: A survey. In C.E. Sherrick et al. (Eds.), *Psychology and the handicapped child* (pp. 109–126). Washington, DC: U.S. Government Printing Office, No. 178-01219.

Swain, M. (1981). Linguistic expectations: Core, extended and immersion programs. *Canadian Modern Language Review, 37,* 486–497.

Swain, M., and Lapkin, S. (1982). *Evaluating bilingual education: A Canadian case study.* Clevedon, England: Multilingual Matters, Ltd.

Taylor, L. (1969). *A language analysis of the writing of deaf children.* Unpublished doctoral dissertation, Florida State University, Tallahassee.

Templin, M. (1950). *Development of reasoning in children with normal and defective hearing.* Minneapolis: University of Minnesota Press.

Thomas, E.S. (1958). A language system. *American Annals of the Deaf, 103,* 510–523.

Tierney, R., and Leys, M. (1984). *What is the value of connecting reading and writing?* (Reading Education Report No. 55). Champaign: University of Illinois, Center for the Study of Reading.

Townson, P. (1978). *Pronoun pages.* Beaverton, OR: Dormac.

Troike, R. (1978). Research evidence for the effectiveness of bilingual education. *NABE Journal, 3,* 13–24.

Troike, R. (1981). Synthesis of research on bilingual education. *Educational Leadership, 38,* 498–504.

Truax, R. (1985). Linking research to teaching to facilitate reading-writing-communication connections. *Volta Review, 87,* 155–169.

Turner, W.W. (1853). On the teaching of grammer to the deaf and dumb. *Proceedings of the third convention of American instructors of the deaf and dumb.* Columbus, Ohio: Steam Press of Smith and Cox, 249–258.

Turnure, C. (1971). Response to voice of mother and stranger by babies in the first year. *Developmental Psychology, 4,* 182–190.

Tweney, R.D., Hoemann, H.W., and Andrews, C.E. (1975). Semantic organization in deaf and hearing subjects. *Journal of Psycholinguistic Research, 4,* 61–73.

Tyack, D., and Ingram, D. (1977). Children's production and comprehension of questions. *Journal of Child Language, 4,* 211–224.

Umiker-Sebeok, J., and Sebeok, T. (1980). Introduction: Questioning apes. In T. Sebeok and J. Umiker-Sebeok (Eds.), *Speaking of apes: A critical anthology of two-way communication with man.* New York: Plenum Press.

Van Uden, A. (1970). *A world of language for deaf children. Part 1. Basic principles: A maternal reflective method.* Rotterdam, Netherlands: Rotterdam University Press.

Waldron, M.B., and Rose, S. (1983). Visual thinking for severe language handicapped children through the use of computer graphics. *Journal of Computer Based Instruction, 9,* 206–210.

Walmsley, S. (1983). Writing disability. In P. Mosenthal, L. Tamor, and S. Walmsley (Eds.), *Research on writing: Principles and methods* (pp. 267–286). New York: Longman.

Walter, G. (1978). Lexical abilities of hearing and hearing-impaired children. *American Annals of the Deaf, 123,* 976–982.

Walter, M., Sr. (1959). The Fitzgerald Key on wheels. *American Annals of the Deaf, 104,* 366–371.

Watson, P. (1979). The utilization of the computer with the hearing impaired and the handicapped. *American Annals of the Deaf, 124,* 670–680.

Watson, T.J. (1967). *The education of hearing-handicapped children.* Manchester, England: Manchester University Press.

Weddell-Monig, J., and Lumley, J.M. (1980). Child deafness and mother-child interaction. *Child Development, 51,* 766–774.

Westervelt, Z., and Peet, H.P. (1880). The natural method. *American Annals of the Deaf, 25,* 212–217.

Wiig E.H. (1982a). *Let's talk: Developing prosocial communication skills.* Columbus, OH: Charles E. Merrill.

Wiig, E.H., and Semel, E.M. (1980). *Language assessment and intervention for the learning disabled.* Columbus, OH: Charles E. Merrill.

Wiig, E.H., and Semel, E. (1984). *Language assessment and intervention for the learning disabled* (2nd ed.). Columbus, OH: Charles E. Merrill.

Wilbur, R. (1977). An explanation of deaf children's difficulty with certain syntactic structures in English. *Volta Review, 79,* 85–92.

Wilbur, R. (1979). *American Sign Language and sign systems.* Baltimore: University Park Press.

Wilbur, R. (1980). The linguistic description of American Sign Language. In H. Lane and F. Grosjean (Eds.), *Recent perspectives on American Sign Language* (pp. 7–31). Hillsdale, NJ: Erlbaum.

Wilbur, R. (1982). The development of morpheme structure constraints in deaf children. *Volta Review, 84,* 1–16.

Wilbur, R., and Jones, M. (1974). Some aspects of the bilingual/bimodal acquisition of sign language and English by three children of deaf parents. In M. LaGaly, R. Fox, and A. Bruck (Eds.), *Papers from the 10th Regional Meeting, Chicago Linguistic Society,* Chicago, IL.

Wilbur, R., Fraser, J., and Fruchter, A. (1981). *Comprehension of idioms by hearing impaired students.* Paper presented at the American Speech-Language-Hearing Association Convention, Los Angeles.

Wilbur, R., Goodhart, W., and Montandon, E. (1983). Comprehension of nine syntactic structures by hearing impaired students. *Volta Review, 85,* 328–345.

Wilbur, R., Montanelli, D., and Quigley, S. (1976). Pronominalization in the language of deaf students. *Journal of Speech and Hearing Research, 19,* 120–140.

Wilbur, R., Quigley, S., and Montanelli, D. (1975). Conjoined structures in the written language of deaf students. *Journal of Speech and Hearing Research, 18,* 319–335.

Wimmer, H. (1980). Children's understanding of stories: Assimilation by a general schema for actions or coordination of temporal relations. In F. Wilkening, J. Becker, and T. Trabasso (Eds.), *Information integration by children* (pp. 267–290). Hillsdale, NJ: Erlbaum.

Wing, G.W. (1887). The theory and practice of grammatical methods. *American Annals of the Deaf, 20,* 84–89.

Winkelman, N. L. (1971). The news story can help students learn to write. *American Annals of the Deaf, 116,* 20–24.

Winner, E., Rosenstiel, A., and Gardner, H. (1976). The development of metaphoric understanding. *Developmental Psychology, 12,* 289–297.

Winzemer, J.A. (1980, October). *A lexical expectation model for children's comprehension of wh-questions.* Paper presented at the Fifth Annual Boston University Conference on Language Development, Boston, MA.

Woodward, J. (1973). Some characteristics of pidgin sign English. *Sign Language Studies, 3,* 39–46.

Woodward, J. (1986, April). *ASL is what it is not: Classroom use of ASL by teachers.* A paper presented at the American Sign Language Research and Learning Conference, Newark, CA.

Wootten, J., Merkin, S., Hood, L., and Bloom, L. (1979, March). *Wh-questions: Linguistic evidence to explain the sequence of acquisition.* Paper presented at the biennial meeting of the Society for Research in Child Development, San Francisco, CA.

Wright, R. (1955). *The abstract reasoning of deaf college students.* Unpublished doctoral dissertation, Northwestern University, Evanston, IL.

Wulbert, M., Inglis, S., Kriegsmann, E., and Mills, B. (1975). Language delay and associated mother-child interactions. *Developmental Psychology, 11,* 61–70.

Wyman, R. (1969). Progress report on the visual response system. *American Annals of the Deaf, 114,* 838–840.

Yoshinaga, C. (1983). Syntactic and semantic characteristics in the written language of hearing impaired and normally hearing school-aged children. Unpublished doctoral dissertation. Northwestern University, Evanston, IL.

Yoshinaga-Itano, C., and Snyder, L. (1985). Form and meaning in the written language of hearing impaired children. *Volta Review, 87,* 75–90.

Yussen, S.R. (1982). Children's impressions of coherence in narratives. In B. Hutson (Ed.), *Advances in reading/language research* (Vol.1), (pp. 245–281). Greenwich, CT: JAI Press.

AUTHOR INDEX

SUBJECT INDEX